THE BEACH FISHERMAN'S COMPENDIUM

John Holden

The Crowood Press

This edition first published in 1990 by
The Crowood Press Ltd
Ramsbury, Marlborough
Wiltshire SN8 2HR

This impression 1991

Originally published in two separate volumes as: *Long Distance Casting*,
1982 (Reprinted 1985, 1986) & *The Beach Fisherman's Tackle Guide*,
1983 (Reprinted 1985)

British Library Cataloguing in Publishing Data

Holden, John, *1947–*
    The beach fisherman's compendium.
    1. Coastal waters. Shore angling
    I. Title
    799.16

    ISBN 1-85223-567-5

Acknowledgement

The photograph on page 103 is reproduced by kind permission of IPC
Magazines

Printed and bound in Great Britain by BPCC Hazell Books, Aylesbury

Contents

PART II

PART I

Introduction to Casting

Casting is the basic skill of rod and line fishing. In fact most people can hide a lot of deficiencies in the way they fish, but no-one can mask an inability to cast properly.

Sometimes a short cast will drop your bait just where you want it, but more often than not you will wish to benefit from the choice of range (e.g. short, medium or long) available to the good caster. In other words good casters switch on the power when necessary; bad casters, on the other hand, struggle . . . and then look for excuses to explain why they went home fishless while other anglers managed to fill their larders with cod, bass, whiting or bluefish!

If you cannot cast as far as you want to, make an effort to learn. Your entire approach to fishing will change: you should enjoy yourself ten times more and should expect to hook at least three times as many fish during the year.

Although many practitioners of long distance casting fail to capitalise on the technique's real advantage, CHOICE OF FISHING RANGE, by continually fishing at maximum range, the un-tamed distance caster is still likely to catch many more fish than the man who cannot top 80 yards with his best effort. For reasons which are not fully understood, there seems to be a band of productive water offshore of most beaches. Putting a figure on it is difficult, but as a rule you will find some of the best fishing lies between 100 and 150 yards out. English cod and bass, American striped bass and red drum, Dutch flatfish all sometimes show a strong preference for the deeper and quieter water well out from the shoreline; tantalisingly close—especially when they are feeding on the surface—yet beyond average casting range for the mass of sportsfishermen. Only one thing is more frustrating than to thrash out your bait 40 yards short of feeding fish, and that is to have another angler stand next to you and cast right into the shoal. A dozen fish for him and none for you is the best catalyst in the world for rethinking your casting technique.

Pure distance however, does not always pay off. A 175 yard cast which impresses everyone around you is pointless if the fish are running through a gulley just 90 yards out. The experienced fisherman is never locked into such a blinding ego-trip that he ignores or simply fails to recognise other factors. Casting skill must be linked to a knowledge of water and of fishes and their habits. Seasons, tides and weather play a major role in fishing of all kinds, and to reap big rewards in terms of fish and personal satisfaction you must learn to think in the context of long range casting, which boils down to knowing when to cast as far as you can and when to toss the bait just a few yards.

'Long distance' is a vague concept. Exactly what is a long cast? 150 yards is a realistic target for the surf fisherman casting 4–6 ounces. Lighter tackle—a 2 or 3 ounce metal lure attached to 12 lb main line, say—travels nearly as far on less powerful equipment used with essentially the same casting style. Baits reduce distance in proportion to their bulk. A 200 yard cast with sinker alone is ripped down to 140 yards on addition of a chunk of fish bait to the hook.

Freshwater fishermen casting plugs and metal lures across rivers and lakes have yet another concept of distance, but tackle for casting less than 1 ounce is still capable of 100 yards in reasonable weather. 2 ounce tackle really flies out there: with appropriate rod, reel and 8–12 lb test line, you could drop a metal lure on a bass some 150 yards away. Progress to a full surf outfit and enjoy easy casting to fishing spots normally accessible only by boat. If you prefer, develop your skills beyond fishing. Tournament casting with surf tackle is a great sport, and although parallels with practical fishing are sometimes hard to relate to these days, there remains an essential link between thrashing a sinker acorss a grass field and casting a bait into water. The skills developed on casting courts make their mark in everyday fishing and some of the best fishing rods and reels on the market have a tournament pedigree.

Tournament distances are phenomenal. The current British record for 5.29 ounces of lead, 0.35 mm main line (about 15 lb test), 0.70 mm shock leader (about 55 lb test) and unrestricted rod and multiplier reel is more than 285 yards. Unofficial practice sessions have produced casts of almost 300 yards. Less than ten years ago a 200 yard cast hit the national headlines. Today, the same distance will not qualify you to cast in the National Finals.

7

The Author, John Holden

Casting long distance on a shingle beach Suffolk, England.

How far can you learn to cast? After years of teaching casting all over the world, I am confident enough to make some predictions. The normally co-ordinated man equipped with basic but efficient surf tackle balanced to 5 ounces of casting weight can develop a reliable, stress-free 150–175 yards without baits. In practical fishing terms, depending on baits and the weather, that equates to an easy 110–150 yards option. You do not have to cast so far, it might be a mistake to do so, but at least you have a choice. Ladies and juniors can expect 100 yards . . . and I have met some powerful, hairy chested female anglers who can add another 50 yards!

Teaching yourself to cast presupposes that you know enough about casting mechanics and methods to interpret various styles and thus form a personal technique of your own. That is not always easy. If you have seen good casters in action, copy what they do until your own experience suggests changes for the better. Best of all, find a coach with a proven record of successful teaching and training. It is a fair bet that he can improve your casting more in one day than you might otherwise achieve on your own in several weeks. But whatever road you travel, be confident. There are thousands of anglers no more talented than you and no more athletic, who can cast a very long way and now catch many more fish than ever before. You can join them. All it takes is determination and commonsense. The idea of this book is to outline mechanics of casting so that you can work out a system for yourself, then polish it to produce those 150 yard casts you

always admired but could never quite manage.

Ernest Hemingway observed that there are many who want to be writers—enjoying the benefits, kudos and riches of the successful novelist—but who do not want actually to sit down and write. Writing is hard work, after all. In a minor way, casting is the same. For every dozen anglers who would like to stand on the beach or lakeside and push out cast after cast—long or short, trouble-free, deadly accurate—only one is prepared to get out there with a fishing rod and actually LEARN. Those who make the effort find that results appear within two months of practising, say, twice a week for an hour. Good tackle is important, yet costs little more than second rate equipment. Apart from the rod or blank, most keen anglers already own the right tackle anyway.

It costs no more in Pounds, Dollars or Yen to be a good caster than a non-starter in the distance race, but it will cost you time, effort and hard work. The rewards are immense; the investment lasts a lifetime.

In this book fishing tackle also comes under the microscope. Although I do not subscribe to the theory that tackle alone makes the caster, I do believe that tuning and selection count heavily in the quest for top results, at whatever stage you are, beginner or expert. The wrong blank, too much handle, no blocks in the multiplier controller or too little line on a spinning reel can create havoc.

9

Distance in Perspective

Excellent fishing distances and tournament record casts are poles apart. For some reason, though, anglers who are interested in better results automatically compare their distances to those of winning competitors. They never stop to consider the vast gulf between beach fishing and pure casting over a grassy court.

Good fishermen are content with 130 yards or so with ordinary beach tackle and baits. Only 130 yards? Well, not one caster in a thousand drops a decent sized cod or drumfish bait that far every cast, and without fear of a backlash. Most distance claims you hear of or read about, are nonsense. 175 yards . . . 190 . . . even the magic 200 yards from a beach? Don't you believe it.

Even the world's champion casters would not try to cast a bait that far unless conditions were absolutely perfect. Yet it is common to read articles which imply that the writer thinks nothing of casting at least 190 yards every time he fishes. I have discussed distance with leading surf fishermen all over the world – men who hit the rod so hard that air friction burns line and who regularly top 250 yards in practice. Which of them claims to cast ordinary bait 200 yards? None of them do. 175 yards, then? Maybe, but it depends on bait size, wind speed, and whether they are on peak form.

You must appreciate that tournament power cannot be switched on regardless of where you go casting. The tremendous speed of a 200 yard-plus cast demands a solid foundation. Just as a rocket needs a launching pad, a monster cast needs firm ground underfoot. You will not find that on sand and shingle where ground clearance of the tournament pendulum arc is limited: unless the beach is flat the sinker will rip out a furrow. Just the extra weight of terminal rig and bait destroy the fine balance you need for perfect co-ordination.

The power input of a 200 yard cast over grass is slightly different from that of a 'normal' fishing cast. There is no time to waste during a full-blooded competition throw. Full power goes into the rod as early as possible. If you drive into the swing as hard as you can, distances certainly will increase which is exactly right for a record cast. The same exaggerated technique in the surf, however, will merely explode the bait.

The consensus opinion on the 200 yard surf casts is this: if you use a tournament rod, competition casting style, big sinker, ultra-thin line and the smallest bait that qualifies for the name, you might just get there. The wind has to be blowing a gale from behind you; the beach must be level and solid underfoot. But even then, do not bet on it. 200 yards with baits soaks up the same power as 250 yards with sinker alone.

Just how far can anyone expect to cast from the beach or across a lake? There is no straight answer because, as any experienced angler appreciates, too much depends on conditions, bait size and tackle specification. 80–90 yards with a whole mackerel or mullet bait is about as much as anyone could reasonably expect whilst casting from the restrictions of a cliff ledge. If the beach is open and you can use compact baits and a powerful style, 160 yards is still exceptionally good going and the very best surf men would not expect more than 175 yards.

Sometimes it's necessary to cast to an exact spot on the seabed. Bass feed in the hot water outlet of Sizewell Power Station on the Suffolk coast. It's a 140 yard cast at high tide. Poor casters don't catch bass here.

10

Less experienced casters lose heart when they hear these figures tossed into the argument. 'If the best casters can't get more than 160 yards', they say, 'what chance do we have? Maybe our present 80 yards isn't so bad after all.'

There is a myth about distance casting. Half as much power on top of that required to reach 100 yards does not result in 150 yards. Doubling initial effort will not produce 200 yards. If it worked that way everyone would fish at 200 yards and tournament records might exceed one mile!

There is a purely scientific method to explain the relationship between casting and effort but I prefer the alternative explanaition which admittedly is a down to earth simplification with technical details reduced to a minimum. The figures are not related directly to pure physics but instead reflect the feeling of power flow I sense when I am casting a surf rod.

Suppose I cast a sinker alone, without baits and terminal rig to reduce distances. 100 yards absorbs 1 Unit of power. 2 Units of power on the next cast increase distance to 150 yards. 3 Units produce 175 yards. You see, the farther you cast the less yards are achieved for the boost in effort.

Progress is smooth enough up to 175 yards but after that you work hard for very little measurable improvement, for at 200 yards, which swallows six times as much effort as 100 yards, the law of diminishing returns bites deep. The extra paces which take you out to 210 yards devour another 3 Units—a 50 per cent premium for a distance increase which, were it applicable to fishing, would make little or no difference to catch rate anyway.

Even in simple terms, the explanation is complicated and concerns an array of factors which interplay every time you cast, but the underlying fact is that many pressures increase as square, cubic or quadratic functions. Double the speed of the sinker as it leaves the rod, and forces holding it back may increase by four, eight or sixteen times. In practical terms, then, your casting distance builds up to a point where it becomes difficlut to wring another yard from the tackle. A slight improvement demands a vast amount of work. I call that point the Distance Barrier.

Cutting line and reel drag to a minimum pushes the barrier back. Taking away line altogether dramatically increases range which is why a cracked-off weight flys so far. In contrast, every time you raise line diameter and consequently must use a larger reel, the Distance Barrier creeps towards you. Problems break into full gallop when you attach even one small baited hook.

Long-casting surf anglers know that casts of

Dick Broomer of Sea Angler Magazine's casting school puts a beach fisherman through the basic mechanics of long range casting. A coach is the short-cut to success.

more than 150 yards with baits impose tremendous demands on man and tackle. You must have a strong rod, free-running reel, split second timing and absolute mastery of casting technique. The outfit usually owes more to casting than to practical fishing; it is heavy and insensitive and out of keeping with bite detection, fishing handling and general precision. Surf fishing is more an assault course than a day's enjoyment and, there is always the spectre of backlash and burned thumbs unless every cast is perfect; and there is also the additional problem that your baits will not stay on the hook.

Set your distance sights just 20 yards lower and return to a better effort/result ratio. Use ordinary fishing tackle which makes for better bite detection—it is more fun when you hook a fish, and exerts less physical strain on you during a prolonged spell on the beach. For these benefits alone it is worth considering 130 yards as a practical target for surf work, or indeed for long range lake and dam fishing as well. Do not bite off more than you can chew. Master the basics, achieve your first 130, then weigh up the pros and cons of learning to cast even farther. The majority of fishermen do not consider the effort worth their while. Having learned to cast a long way—and make no mistake, 130 yards with baits is an impressive performance—they turn their full attention to catching more fish.

I use separate tackle for normal fishing and

ultra-long casting. The fishing outfit has a built-in performance ceiling. I see no reason to destroy my fishing for the sake of a few more yards which are almost surely denied to me in all but exceptional conditions. I go fishing to catch fish rather than to cast as far as possible and I believe that most surf men share the same philosophy. Only on rare occasions will I step up to the most powerful casting tackle in my collection.

Tournament casting is interesting and immensely useful is assessing tackle and casting methods, but that is about as far as it goes. Casting a plain sinker over grass is rewarding, and can be a great ego-trip as well, but I suggest you leave your casting fantasies and over-powered tournament tackle at home when you want to catch fish. It is more enjoyable that way, and in reality your baits will not fall far behind those of your neighbour who is busting a gut to outdo everyone else.

Once you realise that there is a distance trap which affects all casters no matter how good they are, long-range casting assumes the right perspective. To refer back to the point about 80 yards being pretty good, we can see now that it really is unacceptably low. Anyone of normal physique who practices a sound style must boost his distances quite appreciably before running up against the Distance Barrier. Only beyond 130 yards in general fishing conditions will the struggle begin. If you are having to work hard now to top 100 yards, it could be because your technique and tackle are wrong; but more often than not it will be because of your technique alone.

Distances on the beach are hard to assess. What looks like 120 yards may be just 80 yards. Do not fool yourself about your true ability. There is a bitter taste in finding out that your casting needs improvement, but you have to be realistic. Go out to a field or a stretch of dry sandy beach and measure half a dozen of your normal casts. Pace them out—a BIG step is a yard. Now pace out 150 yards from the casting point. There is the target to aim for when you cast without baits to hold back the sinker. Looks a long way, doesn't it? Whoever reckoned that 150 yards is a mediocre performance obviously does not live down here with the rest of us mortals. Truly, in real life 150 yards is a very long way to throw a fishing line and those 250 yard-plus tournament casts do not detract from it one inch. The good news is that YOU can send out cast after cast at least 150 yards on ordinary fishing tackle.

On the other hand, pressures on our sport from pollution and commercial fishing force us to extend horizons. Good distances today may be too short to catch fish in ten years time. With that in mind, dedicated shore fishermen have started work on advanced tackle and techniques which add many yards to everyday beach distances. The 200 mark is still safe from exploitation but a handful of pioneering casters are looking towards 175 yards as a practical range in surf. Their methods—the full tournament pendulum casts especially—and tackle developed for both fishing and competition casting are so intriguing that I have referred to them in several sections of the book. Bear in mind, though, that you must learn to walk before you run; either that or you will need the kind of Band Aid that heals shattered confidence and empty bank accounts.

The Foundations of Good Casting

SELF CONFIDENCE

Right now, you may not be able to cast more than 80 yards. The idea of casting farther interests you; or perhaps your local fishing has changed considerably, forcing you and other anglers to change tactics. You can see that better casters are now picking up fish while you cast all day for little or nothing.

Perhaps you have already tried to cast farther, but without success. It looks so easy when the experts do it. You invested in the finest tackle, but those long casts still elude you. Nothing seems to work; long hours of practice are nothing less than sheer frustration, nothing more than miles of backlashed line and burned thumb.

Or maybe you have improved from 80 yards to a steady 120 yards over grass. Catches are better as well, but something is still missing. If only you could find an extra 30 yards from somewhere. Perhaps you would like to switch to the pendulum style too? Why, even the kids do it these days! The trouble is, you cannot seem to control the swing or the sinker hits the beach every cast.

Self-doubt, misconception and sometimes sheer jealousy prevent potentially good casters from escaping the lower ranks of surf men. They love the idea of casting a long way. Money is no problem: they will happily pay whatever it takes. Time? Well, nobody has too much of that, but keen anglers are willing to find the two or three hours a week it takes to learn a more efficient style. Five out of ten never achieve their target—which for most fishermen is round 150 yards—because when it comes to the crunch they do not really believe in themselves. Even men who are halfway there may give up because they too do not believe they are cut out for really big distances.

YOU can cast 150 yards at least. But you must believe you can do it. It is no good pussyfooting around. Take this casting challenge by the throat and find out just how far you can go. I am not going to kid you into thinking that you (or anyone else picked at random from a million other anglers) are likely to end up World Champion. But I can tell you for certain that unless you suffer some catastrophic physical disability or are numbered among the tiny minority who are just plain dumb and unco-ordinated, you can put out 150 yard casts just as easily as any good caster does.

Physically, it is no harder than riding a bike around the block. If you can figure out how to drive a car, you have more than enough brain and muscular co-ordination to toss a sinker with a surf outfit. What you lack right now is the self confidence to go out and do it.

Confidence is a mixture of believing in your own ability, and knowing what to do. Most fishermen do not know how to cast. They have never thought about it. Casting is just something one does. They copy someone else, learn from Dad, or just pick up a rod and do what comes naturally. Inevitably when they try to cast farther—by doing the same thing harder, or with a different rod and reel—nothing happens and they either forget the whole thing or dream up a neat excuse: 'Those top surf fishermen obviously have some secret formula; they're natural athletes; they're just lucky.' Or maybe 'The rod companies give them special tackle.'

Forget all that. Clear your mind forever about exotic equipment, super strength, years of practice, good luck and talent. None of them has much bearing on long-distance surfcasting. Of course, the naturally adept, physically fit caster will beat you in developing a 150 yard cast. He will probably go on to 200 yards if he works. But because he gets there first, it does not mean you cannot catch up. He may not even know why he does so well—many excellent casters really do not understand much about technique in general or their own in particular.

Natural ability being the sole difference between good and bad casters is an exact parallel to

Two months of occasional field practice adds many yards to the cast. This fisherman raised his distances from 50 yards to 175 yards in just ten weeks.

the theory that enough monkeys bashing type-writers at random would eventually reproduce the works of Shakespeare. It is a neat concept, but does not make sense logically or statistically. Both ideas were dreamed up by frustrated casters or writers who could not come to terms with their own shortcomings.

If you are an 80 yards man, who wants to cast farther, has tried, but cannot manage, I will tell you why you fail. YOU DO NOT KNOW WHAT TO DO. That is all there is to it. It is nothing to

worry about, it does not mean you are stupid, nor will it stop you learning, but it is a statement of fact, since if you DID know what to do, and were then able to put the knowledge into practice, you would be throwing 120 yards at least. It is actually more difficult to keep distances down than to build them up. (I bet you do not believe that one, but you will before long!)

I will bet something else too: you opened this book in the hope of suddenly discovering the secret of casting—just a few words with power to transform you into a super-caster. All right, here they are: THE SECRET OF CASTING IS TO MAKE THE ROD DO THE WORK. That is the single irreplaceable feature of all good casts. Learn to make the rod operate efficiently, and you cannot fail to produce acceptable distances whatever your individual style turns out to be. Where do you find the necessary confidence? You do not. It will find you at the moment you first feel the rod working between your hands.

MAKING A ROD WORK

A fishing rod cannot 'work' in the accepted sense. Without your help it just lies there, inert, unbending, incapable of casting a sinker one inch. When we say that a rod works, we really mean that the muscular speed and strength we put in during the cast is efficiently channelled to the blank and onward to the sinker.

Whatever the strict dictionary definition of work may be, a good rod, cast properly, feels entirely different to one cast by the traditional overhead thump, which is the basic style of millions of untrained anglers. There is no easy way to describe the difference in feel between a 'working' rod and one cast traditionally, but an analogy may help:—

Loop a 3 inch diameter rubber band over your thumb. Draw your hands slowly apart. The band begins by stretching easily, then stiffens up, and finally loses all elasticity. Continue pulling and you will break it. There are three fairly distinct stages then: preliminary extension requiring little effort; mid-stage stretch accompanied by a definite and continually increasing resistance; and the final lock-up where, either you stop pulling or, the rubber snaps. Looking at it subjectively, you will find that the band feels sloppy, springy and then solid. The way in which a fishing rod responds to casting power is almost an exact copy of the band's reaction to thumb pressure.

The rubber strip obviously is not 'working' at all in the first stage of stretching. You can move your thumbs apart as quickly as you like, but the tension between them does not increase because a rubber band in its early stages of extension is incapable of transferring pressure. It does not matter how much force you use either, for as long as the band remains sloppy and rubbery it must act as a shock absorber.

Now, move on to the mid-stage. Here you can feel more tension between your thumbs. Moving your hands rapidly to and fro in this area produces a sensation that the band is 'working', or in other words, acting as a strong spring that resists thumb pressure. Notice that your thumbs seem to be pulling against themselves as well.

However, if you pull the band wide apart, slackness and even elasticity disappear and you can feel the band actually lock solid. It might just as well be a piece of rope. All you can feel is a direct pull. Pull harder and either the band snaps or you get tired. You cannot pull at maximum power unless the band is 'locked' at the end of its elastic limit. Power and speed applied beforehand are merely wasted—the band just absorbs them and elongates.

YOU CANNOT CAST A ROD THAT IS NOT LOCKED. Like a rubber band, every blank starts out with a sloppy shock-absorber action, stiffens up in the mid-compression zone, then locks. The old-style overhead cast applies power and speed too early, so that the blank merely sponges them up and prevents direct transfer of your power to the sinker. The pendulum cast and all other efficient styles extends the casting arc so that the blank is compressed close to lock-up point BEFORE main body power is applied. You feel the rod compress—just as you feel that band stretch—THEN you pour in the power . . . which flows directly to the sinker. On release, the powerful springiness of the blank adds a final flick of acceleration to the sinker and also smooths the flow of line from the reel, hence the lack of backlash on a free-running multiplier.

Now, why does good casting look so relaxed and easy? Simply because a small amount of body power applied to a locked-up blank produces far more sinker speed than ten times as much thrashed into an unlocked rod. The earlier in the cast you apply full power, and the shorter the arc you use, the more of the effort is sponged up by the shock-absorber stage. That is why overhead casters work so hard for so little. Why does the multiplier overrun? That absorbed power has to go somewhere. The rod jerks so badly that line surges off the spool—not too much problem if the sinker is whistling into the air at top speed, taking up the slack line. But it is not, so all those loose coils wrap around each other in a massive bird's nest.

If you blend these observations with the description of zoned action rods, you will see why the design evolved and how neatly it slots into the new casting techniques. Old-fashioned slow taper rods are sloppy, weak rubber bands that never do lock up. Pendulum zoned-action blanks move easily and positively through the three stages, lock up easily and do not have to be 'stretched' half a mile before anything starts to happen.

1 *Ready to go. Sinker hanging near blank, body coiled like a spring.*

2 *Pendulum outswing begins.*

5 *Body fully uncoiled. Weight has transferred to left leg. Rod has just passed the forward limit of the left hand, which is starting to pull down to the rib cage.*

6 *Maximum power generated by the arm punch-pull drives the sinker upward into its flight path.*

3 *Inswing complete. Head turns immediately the sinker pause is felt.*

4 *Body starts to unwind. Rod is pulled forward and blank compression begins.*

7 *Line release point – the rod flicks straight.*

8 *Follow through.*

The Basic Techniques of Casting

BASIC CASTING EXERCISES

Pendulum casts are assembled around four stages of body and rod power. These are:

1. The pendulum swing which positions the sinker correctly relative to the rod and to the caster.
2. A sweeping turn of the body which compresses the rod almost to lock-up point.
3. A full-power javelin-like pull from shoulders and body which, using the leverage of the rigid butt and locked tip, accelerate the sinker powerfully into stage 4.
4. The final punch and pull of the the arms that flick the rod over and hurl the sinker high into the air.

The best way to learn them is in reverse, starting with the flick.

Arm action

Anglers use all kinds of bowling actions, body gyrations and wrist power to flick the rod over at the end of the cast. The only satisfactory technique is a co-ordinated punch and pull with full shoulder weight behind them. The right hand punches the butt upward and forward. The left hand pulls the butt cap down to the lower left side of the rib cage. Both hands act together, with equal power. Anglers who cling to the old notion that using the left hand spells disaster with a multiplier reel should review their ideas because if anything, the left hand action is the more important.

Let us put together a simple exercise for making the arms work correctly. At the same time you will also learn a little of how a rod should feel in mid-cast. We shall not reach full lock-up at this stage, but the system generates enough useful power to bypass initial blank flexibility. In zoned-action terms, you make Zone B work. Expect to cast about 90 yards with standard 5 ounce surf tackle, which is the right equipment for mastering all these exercises. (Use a zoned-action rod, well filled fixed spool or tuned multiplier loaded with 0·35–0·40 mm main line, and a strong shock leader)

Laying out the cast

Draw a line on the beach in the direction you aim to cast. Position your left toe six inches back from the line and your right toe on the mark. Angle your feet slightly towards the casting direction. Suspend the sinker on a 3–4 foot drop, and set the reel ready to cast. Toss the sinker on to the beach directly back from the marked line. Look at the photograph and check these points: that the rod tip is almost touching the beach; that the left hand is high with the elbow raised; that the right hand is straight; and that the leader between rod tip and sinker is taut. This is your starting point. Analyse it carefully because it is to be the foundation for a lot of important work.

1 *Refer to the layout diagram. Set out the tackle with the sinker and leader laid on the beach. Rod tip is low; left elbow is set high. The right arm is comfortably extended in line with the rod.*

18

2 Turn your head and look into the sky. Pull the rod through, javelin throwing fashion, until the left hand reaches its forward and upward limit.

3 Punch and pull the butt so that the rod tip flicks over. Line release will be naturally timed.

4 *Hold the follow through position while the rod reacts to release. Maintain position until the sinker hits the water.*

Settle comfortably into position and turn your head and look high in the air—about 40 degrees elevation—and slightly to the right of casting direction. Now, pull the rod forward ALONG ITS LENGTH, in JAVELIN STYLE, until your left hand is high and well forward, and the right arm doubles up ready to punch. Do not put in any real power. Do not try to lift the sinker off the ground. Just move positively and smoothly and keep your eye on the aerial aiming spot.

As your left arm reaches maximum elevation and extension along the javelin line, the right hand will automatically have bent and moved in closer to your chest. At the precise moment this happens, PUNCH upwards with the right arm, PULL downwards with the left. The right hand should finish at full extension, pushing up towards the aerial mark; the left hand will be close to the bottom of the rib cage. The result of this push-pull action is a firm, powerful but smooth flick over of rod tip, at which stage you release the line. You will find that release takes place automatically. Do not force it . . . just let it happen. The sinker flies off, and you do nothing until it hits the sea. Then stop the reel.

The important point is that the transition from javelin pull to arm action is not a one-two movement with a gap in between. The two should blend together with no perceptible hesitation, no sudden acceleration and no loss of confidence. Just practise this simple exercise until it feels right. Aim for good direction and height. Forget all about distance as that will come later. Feel the butt starting to work between your hands and sense the controlled springiness of the blank. You are actually using a much bigger rod arc than you probably suspect. Laying the weight on the beach overrides most weaknesses of the overhead style and its stunted rod action.

Adding extra body power and casting arc
Your arms have a relatively short operating zone, and they are nowhere near as strong as leg, back and shoulder muscles. You cannot generate a massive amount of speed and power on that final punch-pull flick even if you were to try, for it would be wasted due to blank's failure to lock. The road to longer casts lies in another direction: that of using your body, and extending the total arc of the cast. Do that by re-thinking the start of the previous casting exercise. Now let us add the power necessary to take the distances up to 130 yards or more, again, with no sense of physical strain, no backlashes, no self-doubt.

The diagram is a plan view of the cast's layout. We have been working on rod and sinker alignment 'A'. Now it is time to investigate the extra power available in the shaded area 'B'–'C'. Rod tip and sinker lay-out move clockwise from 'A', and as they progress into the new region you will notice that the sinker shifts around relatively farther than the rod tip, thus altering the leader angle. This is not strictly necessary but will help smooth the cast later on when you increase speed and acceleration.

There are two ways to position yourself and the sinker/rod tip. First—and most common—is to lay out the tackle, then set your feet. Learn to work the other way around: pick out your aerial target, align your feet, then SWIVEL AROUND at the waist and shoulders to drop the sinker to the beach. This may seem an academic point, but it is actually crucial to the whole cast.

By working from the sinker position, you do not feel anything happening to your waist, leg and back muscles. The cast tends to be too much overhead, bypasses the body muscles and reduces the arc. But if you set your feet and aiming mark, then deliberately swivel around from hips, knees and shoulders to drop the sinker on the beach, your body coils like a spring . . . and more important you can feel it doing so. Run a few tests each way and see how much more positive the second technique really is. Do not bite off too much arc to start with—lay the sinker somewhere in the middle of the shaded area.

Check the photograph. Note that the right and left arms are relaxed but straight, holding the rod butt comfortably away from the chest. All the body weight is on the right leg, which is bent at the knee. The whole upper body is coiled and ready to unwind; the rod tip is low. In all, the starting position is similar to the body rotation of discus throwing.

The cast itself is very easy; it is so easy that you might be tricked into over-analysing the movements. All you do is turn your head to face the aerial target (yes, it is going to make your neck stiff the first few times) and uncoil your body through into the javelin-like pull and arm action used in the preliminary exercise. Do not flick the rod too soon, or you will end up with a sideswipe which misses out on control and power. If you get your head right round, then uncoil your body like a spiral spring, the rod seems to follow you rather than move around at exactly the same time—you will sense it coming from somewhere behind your right shoulder. Pull it through, javelin-style and flick the butt over. That is all there is to it.

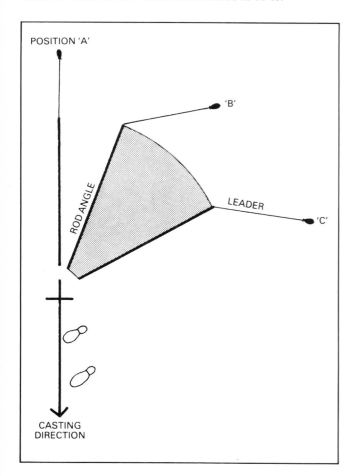

POSITION 'A'

'B'

ROD ANGLE

LEADER

'C'

CASTING
DIRECTION

Spend plenty of time on this exercise, which is a good cast in its own right and quite capable of exceeding 175 yards. Experiment with various sinker drops and lay-out angles. See what happens when you reduce or increase the body rotation; feel the effect of transferring body weight from the right to the left leg as the cast progresses.

These two exercises are the foundation of good casting. After a couple of weeks practising the second technique with its extended power arc, you will be casting at least 110 yards easily and without backlash. Keep working, add power and speed, and you will top 130 yards. Then you can switch to the pendulum style, which in its simplest form is the same cast prefaced with a sinker swing rather than a ground lay-out. But most important—far more useful than pure distance right now—learn to control the cast. Aim for height, consistency and accuracy and at the same time get the feel of the rod working.

When you unwind your body, you will feel the blank start to bend smoothly. As the rod drives forward from behind your right shoulder and into the javelin-pull, the butt stiffens between your hands and the whole rod seems to tense up. That is the effect of body power flowing into the blank and locking down sections 'A' and 'B' of the zoned construction. A fraction of a second later, just as the arms take over, the whole rod seems to lock solid . . . and of course that means you punch and pull against the full rigidity of the butt section. It is a great sensation which guarantees excellent results. In fact if you do produce lock-up and solid leverage, the cast cannot go much under 130 yards, and the chances of a well tuned multiplier backlashing are minimal.

You have now learned to make a rod 'work' which is 90 per cent of good surfcasting technique.

Developing the off-ground cast

Extend the body rotation and rod arc until the sinker pulls around through 270 degrees or more, boost sinker speed with a long rod, and you have the South African style, the most powerful off-ground cast of them all, easily capable of hurling a 5 ounce sinker over 200 yards. If you fish clean, flat beaches where you can stand back from the water to cast, there is no overriding obligation to learn the pendulum cast. Just work through the original two exercises, and then build up to a full South African lay-out. When real power develops, switch to at least 12·5 feet of rod. This cast is slower than the pendulum but very powerful. In order to reap the benefit of the extra leverage, most South African experts prefer 13–13·5 foot surf rods.

1 Sinker and rod laid out. Left hand at shoulder level, right hand extended. The cast is ready to begin.

2 Turn your head and look upward toward the aerial aiming mark. Pull the rod forward javelin-throwing fashion. The left hand rises, the right begins to double up comfortably close to the chest.

3 Continue the direct javelin pull until the left hand drives to its foward limit. Notice that the rod hasn't swung around yet – the butt cap still points into the sky.

Action

4 The arm action begins. Left hand pulls down while *AT THE SAME TIME* the right hand punches upward.

5 The punch-pull continues, smoothly yet ever faster as the tip flicks over toward release point.

6 The punch-pull is complete. Line runs from the reel. You naturally follow through until the right hand is fully extended and the left stops close to the bottom left of the rib cage.

Body Rotation

1 *Refer to the layout diagram. The sinker and leader are at position 'B'. Note that the body is positively coiled—rather like a spiral spring.*

2 *The cast begins as usual with the head turning. This time, the forward and upward pull of the left hand and rod handle is accompanied by a powerful unwinding of the body.*

The Key to

3 The longer rod and sinker arc, extra power from the body's uncoiling action, plus even more power drawn from the transfer of body weight from the right leg to the left to produce far more casting speed, which is felt as a positive 'tightening' in the butt as the left hand reaches its upward limit.

4 The cast ends as normal with a smooth, powerful punch and pull of the arms. Don't forget to hold the follow through position.

Better Distances

Casting with the Pendulum Swing

Off-ground casts are of limited value in beach fishing and almost useless from lake and riverside. Undergrowth, weeds, boulders or swirling water prevent a neat lay-out and clean lift off. Yet good results depend on maintaining that long arc of movement that pre-loads the blanks. The pendulum swing overcomes all the drawbacks of the off-ground casts and also adds a little more speed and power. However, you should regard the pendulum swing primarily as the means of positioning the sinker, not as a power source.

The style is versatile and thoroughly practical, and overcomes the limitations of the cast already developed by the previous two exercises. You already have sufficient power and control to cast 150 yards at least. All the pendulum swing does is release that expertise for all-round fishing. The main power stroke and loading pattern of the new cast remains the same; all we do is to substitute a simple pendulum swing for the ground lay-out.

The new Sinker Position

Control of the pendulum is easier if you understand exactly what you are trying to achieve by swinging the sinker. The speed and momentum of the lead itself are secondary at this stage. Concentrate on sinker position and leader angle relative to the rod. Get them right, and the sinker itself automatically produces the inertia necessary to make the latter part of the cast flow smoothly and powerfully.

Set yourself up as if for the full off-ground cast with its extended casting arc. Lay out the sinker and leader as before. Make sure your body is fully coiled and ready to sweep the sinker into the air. Do not cast but imagine that instead of lying on the beach, the sinker is hovering in mid air, just out of sight, above and to the right of your head. Just visualise how it would sweep down to follow the sinker as you uncoil your body and pull the rod through to the final punch and pull. That is all there is to a pendulum cast . . . so let us make it happen. But first, note the exact position of the rod tip in the off-ground cast position. Do not

guess at it but lay out a cast and then mark the spot with a handkerchief or coin. It is an essential reference point for the pendulum swing.

Re-adjusting the leader drop

Experiments during the preliminary exercises probably suggested a sinker drop of 5–7 feet between the tip and the sinker. This is about the right length of leader for most casters using an 11·5 foot surf rod, but it will not do for pendulum casting. Logically, you would conclude that the sinker must be swung on the shortest possible drop to avoid hitting the beach during the second half of the cast. Actually, the drop must be extended to permit adequate ground clearance. Most 11·5 foot pendulum rods work well with about 8 feet of free leader; and if in doubt, you are better off lengthening the drop rather than cutting back. Good casters always use very long drops on powerful rods, even with a standard length surf rod the working pendulum drop might be 9 or 10 feet. Some casters use a drop longer than the rod itself. To start, though, practise with 8 feet.

Producing a clean, smooth pendulum swing

Stand in your usual position on the casting line, coil your body around and down as if you were going to cast with the sinker on the beach, but this time hold the rod vertically in front of your face at a comfortable arm's length. The sinker, on the full 8 foot drop this time, will hang parallel to the blank. It may help later in the cast if you now adjust the rod position so that the reel is slightly above eye level.

If you have set yourself up exactly as before, except for rod grip and blank angle, the mark on the beach indicating the previous rod tip position will now appear slightly to the right of the vertical rod as you sight through. If it does not, swivel the whole upper body/rod unit right or left until it is correct. Do not move your arms and rod alone. Make a determined effort to rotate at the waist. Now you are ready to start the pendulum.

1 *The full extent of the outward swing should carry the sinker above eye level.*

2 *The inswing takes the sinker high behind the caster's head. The main cast begins when you feel the distinct pause in the pendulum action.*

PUSH the right hand firmly away from you, directly towards the mark on the beach. Move smoothly and quickly—but do not jerk—and you will generate enough force to lift the sinker well away from the rod on an outward pendulum swing which rises to at least eye level. As the sinker reaches the peak of its arc and hovers, PUSH DOWN WITH YOUR LEFT HAND AND LEAVE THE RIGHT ARM OUT-STRETCHED. Even a small downward press on the rod butt sweeps the sinker powerfully through a complete pendulum arc which takes the leader close to the right hand side of the rod, up past your right shoulder and out of sight. At the peak of its inswing, which you do not need to watch, you will feel a definite loss of tension on the rod tip. This pause indicates that the sinker has stopped climbing and hovers in exactly the right position for casting. It is your signal to GO on the rest of the cast.

It is worth practising the pendulum swing before adding the second half of the cast. Get used to setting up the rod and body, see how the right and left hands operate, feel for that definite pause in the inswing. Above all, make sure you work to a pattern. Too many anglers swing the sinker haphazardly to and fro, at any old angle, any height, in the hope that it will eventually hit the right spot and pause. That system never works. Aim for one clean outswing controlled by the right hand, a single inswing powered by the left hand pushing down: then you are ready to cast. Should something go wrong, drop the sinker to the ground by lowering the rod tip and then set up and start the whole rhythm again. Consistency is the key to pendulum smoothness and control. If necessary FORCE yourself to do it right. Lessons learned now are worth a fortune later in your casting career.

Putting it all together
This time, make your full pendulum swing, and as the sinker rises to the limit of its inswing and YOU FEEL THE PAUSE, turn your head, imagine the rod falling into the starting position used in the ground-cast exercise, AND CAST EXACTLY AS YOU DID THEN. Feel your body uncoil to load the rod then pull the butt forward, javelin throwing style, until your arms are in the correct position to flick the rod over. Do not rush because there is all the time in the world to get that sinker around and into the sky. The full cast is actually quite slow, especially at the start of the power flow which guides the sinker down from its pendulum position.

That is all there is to it. Does it sound like an anticlimax? Good because that is exactly what a pendulum swing should be. Thousands of casters look for problems which simply do not exist. By positioning that sinker where you want it, relying on the pause to trigger the next stage, and then falling into the now subconscious flow of the off-ground cast you practised to perfection, you eliminate the problems that inevitably plague casters who try to learn the whole technique in one piece. Think simple thoughts and just DO it. Of course you will need to practise. Take it easy, first get the feel of it, then turn up the power. Distance takes care of itself if you concentrate on smooth, relaxed flow. As in the earlier casting exercises, learn to feel how the rod reacts and loads during the entire casting arc. Also, remember that it is a waste of time to put in the final surge of acceleration until you feel the rod has locked up.

PENDULUM CASTING WITH LIGHT TACKLE

Casting under 2 ounce sinkers, especially on light rods, follows the same principles as those necessary to hurl big surf weights. There is one small change in technique: you do not need so much lower body power because the sinker just does not require that much arc or speed to produce good results. Most adults can simply reach a little farther back into the cast by straightening their arms, then bring the rod through the javelin pull and final flick on arm muscles' power alone, or with the addition of a positive weight transfer from right to left foot, which itself adds a significant boost to any cast. Run a few tests to see just how much body rotation and uncoiling action can be incorporated into your light tackle style. Under 1 ounce is virtually all arm power, but do not forget to extend the arc, especially if you use a baitcaster reel. 2 ounces is about the limit for pure arm action; 3 ounces is usually a full-power surf casting swing but you may not need quite as much sinker drop as for the 4 ounce-plus weights.

THE FULL TOURNAMENT PENDULUM STYLE

In principle the tournament style is an extension of the normal pendulum cast used for surfcasting. More power is derived from an extended body rotation and exaggerated pendulum swing. Top competitors use the same full 270 degree body rotation favoured by the South Africans. The sinker drop on an 11·5 foot surf blank would be at least 9·5 feet, and probably almost as long as the entire rod. Power build-up is rapid, so that the rod fully locks as early as possible, leaving room for terrific acceleration and leverage throughout the remaining arc.

1 Begin by raising the rod slowly to vertical. The sinker hangs close to the blank. Make sure you know the outswing direction—see text for details.

2 PUSH the right hand away. A firm push outward will carry the sinker into its full upward arc.

3 Drive the sinker into the next phase of the pendulum arc with a firm PUSH with the left hand. Ideally, the right arm should remain straight, but you'll find it normally drifts backward a little. DO NOT deliberately PULL with the right hand—that would almost certainly result in loss of casting arc and reduced pendulum control. The sinker now climbs to its inswing limit.

Inevitably, theory does not reflect the practice, time and effort necessary to hit those 230 yard-plus distances, and no two casters of that standard cast exactly the same way. The pendulum cast, tournament style, is therefore an ideal which the individual caster interprets as best he can. Learning the technique is a slow, steady process of trial and error using the simple fishing pendulum cast as the launching pad for personal development. I do not believe anyone can tell you exactly how to excel with these advanced techniques because to start with, this level of skill is self generating. Almost by definition, the winning casts result from new ideas and greater physical and mental conditioning. A coach can certainly pick out obvious flaws and bring out the best in a caster, but when it comes to the crunch, everything depends on the man who holds the rod. The greatest asset a tournament caster can have is an open mind.

THE MAJOR FAULTS IN CASTING

Negative feedback is the biggest block in casting. Too many anglers overanalyse their tackle and casting style. Instead of making it simple—and casting really is simple—they make life unnecessarily difficult by looking for faults that do not exist. I believe that if you understand the object of the exercise, which is to make the rod work properly, you can soon develop your own casting style. An individual's style is always a variation on a theme, never a carbon copy. Provided the theme is sound, the results have to be pretty good. However, there are a few faults which arise all the time, often with anglers whose techniques are basically healthy. For whatever value they may be to you, here they are, but please do not *imagine* you have them . . . get someone to watch you cast. We are all our own worst—and most innacurate—critics.

Most poor results are directly attributable to your failing to make the rod work properly. 90 per cent of the casters I meet with, or coach, suffer from this elementary mistake. Unless it is corrected, they never do cast properly. The main reasons are (roughly in order of likelihood):

1. *Too much power applied too soon through too short an arc.* Basically, this means you are using an overhead cast that relies almost exclusively on arm action.

2. *Not waiting for the rod to lock before applying full power.* Even if the off-ground lay-out of pendulum swings are correct, you lose out by snatching at the cast too early. Start slowly, build up smoothly until you feel the rod lock, then hit it.

3. *Directing the cast along rather than upwards.* This is a subtle one. When you cast easily, without trying for sheer distance, the cast flies high and straight. Add extra speed to the cast, and you start hitting low left casts, which may overrun or burn your thumb. The main reason is misalignment of the power line with the necessary angle of elevation, and that is caused by a progressively lazier left arm. If the left elbow drops, the cast flies low left. Correct it by making a positive effort to turn your head early in the cast and LOOK UP toward the aerial aiming mark. Drive the full power of the cast up into the air. That is how you gain those extra yards.

4. *Cutting the corner on the pendulum* is a serious fault. Rather than fall back toward the original off-ground cast rod position immediately after the pendulum swing, some casters hold the rod too high, then cut the corner of the cast, so that it finishes as a directly overhead thrash, almost like a vertical slice with a double-handed broadsword. The results include low left casts and burned thumbs (so you will need to decide between this fault and Number 3), snapped leaders and, in extreme cases, literally twisting the rod blank apart. The solution is obvious: regain the full casting arc.

5. *Misaligned pendulum swings* ruin any chances of a good cast. The most common error is to swing the sinker through an arc that lies at right angles to the rod, rather than almost parallel. This is a nasty problem, and frequently the destruction of an otherwise perfect cast. It is particularly prevalent in casters who use more body rotation than they can handle. In the same category come overshort leader drops they are a real menace. If you lose the cast or hit the ground, lengthen the drop and slow down.

Power Flow

1 *The sinker is poised at the top of the pendulum inswing. When you feel the pause, turn your head and look at the aerial target. You should have the impression of leaving the rod behind you—somewhere behind your right shoulder.*

2 *Pull the rod through JAVELIN STYLE, as before, and allow the tip to drop towards the mark on the ground (refer to text). Don't force it down; let it go there naturally . . .*

3 *. . . and you'll find yourself back in virtually the same position used in the off-ground cast. Continue the normal pull forward until the left hand is fully forward.*

4 *Then punch and pull as before. Compare this sequence with that of the off-ground cast. Pick out the common factors, and you'll see that the pendulum is only a substitute for the initial beach layout of sinker and leader. The power flow is almost identical.*

Choosing a Rod for Pendulum Casting

Rods are everyone's favourite talking point. Hundreds of rods, blanks and fittings on the market offer surf and freshwater fishermen a bewildering choice. Yet the majority of rods are unsuitable for high-performance casting. Even in Britain, where the angling world is well versed in pendulum techniques and custom rod building, the average tackle shop stocks surf rods which are physically incapable of casting a long way. Most of them would snap or feel rubbery if hit hard with a pendulum-style swing.

The continuous stream of beginners and inexperienced anglers ensures that second-rate tackle eventually finds a home, usually with a man who had no initial idea of his poor investment. It is said that, in the British tackle trade especially, you can sell just about anything. Hundreds of uncaring, unknowledgeable dealers outsmart the angling public time after time.

Unless you know precisely what to look for in a distance casting rod or do-it-yourself kit, the odds are that you will end up with a pile of junk. However, this need not be the case, since good tackle costs no more than inferior tackle, and often is cheaper.

Specialist tackle shops all over the world offer excellent advice whether you aim to buy a ready-made rod or a set of parts. Leading dealers almost certainly offer a custom-building service—rods usually designed and finished to a standard far in excess of anything found in mass production. On the other hand, there are sharks in these waters as well.

Recommendation—product, manufacturuer and dealer—cannot be beaten. It pays in both time and money to search for a good supplier who understands your personal requirements. Some argue that it takes a good caster to know good tackle and it is no coincidence that the best shops are owned or staffed by anglers who spend as much time on the beach as behind the counter. Every tackle shop, wholesaler and manufactuer I have ever met who makes and stocks the best surf and general casting equipment has at least one man on the staff who speaks the right language.

The converse is also true: big, impersonal companies who produce and market second-rate equipment usually have nobody who really understands your problems. You get an answer all right, but it is obviously not born of experience or even of interest: 'Take it or leave it.'

Angling clubs, casting tournaments and fishing matches are an excellent source of basic information. If you want to know more about tackle, go there and ask. You will be surprised just how helpful other anglers can be. Most are quite happy to lend you their tackle for a few casts. Look out for manufacturer's demonstrations, magazine teach-ins (like the ambitious and highly acclaimed scheme run by Sea Angler magazine) and club lectures given by leading casters and fishermen. There is plenty of assistance available if you go and find it. Do not be afraid to write to columnists in the angling press or to consultants and field staff retained by the best manufacturers, but do remember to enclose a stamped addressed envelope for their reply.

Suppose you want to buy a new rod or kit right now. You do not know anyone who can lend you their tackle to try; local tackle shops are well stocked but not too helpful because chiefly there is nobody who really understands the difference between old and new-style casting tackle. A handful of simple tests applied to any blank or completed rod will eliminate trash and leave behind equipment which though perhaps not perfect, is at least capable of producing the right results. You do not risk spending good money on a soft, weak blank that is incapable of withstanding the power of a hard pendulum cast.

How to select a suitable blank for surfcasting
The tackle shop is filled with dozens of rods, both long and short, powerful and whippy, brightly finished and in kit form. All of them are labelled 'Surfcaster'. 'Take your pick', the dealer says. 'Carbon fibre rods are on the end of the line. Don't miss this week's special offer on Daiwa. I'll be in the back if you want me, but don't ask me about surf rods. Freshwater fishing's my scene.'

Custom-builders offer a fine range of casting rods for long-distance surfcasting. You can specify a blank action which exactly matches your physique and style.

Despite knowing little about surf rods, you can take some shortcuts. First, put all the carbon fibre rods to one side. Discard all those with carbon fibre tip sections. Glassfibre is a better choice for learning to cast and fish in the surf. Carbon (graphite) is actually superior in nearly every respect, but it is less tolerant of varying sinker weight and line test, and makes more demands on the angler, who must specify exactly which length, action and power of blank suits him and the way he fishes. Later on you may switch to a carbon rod. To begin with, ordinary 'E' glassfibre or, better still 'S' glassfibre, are just fine. They are versatile, virtually unbreakable, forgiving of error, and much cheaper than carbon fibre. The only exception is where the rod is made up of glassfibre tip and a carbonfibre butt. This is an excellent combination for any surf angler, experienced or beginner. The extra cost of a carbon butt is fully justified in terms of performance, weight saving and overall sensitivity. Fenwick Surf Sticks—in blank and rod version—are all made this way, and there is an optional carbonfibre butt now available for Conoflex and Carroll Zziplex blanks.

The majority of glassfibre blanks have either glassfibre or tubular aluminium butts, both adequate for surfcasting. Glassfibre will not corrode and usually imparts a little more 'feel' to the cast. Aluminium is the cheapest way to make a butt rigid and thus offers top-level casting performance (almost as high as a carbon fibre butt) at low cost. Drawbacks are lack of 'feel' during the build up of the pendulum cast, harshness and corrosion. Aluminium butts have a nasty habit of snapping in mid-cast because saltwater has eaten away the walls of the tube, but it is nothing that cannot be repaired with a new length of tube glued to the bottom of the rod. Most surf rods fitted with aluminium butts are very powerful and fast-actioned. Though not impossible for a beginner to master, they still present a few problems—mainly harshness and magnification of errors in style. When the choice falls between two equally good tip sections, one with a glass butt·the other of aluminium, choose the former. If necessary you can always upgrade the rod by cutting off the glassfibre and glueing on a piece of alloy.

Line up all the glass/carbon, all-glass and glass/aluminium rods and blanks. Now check length.

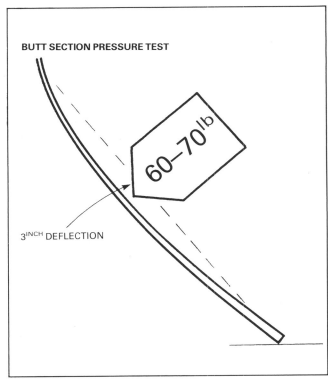

BUTT SECTION PRESSURE TEST

60–70^{lb}

3^{INCH} DEFLECTION

The butt pressure test—a simple method to determine the casting power of a beach rod.

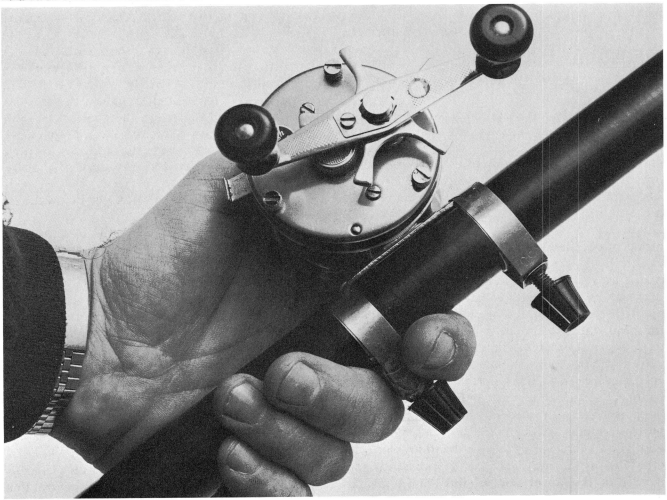

Plain parallel handles with hosepipe clips are excellent for multiplier reel casting. The adjusting screw is a handy trigger for extra security.

Over the years, 11·5 feet has become the standard length for surf rods balanced to cast 5 ounces of lead, pendulum style. A few inches on top does not make much difference, so you should discard from the collection all those over 12 feet long or under 11·25 feet. It is a great mistake to take on more rod than you can handle. Too short a rod lacks power and feel, and is more difficult to time.

Now we are left with a handful of rods and blanks that are of the right materials, and either ideal length or close to it. Let us assess the blank (i.e. the tip and handle complete). It does not matter if the rod is made up of two equal-length sections or as long tip (usually about 8 feet long) plus detachable butt. Consider the whole unit at this stage. Put each rod together. Support the centre of the blank with your left hand and rest the butt on the ground. Now push down on the blank midway between left hand and floor. A firm shove with your right hand—say 50–70 lbs pressure—should flex that part of the rod some 3 inches. Discard all rods that flex like longbows under this test because they lack sufficient backbone for 5 ounce surfcasting. Make a note of those with butts so stiff that you cannot bend them more than an inch or so, however do not rule them out at this point. Although they are a little too rigid, they are far better than a soft rod. The chances are that a handful of rods and blanks pass this test with flying colours and that one of them is probably right for you.

The simple butt-pressure test is designed for powerful surfcasting tackle rather than freshwater rods and blanks. It can be modified to give a reasonable idea of the potential performance of lightweight surf and freshwater blanks as well. The formula for surf rods is used to calculate a ratio between hand pressure and casting weight. Divide the pressure necessary to flex the rod 3 inches out of line, by the sinker weight you intend to use. In the case of the surf rod just described, the figure works out to be 12—that is, 60 pounds divided by 5 ounces (forget the pounds and ounces). The factor 12 represents a stiffness ratio for a rod which casts extremly well (though not to tournament standards), but is still very nice to fish with. It will not explode baits, is light and sensitive and forgives many casting mistakes. Use that same factor to calculate the pressure for a lighter blank. Suppose you want a rod to cast 2 ounces. The pressure factor stays at 12, but this time you multiply by 2 instead of 5 to get hand pressure. In other words, a 24 pound push applied to the middle of the lower half of the blank, just as before, should produce a 3 inch flex.

The factor 12 is close to perfect for a beginner. Avoid rods which produce a factor of 10 (50 pounds pressure with 5 ounces, 20 pounds with 2 ounces) because they are just a little too soft in the butt to accommodate a hard pendulum cast. Go as high as 15 (75 and 30 pounds pressure for a 3 inch flex) without worrying whether the butt is too stiff. Full-power tournament blanks for 5–6 ounces will not bend 3 inches with less than 100 pounds and some you just cannot bend that far anyway. These ultra-stiff butts are too critical for a beginner and may even be too stiff for good fishing. Although sloppiness in the butt is impossible to live with whatever kind of caster you are, the stiffest rods do not necessarily produce better distances in surf. You cannot exploit their full potential without drilling yourself into the sand or smashing off baits. So overall, a factor of 12–15 should suit 99 per cent of all casters who practice on surf, lake, dam or river.

The rod butt provides leverage and resilience to drive the mid-section of the blank. The mid-section in turn accelerates sinker and terminal rig. The final 18–24 inches of the blank immediately below the tip ring help control that flow of power and also link the main part of the rod to sinker and shock leader. You should think of the end of the rod as being a flexible joint. These three zones of the complete blank determine the performance of a rod and complement the arc and power flow of the pendulum cast. Zoned action is fully described in another chapter, so for the moment all you need to know is how to identify a rod of that kind. The butt pressure test identifies all rods with a suitable zoned butt action. Now turn your attention to tip zones.

Outside diameter of the blank just below the tip ring should be approximately ⅛ inch. ³/₁₆ inch is probably acceptable, but ¼ inch or more rules out that blank altogether. Traditional surf men, particularly those brought up with American-style surf rods, always have initial reservations about such a flimsy tip, but they should not worry about it for the rod is nowhere near as underpowered as it seems. Fine diameter makes casting easier and actually protects the tip of the rod from overload. You cannot cast properly, pendulum style, with a large diameter, hard tip.

If the butt is right, and the tip diameter measures up to specification, it is almost inevitable that the mid-section of the blank is of correct wall thickness, taper rate and power. With thin diameter of upper blank and stiffness of butt virtually dictating upper and lower limits of the centre, that section cannot be too far off the mark whatever the precise design might be. There are subtle differences between rods with identical tip diameters and butt pressures, but as far as learning to cast is concerned, the individual characteristics of such blanks count for little. Later on you will probably come to like one type more than the rest, but by then you will know exactly what to look for anyway.

All rods and blanks on your list are fundamentally sound as BLANKS go. Prices are likely to range between £25 and £90. Generally, you get what you pay for. Expensive tackle is better made and finished, and, if in rod form, has fittings and rings which will last a long time. An excellent rod is always a good investment. Even if you do not like it or soon outgrow it, secondhand value remains high. On the other hand, some would say that it makes more sense to buy a cheap but serviceable blank and build it for yourself. Another option, which I personally favour for anyone who does not want to go for a top-quality rod in the first place, is a cheap production rod. It is worth buying a good blank with poor rings, but only if the price is right. These days some of the better mass-production rods are actually cheaper than a bare blank. The Daiwa Fast Tip, for example, is well made and fitted with reasonably durable rings. It is worth buying for the blank alone, which offers plenty of casting power along with ease of handling and forgiveness of mistakes. The Fast Tip is the economy beachcaster by which all others are judged.

Mass produced beachcasters are a poor bunch on the whole mainly because they do not conform to the design and performance factors now regarded as essential for modern distance casting. Thus, there is an obvious gap in the market between the Fast Tip at the bottom and established thoroughbreds costing £150 or more.

Of the few middle ranking rods available, the Zziplex 2500 reigns supreme. Semi-carbon versions of the Conoflex Cod 5 or Cod 6 are worth considering, as are the softer blanks in the Century Formula range. All combine enhanced casting ability with vice-free handling and a wide power band.

Up-market Zziplex, Conoflex and Century surfcasting blanks range from specialist match rods to all-out tournament poles quite unsuited to everyday fishing. Length, stiffness and action must be carefully matched to the caster's individual physique and requirements. Mistakes can be very expensive, and at worst can destroy a caster's technique and confidence. For beginners who do not yet understand rod technology, they are better avoided regardless of their excellence.

All the blank jointing systems are satisfactory for routine beach casting. The Fenwick Feralite joint on this surf rod is particularly strong and reliable.

Handgrips spaced 30–32 inches apart encourage smooth, fast arm acceleration during the final flick of the cast.

Zoned-Action Rods for Pendulum Casting

Modern casting rods capable of working baits and lures efficiently, playing big fish and casting to maximum range using the pendulum style, are designed to compromise between casting and fishing characteristics. Anglers brought up on old-fashioned slow action surf and spinning tackle nurse sore fingers and thumbs after trying the new breed of surf tackle. Pick up one of those stiff butt/whippy tip blanks and you are in trouble if you cast traditionally with a direct overhead thump. Even tournament casters suffer: the speed of blank is alien and does not react to casts that excel with through action rods and Hatteras Heavers.

Blanks and rods orignally produced for surf fishing and tournament casting in Britain, and now available in America and Europe, certainly do appear fast and powerful. But if you adopt a pendulum cast with its long sinker drop of at least 8 feet between sinker and rod tip, the rod feels ultra-smooth, precise and downright easy to handle. It is not unusual for a surf or freshwater angler to add 50–100 feet to his previous best cast and sometimes within minutes of changing tackle and technique. What is the secret formula? How can an experienced surf man who cast traditional tackle for twenty years be beaten by a newcomer in his first season on the beach?

Some call it cheating. And if exploiting space-age materials, less critical timing and lower physical effort does add up to bending rules, there are thousands of fishermen happy to live with it. Those who reach elusive fish 130–150 yards out in the surf or around the margins of a dam certainly never complain.

Who cares if you do not need years of practice to handle a multiplier (conventional) reel? On the new rods you set your reel to run freely on its bearings, with just a pair of small brake blocks or a magnetic controller to tame the initial surge of acceleration. Cast as hard as you like; tie on the weight of sinker or lure that best suits you and the fishing. The cast stays the same. Only minor alterations are necessary in sinker drop, timing and power flow. More to the point, just a couple of rods, light and heavy, master an entire range of baits and lures from ultra-light to heavy-duty surf.

Good pendulum blanks incorporate three distinct action zones which are married together in a single blank and handle. There is a flexible tip, powerful and responsive centre, and a stiff butt. No matter what length and casting weight the rod may be, design still conforms to this zoned, programmed action.

Zoned action blanks cast further for less effort. The same action formula also operates to your advantage when you work a lure, set the rod in a sandspike to detect bites, drive in the hook and fight a heavy fish. The blank cushions errors and insures line against snapping to a degree impossible with old-style rods. You cast better, detect more bites, and beat heavier fish on lighter tackle. It all adds up to more enjoyable sport.

ZONED-ACTION IN CLOSE-UP

Let us examine the structure of a typical 11·5 ft pendulum rod for casting 3–8 ounces. The same theory applies to all weights of high-performance tackle—freshwater and ultra-light surf rods are variations on the theme.

Zone A: The flexible tip of the blank is roughly 18–24 inches long and extends down from the tip guide to blend with the next zone. Extreme tip diameter is usually ⅛ in 'E' and 'S' glassfibre. Internal taper of the blank is quite slow—say 80 thousandths of an inch per foot on a multi-taper mandrel.

Zone B: The power zone lies in the centre of the bank, starts at the 18 inch limit of the tip and covers the next 72 inches of the rod. On most surf rods you will not detect any surface clues that herald the switch from ZONE A to B. Cheaper rods do not change internal taper anyway. Here the tip is flexible because blank walls and diameter are particularly thin at that point. Only advanced manufacturers like Fenwick-Woodstream have the technical ability to shift taper rates on the mandrel, which is the best method of building up the zones. Today's carbon-reinforced straight taper blanks are of equally high performance.

The power zone always features a medium-fast or fast taper rate which develops strength and blank speed progressively but rapidly within the centre section of the blank. Here casting power is loaded, stored and released during a pendulum cast. You need plenty of material to withstand pressure so the blank is usually around 1 inch diameter at the lower end of this zone, and may be reinforced with graphite.

Zone C: The leverage unit, approximately 42 inches of graphite, aluminium alloy tube or thick-walled fibreglass completes the blank. The Power Unit may be spigotted to the upper section of the rod, permanently jointed, or made detachable by the Feralite process, as on Fenwick's Surf Stick range.

Compared to a traditional surf rod, the butt of a modern pendulum rod is very stiff indeed and virtually unbendable on a powerful 5–8 ounce surf blank. Long 'S' or 'E' glass tips (zones A and B combined) plus detachable butt or spigotted handle are an ideal balance between materials technology, strength and performance.

HOW THE ZONES OPERATE DURING A PENDULUM CAST

Zones work both independently and in unison from the initial pendulum swing of lure or sinker until moments after line is released. Let us stop the cast in stages and analyse power transfer.

Diagram 1: The preliminary outswing of the sinker on its leader drop should be slow but still hard enough to lift the sinker to at least eye level. Zones B and C form a solid foundation for the tip, Zone A, which flexes gently. Zoned action buffers a pendulum swing against slight mistakes in timing and direction and generally smooths the start of a cast. It is extremely difficult to control an extended pendulum swing on a stiff-tipped blank.

Diagram 2: A gentle push down with the left hand transmits enough tip speed through the butt and centre zones to flip the sinker into its backswing. Again, only Zone A flexes.

Diagram 3: As the caster's body begins to rotate, the sinker tries to maintain its position at the peak of the pendulum inswing. Its inertia draws Zone A into compression and then directs power down into Zone B. All you actually feel is a slight resistance between the handgrips—as if you were pulling the rod along its length, javelin style. As body rotation progresses and builds more power and speed into the cast, Zone B begins to work hard. The more you load it, the more it bends.

Diagram 4: Shoulders swing around to face almost squarely towards the sea. Muscle strength pours from legs, waist and back, and is channelled into Zone B by way of the upper tip. The harder the cast and the heavier a sinker and bait, the more Zone B is compressed and loaded. The tip zone, A, is actually bypassed and STRAIGHTENS TO FORM A LOOSE LINK BETWEEN THE LEADER AND THE CENTRE ZONE OF THE BLANK.

Now you feel stiffness and resilience between your hands. Having soaked up its full complement of bend and workload, the upper blank channels extra power and speed directly to the stiff butt. As you punch and pull with your arms you should notice that the rod feels 'locked'—is unable to bend any more and thus becomes a solid lever. Lock-up point is a critical factor in rod design and extends beyond surf tackle to boat, fly and fresh-water casting.

There is a paradox here. The sensation you feel during a good cast is of power being fed DOWN the rod, towards you. The tip loads, Zone B flexes and locks, then the butt stiffens between your hands. In fact, power is transmitted UP the rod, while inertia of the sinker provides an opposing force. It is important to understand that despite this clash with pure physics, that is how a rod should actually feel in mid cast. I stress the point because, during a bad cast, power really does seem to flow upwards from your hands all through the cast. It is an obscure phenomenon that good casters take for granted and poor performers never experience, and concerns the mechanics of making a rod 'work', an exercise described in the casting section of the book.

Diagram 5: At the precise moment of line release, the unyielding butt zone magnifies and directs the final power surge and acceleration of Zone B. The middle of the blank unleashes a massive propulsive force, but it is *smooth and controlled* and nothing like the haphazard response of a traditional surf rod. As Zone B flicks straight, Zone A recompresses slightly, adding a marginal boost to sinker speed, ironing out minor errors in the cast.

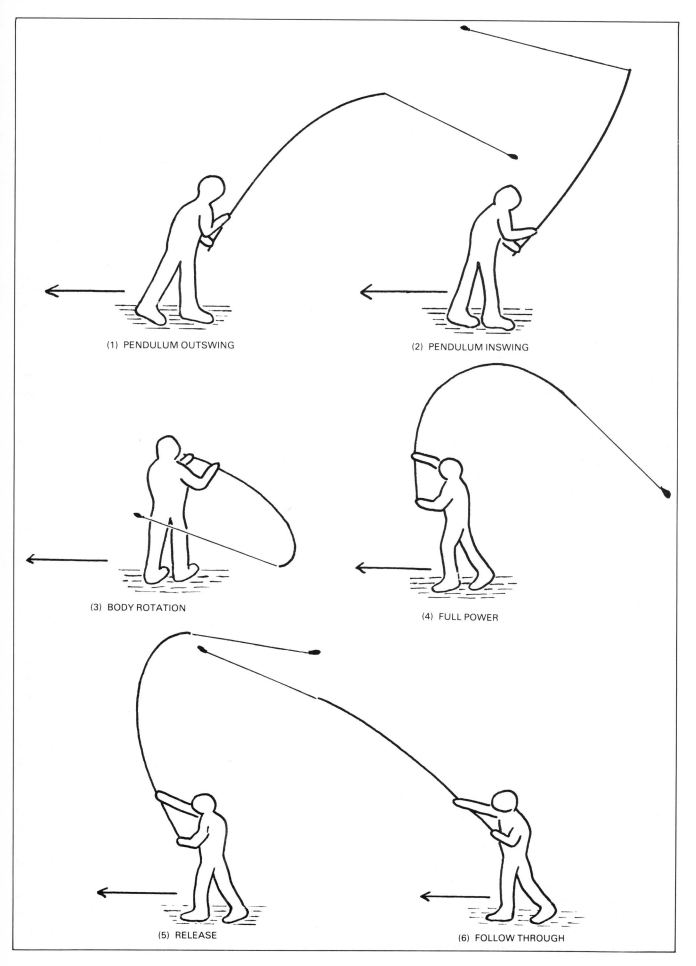

(1) PENDULUM OUTSWING

(2) PENDULUM INSWING

(3) BODY ROTATION

(4) FULL POWER

(5) RELEASE

(6) FOLLOW THROUGH

Diagram 6: Zones B and C are now relaxed, straight and virtually stationary. Zone A follows through to maintain smoothness and control, an important phase which helps eliminate backlash on a multiplier reel and eases the passage of leader knot through rings. The tip is so light and responsive that it straightens and stops dead. Heavy-tipped blanks oscillate for a long time which is a distinct hazard to multiplier control, and often the cause of leader knots wrapping around the rings.

Once you master a pendulum cast and have tuned your reel to the blank, you will discover that something like 30 per cent of the effort previously expended in casting an old-fashioned rod 80 yards now produces 120 yards or more. Modern blank action, along with full power drawn from legs, waist and shoulders, reduces the load on your arms by an almost unbelievable amount. It can be calculated that the reward for effort ratio of a zoned blank is vastly superior. About 45 per cent of the power intake of a Hatteras Heaver is wasted because of the rod's inherent mechanical limitations, further restricted by heavy control necessary to keep a multiplier from backlashing. Pendulum casting with a zoned blank transfers around 90 per cent of your muscle input to the sinker. Minimal reel control, and, if you like, lighter running line on the spool, sponge up only a fraction of the sinker's available kinetic energy. You cast farther, more easily and with full confidence.

THE FISHING QUALITIES OF ZONED ACTION BLANKS

Zoned-action blanks are equally good for working lures, detecting tiny bites at long range and for battling strong fish in heavy water. The same programmed sections of blank that smooth the cast and release full body power still operate when the bait is in the water but in reverse.

Zone A: The tip of the blank is so sensitive to line vibration that you feel the slightest bite. With the rod in a sandspike and line pulled tight between sinker and tip ring, Zone A flexes and remains compressed against the pull of wind and tide. Pre-stressed, the tip irons out wind and wave movement—which may signal false bites—and picks up tremors you would not notice on an ordinary rod.

Super-sensitive bite detection is not necessary all the time, but there are many occasions in surf and freshwater when a fish takes bait so gently you feel nothing. Those are the days you wind in to find bait gone. Maybe it really was crabs and shrimps . . . could be it was a sneaky cod or bass. Some of the biggest fish are hardest to detect: a 20 pound-plus cod in Britain's winter surf will sometimes flicker the rod tip just a couple of inches. On a zoned rod you can feel six inch flounders chew a bait 500 feet out in rough water. If anything, tip sensitivity is too high for beginners who snatch the rod at the slightest sign of life.

Zone B: The centre of the rod is progressively powerful and stiff. As you strike the fish, the bend of the rod gradually transfers from Zone A to B. The harder you and the fish work out, the more of B is brought into play. Lower sections of the rod start to work while the very tip is gradually bypassed.

Traditional heavy surf rods have a narrow power band. The blank does little until line tension is high. A pendulum rod responds to very small tip pressures, yet still has the backbone to haul on 25–40 lb test line when necessary. More 'feel' is transmitted down to the handle. The rod greatly improves response time of the reel's drag plates.

Wide power band and its built-in cushion mean you can afford to push yourself and the tackle to their limits without risking a snapped line. You can either kill fish quickly on heavy line or reduce breaking strain and go for pure sport, along with a significant increase in casting range.

Zone C: The rigid butt (rigid on a surf rod, that is—lighter rods do have more flexibility to accommodate lower line test and smaller casting weights) is a solid lever for you to work against. There is nothing more disconcerting than a butt which 'gives' under your hands when power is turned on. There is input to consider as well: a stiff, light handle, especially graphite, transmits every tremor and change in line pressure as they run down the line and through the blank. You sense the lure working through the water and can almost visualise a fish grate its teeth on the hooks. Monitoring line pressure during the fight is ten times more precise on a zoned rod. In all, the stiff butt adds up to enhanced control.

Zoned action rods—the popular questions

Why do these rods rip the skin off my thumb when I cast traditionally?
The blank is designed to load and release its power over a long, smooth arc. If you cast overhead-style, the blank part-loads then releases like lightning and you just cannot control it.

Why doesn't that flimsy tip snap off?
Zone A cannot overload enough to break off unless you abuse the rod. When it encounters

Zoned blanks won't operate with old-style casting methods. Pendulum cast and an exaggerated sinker drop are important—the drop is the MINIMUM for smooth results with 5 ounces of lead.

The tip section is extremely sensitive to bites. When line is pulled taut against the inertia of a grip-wired sinker, you can feel the smallest of fish at long distance.

A split second before line release: the powerful mid-section unleashes its force while the flexible tip buffers the cast from errors. The top 18 inches of blank reduce backlash on multipliers.

Powerful Zone B exerts full pressure on a heavy fish. A good zoned blank balanced for 5 ounce casting handles lines between 12 and 35 lb test.

41

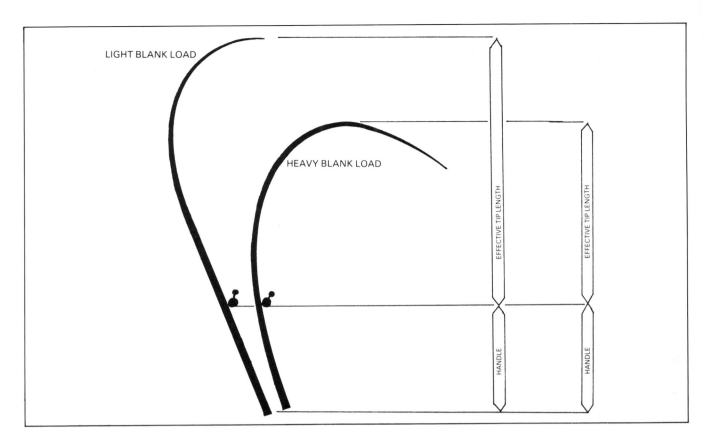

LIGHT BLANK LOAD

HEAVY BLANK LOAD

EFFECTIVE TIP LENGTH

EFFECTIVE TIP LENGTH

HANDLE

HANDLE

too much stress, whether from casting or fishing, the blank automatically shifts load from Zone A to B. It may look downwright cruel to pendulum cast 8 ounces and half a mackeral on a ⅛ inch diameter tip, but it is perfectly safe and easier than on a thick tip.

Why not cut off the tip anyway?
Zone A is a vital link between the main power-house of the rod, line and fish/sinker. Just 18 inches of flexible glassfibre blended to a progressive middle and butt make a vast difference to handling and performance. You notice enhanced smoothness and control, freedom from backlash and supreme bite detection. Zone A is an inbuilt computer which does a lot of the thinking for you.

How can the same blank handle such a wide sinker range—say, 3 to 8 ounces on a surf model?
Because it is many rods in one. The harder you cast and the greater the sinker load, the more you compress Zones A and B. Zone B is quickly bypassed, straightens out, then follows through during the main power stroke of a pendulum cast. You 'dial in' lower sections of rod and utilise the rigidity of butt for leverage.

In contrast, a light sinker is flicked away by the flexible tip and upper section of Zone B. The diagram shows how a pendulum rod com-pensates for light and heavy loads. You see how the rod effectively shortens as pressures and load increase? You cast 3 ounces on an effective 11·5 feet, 5 ounces on the lower 10 feet, 8 ounces on the bottom 8 feet, by which time Zone A and a small part of Zone B are bypassed. Given a constant distance between your hands, effective reduction in tip length raises mechanical advantage in your favour. You cast a heavy sinker as easily as a small one. Timing and speed of cast vary, but sensation of power flow is relatively unchanged between sinker weights.

By the same token, the blank exploits a wider range of line tests: say, 12–40 lb on a heavy-duty surf model. The harder you and the fish pull, the more the leverage ratio swings in your favour. Set the reel's drag to protect line, and you are unlikely to snap off even if the fish momentarily gets the better of you.

Which is better—multiplier or spinning (fixed spool) reel?
It makes no difference to a zoned action rod since timing the cast is the same for each reel. Multipliers require no special tuning, spool thumbing or over-tightening of bearing caps. You need never touch the spool from release to splash down. A zoned rod is a marvellous confidence builder for surf men who have always dreamed of mastering the multiplier reel but never could.

42

Rod Materials and Blank Design

Zoned action blanks offer the best casting performance along with good fishing characteristics. Glassfibre rods are perfectly adequate for most surf fishing and long-range freshwater applications. On the face of it, then, there is no need to look deeper into either materials or alternative designs of blanks. If you aim to learn pendulum technique, the zoned blank theory and the guide to choosing a suitable rod are everything you need to know about rod design. However, the more involved angler likes to understand carbon fibre, alternative actions and lengths of rods. New materials and specialised blanks really do help develop more advanced fishing methods, and they may offer significant improvements in distance with lightweight plugs and lures. Argument for lighter tackle grows stronger as quality of fishing generally deteriorates. To exploit 8 lb test nylon instead of standard 12–15 lb surf line, action and power of rod must be altered, otherwise the line will snap on almost every cast. At the moment you might not need a 13 foot surf rod. Next year, however, your casting could benefit and you may possibly want to enter distance tournaments, where the extra 15 yards provided by a longer blank could help you set new World Records.

GLASSFIBRE

As a material for rod building, glassfibre offers a good blend of performance, sensitivity and cost. The vast majority of surf and casting rods for weights over 2 ounces are still glassfibre despite the rapid advance of more exotic blanks in freshwater lure and fly fishing. Glassfibre in an easy material to manufacture, store and work. Simple mandrels produce a variety of actions, and to build in more power you can thicken the walls a little which is a cheap way to upgrade existing designs. A fairly high percentage of glassfibre is essential in your first casting rod, especially at the tip. The Daiwa Fast Tip is an excellent example of what can be achieved without resorting to carbonfibre – it casts almost 200 yards with ease. Ordinary 'E' glass rods will soon be obsolete because carbon-based reinforced plastics are growing cheaper. Already it has become standard practice to add a little carbonfibre to the cheapest of rods in order to boost performance, so in this respect ordinary glassfibre rods have no future. This is far from the case with 'S' glassfibre (also alled 'R' glass).

Yes, modern bottom and mid-market glassfibre rods are fairly primitive but any blank which passes the tip and hand pressure tests outlined elsewhere in the book will cast well enough for learning to cast pendulum style. But the blank is not as sensitive, lively and powerful as highest-grade glassfibre. With prices ranging upward of £20 for a blank or £30 for a built rod, you cannot really expect much more for your money. You may outgrow the rod, learn to hate its weight and bad balance, or curse it every time a ring breaks off, but you still learned to cast 150 yards or more and the investment paid off.

The economics of manufacturing rods and blanks is fast polarising the industry: mass-production in the Far East undercuts high labour costs in Europe and America and the West simply cannot compete at the cheaper end of the market. The result is that more and more glassfibre rods are imported. The bulk of them are mediocre—as far as long-casting is concerned—yet there are a few that pass tests outlined in the section 'Choosing a rod'.

Blank makers can still afford to pour realistic design and quality into ordinary 'E' glassfibre. Custom rod builders turn out reasonable surf rods. You can make up your own casting rod. It is in mass-production that standards are lower, and falling. The writing is on the wall: low-cast glassfibre rods for long-distance work are obsolescent, and blanks will follow.

'S' grade glassfibre is quite different from ordinary rod material. It is faster, lighter, more sensitive and of significantly better casting potential. In many respects it rivals carbonfibre for surf and heavy casting rods. Add its amazing toughness and lower price, and you have a material which presently outstrips carbon in the race towards the perfect all-round surf blank. The drawback is manufacturing technology: 'S' glassfibre does not give its best performance without advanced design, very careful manufacture and multi-tapered mandrels. Fenwick Woodstream are the only company to fully exploit theoretical advantages of 'S' glass for surf work and lighter freshwater distance. Surf Sticks are in a class of their own—the only zoned action, high-performance blanks and rods on the market.

CARBON FIBRE

This space-age material is even faster, lighter and better casting than 'S' glass. Specialised raw materials for the tackle industry are more advanced than cloth employed in the first carbonfibre rods, which were unreliable, to say the least. The remaining bugbear is price—very few surf men are prepared to invest in a blank which costs at least three times as much as good glass.

Actually, that is a blinkered view. Carbonfibre holds the key to the future of surf and general distance casting. It does cast farther for the same effort, handles lighter lines, enhances bite detection and weighs far less. In a word, carbonfibre is precise – to a degree impossible to achieve in glassfibre. BUT, that very precision imposes extra responsibilities on the angler. He too must be specific – must select a rod for a range of sinker weights and line tests, of exact action and length and for a particular style of casting. A 'normal' glass surf rod should handle 4–8 ounces of lead, 12–40 lb line, allow reasonable results with any efficient casting style, and be tolerant of an angler's exact length and action requirements. A top-grade carbon beach rod may cast 4-ounces on 10–12 lb line with a fishing pendulum cast. At 12 feet long, it would not suit a man whose physique is better matched to 11 feet. Parameters are strict; though of course it is possible to design a rod for virtually any combination of sinker weight, action, line test and style. Anglers who dabbled in carbonfibre with poor results usually chose inferior grade blanks and failed to narrow down the specifications. This material trades off superior performance against diminished versatility.

Glassfibre rods are highly recommended to beginners because they will handle such a range of tackle and can accommodate stresses which inevitably occur when you are learning to cast. A pendulum cast that loses control and direction can savagely twist the blank through two or three opposing planes. Carbonfibre will not forgive these mistakes, and the cast is sure to go astray. The rod may eventually pull itself apart if the error is ingrained in the caster's style.

Design and materials specification are critical in modern surf rods. Jim Bruce, of Bruce & Walker, checks out a sample of carbon fibre before cutting it to shape for the mandrel.

Wrapping and taping the raw material to the mandrel before curing the blank. Blank quality is dependant on careful workmanship.

Suppose, after mastering a pendulum style, you settle on 5 ounces of lead, 12 lb test main line, multiplier reel and a 12 foot rod and you normally cast 125 yards (the ideal distance for the beaches you fish) would carbon fibre add to your expertise?

A carbon blank weighs about half as much as a glassfibre one. The action is sweeter yet somehow more powerful—a difficult characteristic to define and typical of the finest carbon rods. Either you would cast the same distances with noticeably less effort, or the same casting power as before would add another 10–15 yards. Another alternative is to choose a slightly slower blank action with a few pounds less pressure on the butt (see the hand pressure detailed elsewhere) which would retain the casting distance of the old glass rod but allow you to cast much softer baits. This could well be the deciding factor if you fish a lot with peeler crab or shrimp, which are notoriously difficult to throw a long way unless they are wrapped up in shearing elastic or even frozen to the trace. The cast would be even more protected from backlash—carbon fibre delivers its power and acceleration more progressively than glass.

Bite sensitivity is in a class of its own. You would almost certainly need to rethink your fishing style, otherwise you could easily spend all day striking at bites from crabs and tiny fish too small to swallow bait. A good carbon blank is so light at the tip (and lightness counts more than pure flexibility in bite detection) that even a sinker shifting a few inches in the current is clearly signalled. Advantage goes beyond bites: as you reel in, the blank transmits every last vibration to your hands. A good carbon rod feels change of seabed as the sinker rolls along—you sense a clear difference between sand, mud and shingle even at 150 yards-plus. When you fight a big fish, carbonfibre completely outclasses glassfibre. Overall, the RIGHT carbon rod is so much better that you would never want to fish again with a glass surf blank.

Versatility is more important for anglers who travel to different beaches, fish for a variety of species, or who must sometimes change the sinker weight to suit the prevailing weather conditions. Those considerations tip the balance back to glassfibre for general surf fishing. One alternative for the non-specialist is a set of carbonfibre rods . . . but that is a very big investment. Another would be to use a glass rod for all-round sport and one or two carbons for the fishing you enjoy most.

I use an 'S' glass tip/graphite butt surf rod for its versatility: I cast 3–8 ounces on a range of lines, with all kinds of baits and tackle. This is the rod for conger eels, flatfish, bluefish, channel bass and cod. I could take it medium-heavyweight surfcasting anywhere in the world confident in its ability to cast well and handle whatever species I hooked. If I have room for only one rod, that is the one for me unless I am going to fish for a single species in unique conditions.

I greatly enjoy light fishing—lines down to 6 lb test, sinkers less than 4 ounces, and here I switch to a 12 or 13 foot carbon rod specially designed and built for this kind of fishing. It far outperforms the 'S' glass tip, casts extremely well with such small weights and feels ten times more sensitive and better balanced. I can easily justify the cost; and, in fact, I could argue that unless I owned these rods, I could not fish this way at all.

I also have a 13·75 foot rod for casting 5–5·5 ounces on heavy shock leader and 0·35 mm tournament grade line. It is invaluable for casting over grass for pure distance, and for blasting out a bait to spring cod which, in my part of the world, are shy of clear, sunlit water. Without bait close to 175 yards out from the surfline I am not likely to hook a fish all day. Again the special qualities of carbonfibre are worth the expense: the rod blank weighs just 12 ounces, is deceptively powerful and smooth to cast, yet handles relatively light lines with safety. Bite detection is superb – a prerequisite for fishing at these extreme ranges. I could get acceptable results with the 'S' glass rod but for me it is a personal preference to fish carbonfibre in these conditions.

CARBON-REINFORCED

Because a good rod action benefits from the specific characteristics of both glassfibre and carbon, it is hardly surprising that high performance blanks can be produced by combining both materials within the blank wall. Most of the best rods are manufactured this way, the very latest being further improved by adding an aramid fibre (Kevlar, for example) to provide extra protection from distortion and shock.

Carbonfibre has the enormous advantage of stiffening chosen areas of the blank without adding surplus mass or diameter. The exact balance between strength and recovery speed is controlled by choosing high modulus or high tensile types of carbon, or even by mixing the two to achieve the desired action and power.

Note that the 18-24 inches at the very top of the blank are not reinforced: even a small amount of carbon can destroy the smooth flexibility of a well designed 'E' or 'S' glass tip.

45

blanks offer extremely high performance with great toughness and for the most part quite docile handling.

One drawback remains: the higher the casting power, the narrower the power band and the less room for error. It is also much more difficult to retain excellent fishing characteristics in a very powerful casting weapon. This underlines why it is so important to avoid tournament and other high-power blanks until you have learned to cast very well. On the other hand the skilful blending of carbonfibre and aramids can also widen a blank's power band, make it virtually idiot proof and enhance bite detection to an almost unbelievable level.

'Carbon-reinforced' and 'semi-carbon' cannot therefore be regarded as necessarily synonymous with the highest casting performance. Check with the manufacturer or a specialist dealer what the particular rod has been designed to do. Nor should you assume that the addition of carbonfibre automatically improves a rod. In reality, only a handful of designers can really exploit the material. Of these, Terry Carroll of Zziplex stands supreme.

Butt materials

Many of today's surf and long range casting rods are manufactured as long tips and short butts. The typical format is an 8.5 foot tip spigotted or Feralite-jointed to a handle long enough to bring total rod length up the desired 11.5–12 feet. Some rods are permanently spliced together at the butt, then cut and spigotted in the middle for easier transportation and storage. Diehard surfmen prefer a detachable butt and one-piece tip.

Glassfibre blanks may have aluminium alloy, graphite or glassfibre butts, usually in parallel tube form. Glass butts are acceptable for long distance work although they tend to run out of steam beyond 175 yards; by then walls and diameter are so great (for stiffness) that the handle is too thick to grip and so heavy it unbalances the whole rod. In the lower ranks of distance, glass butts are excellent for their 'feel' and forgiveness of error. Beginners like them very much.

Aluminium alloy adds stiffness without weight. Stiffness is important with a high-power glass tip and cannot be compromised on semi-carbons and some all-carbon tips. One inch diameter, 16SWG wall high-tensile aluminium drives an 11·5 foot surf rod to new performance levels. It may bend if used on longer rods cast with more than 5 ounces. Here 1.125 inch diameter or more, same wall thickness and alloy specification, answers the needs of the best casters and anglers. The snag

Just at the point of locking-up in mid-cast, a zoned action rod stiffens under the caster's hands in a smooth surge of leverage and acceleration. Soft butts are useless for this style of long range fishing.

Rods of this type are derived from the crude semi-carbon blanks which were at the forerunners of modern design. Through experience, better manufacturing processes and above all by far superior materials, today's carbon-reinforced

Medium-fast, lightweight action blanks are fine for lure work. The correct zoned-action blank throws a small metal lure well over 100 yards on 10 lb line.

Brute power is the key to some forms of beachcasting. Conger eel fishing into deep water obstructed by rocks and weeds requires a robust rod with the design emphasis more on retrieve power than on sheer distance.

with aluminium is loss of 'feel'. Absolute rigidity takes its toll of bad casts and poor style.

Carbon fibre tubular butts are the only serious choice for carbon tips although aluminium alloy handles are acceptable as far as performance goes, but ruin the balance and lightness of carbon— factors which head the reasons to buy carbon in the first place. Carbon tube is immensely valuable on 'S' glass and semi-carbon tips as well. It is a beautifully powerful material and at least as powerful as alloy. The real advantage is increased tip acceleration and 'feel'.

Carbon fibre has the characteristic of bending a little, then locking solid. You notice a smoother power load in the cast, and the sinker gets away considerably faster. Locked carbon tube unleashes powerful spring-like acceleration when you release the line. Unlike the 'dead' drive of rigid alloy, carbon imparts the same leverage PLUS a final boost. You can measure the extra performance – smoother casts, less backlash with reels tuned to the limit, and around 10 per cent more distance than with an alloy butt and 20 per cent more than with plain glassfibre.

It is possible that boron fibres will add more butt performance to surf rods and spinning tackle. Experiments show that a stiff boron butt is slimmer

than carbonfibre, and is thus easier to hold. Other alternatives loom on the edges of rod design. New generation plastics, among them advanced polycarbonates, might offer stiff, lively butts at relatively low cost. At the moment, choose carbonfibre if you can justify the extra expense. The standard you cast is unimportant— the material adds distance, precision and control to any surf tip. Beginners and experienced anglers cast better and enjoy their fishing even more.

OTHER BLANK ACTIONS

A fast, zoned action blank with stiff butt is superior for everyday long distance fishing with lures and baits. Most surf and freshwater anglers are happy to remain loyal to the design, which has proved itself over millions of fish on thousands of beaches, lakes and rivers. In more specialised fishing you can switch designs with advantage.

A slower action blank without quite as much butt power relative to tip speed (say a stiffness factor of 8–10) is perfect for casting baits and artificials, which by virtue of their specific gravity and shape cannot cast a long way, no matter how hard you try, or are so soft that a modest cast on a stiff zoned-action rod tears them to shreds.

47

Crabs are an excellent example of baits which cannot be cast a long way unless bound to the hook with a maze of elasticated thread. Some fish are happy to eat such bait, others, like shy-feeding bass in rocky ground, will not touch them unless appearance also is right. A soft rod lobs crab plenty far enough, whereas the standard surf rod either smashes the bait or is difficult to control. (All high-performance blanks, zoned models too, suffer to some degree from control loss on short range casts which do not allow the blank to operate as it should.) A slower rod may begin to 'work' really well at 75 yards range. Crab fishing for bass is almost exclusively a short-range sport, so you gain nothing by using a rod with high-performance capability.

Plug baits—especially surface lures and poppers—are extremely hard to cast a long way. You can hit the cast as hard as you like, but the bait is so light and bulky that it simply cannot tolerate so much acceleration and speed. A slightly less powerful butt and softer mid-action produce casts which fall within 90 per cent of those possible with the most powerful casting weapon, and with much less effort and greater control. A plug rod roughly conforming to zoned action still outcasts a standard sloppy-actioned surf or freshwater rod. A return to old-style surf and freshwater blanks is not the answer.

Fixed spool casters may benefit from a slightly heavier tip zone. Stiffness and additional power are irrelevant, although you may need them to compensate for specialised rod rings preferred by some casters. Slight extra weight in the tip helps smooth line flow immediately after release and resolves the eternal headache of leader knots and line tangles which always seem to accompany high-power fixed spool work.

Heavier tip plus three or four weighty, large diameter rings spaced well up the rod are one way to improve fixed spool casting. Another method is to soften the mid-section by around 15 per cent while boosting the top two feet by a few sixteenths of an inch in diameter. Then you can use a set of lighter but still moderately large diameter rings set evenly along the tip. Spanish casters, who excel with fixed spool reels, favour a quite soft action rod with a limited zone action, BUT they make up for lower efficiency in the blank by raising its length beyond 14 feet. The enhanced cushioning action of such a long rod also permits better casting and safer fishing with very light lines. As a general rule, whatever type of fishing you prefer, use progressively softer and longer rods in step with a decrease in line test.

ROD LENGTH

Everyone develops pet ideas about fishing tackle. No two anglers agree on every aspect of tackle, but on rod length for all-round surf fishing a concensus does arise. 11·5 feet seems perfect for most anglers casting pendulum style with 3–8 ounce zoned action rods.

It is highly unlikely that 11·5 feet will seriously hamper your attempts to learn good casting. Another rod may add distance, but initially that is not the issue at stake. You need the best possible chance to master the skills of pendulum cast and reel control. Statistically, it seems you are more likely to get the best results with an 11·5 foot surf blank. I strongly advise you not to stray under 11 feet or over 12 until you know exactly how to assess rod length as it applies to you personally.

No matter how well you cast, the direct rewards of modified rod length are hard to measure from the surf. You will not cast a bait significantly farther. Even if your casts with baits averaged ten yards more, only once or twice a year would that show an extra fish in the bag. Long rods are generally no more senstitive to bites, nor does the tip hold line farther away from surf and back-wash—at least, not far enough to make any real difference to wave action's effect on the rod tip. Longer rods are actually slightly less efficient at hauling in big fish. Shorter rods do not make casting any easier with heavy sinkers, even though theorectically they should. The more common result of shortening the rod from 11·5 feet is to exaggerate timing mistakes in pendulum swing and power arc.

Those observations are aimed at normal casting with standard surf tackle. You do not need such a long rod with the lighter weights. 10 feet is perfectly acceptable with 2–4 ounce lures; 9·25 feet balances nicely to ⅝–1 ounce, (although you can use a longer, lighter rod if you like) and as we have seen in relation to light line casting, a rod longer than 11·5 feet is fine with as much as 4–5 ounces, provided you compensate for extra length with a slower taper and less backbone.

In pure distance terms—almost specifically in tournament casting terms—you should experiment with longer surf rods. Basically, there are two types of caster: slow and fast. A slow, average strength man gets his best results with an 'average' 11·5 foot rod whilst a slow but extremely strong caster can afford to lengthen his rod. He has the necessary muscle to swing the beast. Sinker speed is produced by generating high tip speed in the rod. There are two ways to arrive at the same result: a long rod moved slowly, or a short one

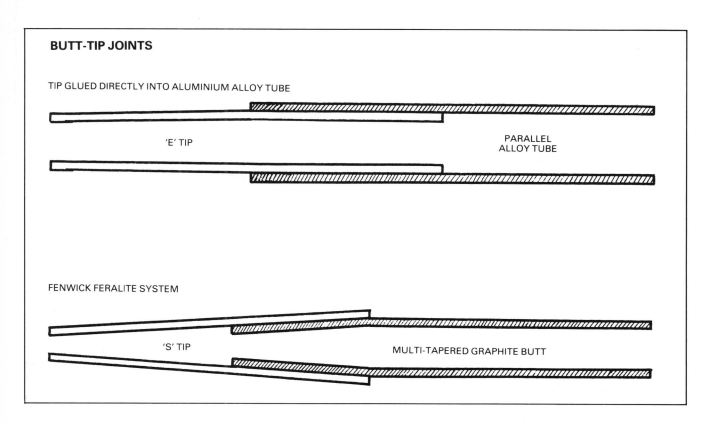

BUTT-TIP JOINTS

TIP GLUED DIRECTLY INTO ALUMINIUM ALLOY TUBE

'E' TIP

PARALLEL ALLOY TUBE

FENWICK FERALITE SYSTEM

'S' TIP

MULTI-TAPERED GRAPHITE BUTT

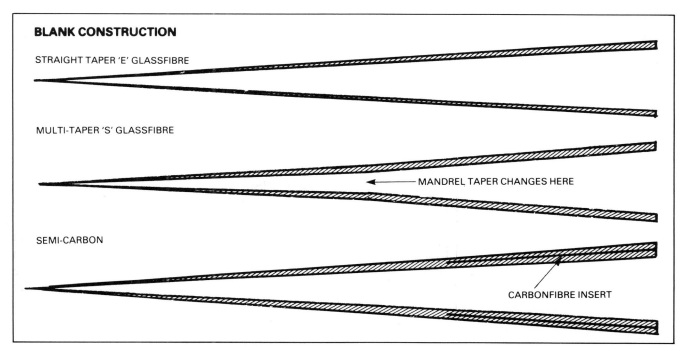

BLANK CONSTRUCTION

STRAIGHT TAPER 'E' GLASSFIBRE

MULTI-TAPER 'S' GLASSFIBRE

MANDREL TAPER CHANGES HERE

SEMI-CARBON

CARBONFIBRE INSERT

moved quickly. It takes more physical effort to push a big and inevitably heavier rod, which is also fighting air pressure as it rotates through the casting arc. A strong man who cannot move fast uses a longer rod to generate the same tip speed as a faster, less powerful caster who can really swish a short blank but is unable to do half as well with, say, a 13·5 foot blank.

The theory works well. Slow, powerful casters really do benefit from an extra couple of feet. If you fit this category, make a few tests—the results might be an extra 20 yards. The perfect caster would be both fast and powerful—strong enough to handle a long rod and fast enough to bring it through at the same speed as a shorter rod. With such qualities record casts are made. It is no coincidence that many leading British and South African tournament casters use long rods. The winners are big, fast men in a sport that is becoming the stronghold of the athlete angler.

Rod Rings and Fittings

ROD RINGS

It pays to invest in the best rod rings (guides). Many a good rod is ruined by cheap rings which reduce distances, strain the blank and chew line to pieces. The reverse is also true: a mediocre blank upgrades into an acceptable fishing rod by whipping on a set of top-quality rings. Check your surf rod to see exactly how the rings affect the bend and power of the blank. You might cast 20 yards farther by repositioning the intermediates. Moving the butt ring a foot farther away from a fixed spool reel reduces wind knots and trapped leaders.

Rod rings share two responsibilities: they correctly align leader with the compressed blank and they form a tunnel for inward and outward line flow. The right set of rings, correctly positioned on the blank, helps wring the ultimate performance from fixed spool and multiplier reels, each of which requires a specific ring pattern for peak results. However, it is not strictly necessary to switch to a special fixed spool or multiplier rod until your distances exceed 175 yards. Even 200 yard casts are easily accommodated on rods ringed for both reels. In fact, the surf angler who selects reels according to beach conditions usually prefers a rod that casts nicely with both. It makes sense to use versatile tackle when you can—and of course it is cheaper to have one rod instead of two.

Rings for multiplier casting. The zoned action surf rod, 11·5 feet long and matched to 0·35–0.40 mm diameter main line, probably requires at least six intermediate rings. Ideally, the number of rings should be cut to the bare minimum that spreads the load of casting and fishing over the full working length of glass or carbonfibre. Tournament casters sometimes prefer the same pattern even if it results in limited contact between line and blank when the rod is under full compression with a fish on the hook. Flexibility of the tip two feet of a pendulum blank fished with the reel on top of the handle certainly encourages line to hang in chords between rings.

In my experience you should balance theoretically correct ring spacing, which prevents line touching the blank, against weight saved by cutting out one or two rings near the top of the rod. I have never found that it has made any difference to the rod if line did make contact here and there. I have not lost any fish through friction burns. As long as you do not allow great gaps between rings, and therefore overload the blank unnecessarily, the rod never suffers.

By whipping, say, three rings instead of four on the top zone of the blank, some rods cast more smoothly. The more sensitive the blank tip to excessive weight, the more important it is to reduce ring size and numbers, even at risk of losing perfect line flow along the rod. There is no single formula to calculate the best ring spacings and numbers on this or any other fishing rod. Tape on a set of rings, then cast and fish until trial and error determines the best compromise.

Where rings are closely spaced on a flexible tip to preserve blank action, choose small, lightweight rings. If the tip is stiffer, which makes it less sensitive to extra weight and fairly immune to line drop between the rings, you have the option of whipping on three or four large diameter, high-standing rings like the Fuji BSHGs, or five or six low-set, smaller diameter rings—Fuji BNHG, Seymo or Daiwa Dynaflo. Use which one you prefer, but remember that small rings soon clog with weed.

The mid-section of the blank (Zone B) does not flex enough to bring line into contact. Use as few rings as necessary to spread the load. Some rods need only two rings—but if you are in doubt, add another for luck. This zone of the rod is so stiff that the weight of one more ring will not be noticed. The lowest ring—the butt ring which collects line directly from the reel—should be at least 25 mm in diameter. 30 mm is better if you use 40 pound-plus shock leader. Height of ring also aids line flow. Ideally its centre should be at spool level so that the line neither rises nor dives into the ring. BSHG rings may be better than BSHG-type for large capacity reels like the ABU 9000C and Penn 970. Aim to have around 30 inches minimum between reel and butt ring regardless of ring and spool dimensions.

Rings for fixed spool casting. A fixed spool is fished under the rod. The line never drifts close to the blank when the rod is pulled heavily on a fish. In fact the opposite may occur—line creeps too far from the blank and jumps in such big chords between rings that the blank is not correctly loaded. This is a particular hazard on fixed spool rods fitted with three or four rings only, all whipped on the upper half of the blank.

The idea of a few, large diameter rings is to eliminate line friction and to prevent the leader knot catching in the butt ring or tip immediately after line release on a powerful cast. In general the scheme works well but it can strain the tip. Tournament casters use a slightly stiffer tip to support the extra weight and torsion of the rings, and to produce a smoother line delivery. A typical high-performance surf rod between 11 and 12 feet long, used with the reel in the high butt position, would feature a 16 mm tip ring, 20, 30, 40 and 50 mm intermediates on the top 6 feet of the blank, and a gap of at least 40 inches between the 50 mm ring and the reel. Line flow is excellent, yet the rod still fishes quite well, Fuji BSHG rings are universally accepted for fixed spool work, chiefly because they sit nice and high off the blank.

Space between reel spool and butt ring is more critical than any other dimension in fixed spool ringing. Without an appreciable free-flow area before the shock leader passes into the butt ring, the chances of a tangle escalate; a butt ring 18 inches from the spool traps the leader every cast. Under no circumstances should you reduce the gap below 30 inches.

One school of thought says that the butt ring should be small to break up the coned flow of line leaving a spool. The idea has merit, but few surf anglers travel that road. The alternative philosophy—to whip on large diameter rings to reduce friction—is still popular. The friction side of the argument is not watertight: in either case direct ring friction is minimal on surf tackle. What counts is lack of line obstruction. Larger rings, widely spaced and with the butt ring well up the rod, make a lot more sense. How large is large? Well, that too is a question of personal interpretation. You are unlikely to find much benefit in a butt ring over 50 mm diameter. Selecting the rest of the set is a matter of progressively grading down the intermediates to produce a neat funnel for flowing line.

Hybrid multiplier/fixed spool ringing. Whip a 40 mm or 50 mm butt ring to Zone B so that there is at least 33 inches between the reel seat and the ring itself. (On most 11·5 foot blanks with the reel seat set at 30–32 inches you can usually afford a 36–39 inch gap). Glue on a 16 mm tip ring. Now space in 12, 16, 20, 25 and 30 mm intermediate rings so that the holes in the rings align into a

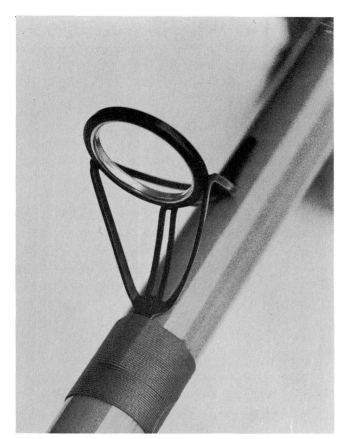

Daiwa's Dynaflo stainless steel insert ring.

conical tunnel as you look through the butt ring. The rod will handle both fixed spool and multiplier reels with no flow problems at all up to 200 yards. Load of casting and fishing is neatly absorbed by the entire working length of the rod. Turn the rod upside down—multiplier style—and you will find that line hardly touches the blank under full compression. Even on flexible tips which do exaggerate line drop, contact is of no consequence.

Fuji BSHG and Dynaflo rings are excellent. The butt ring may be a BSHG or the slightly lower BNHG depending on the height of the fixed spool face. A butt BNHG mixes nicely with a set of BSHG fitted higher on the rod—many custom builders think it looks neater than a complete set of BSHGs. Seymo rings are not quite high enough, nor are they yet available in large sizes. When these limitations are resolved this British ring will make its mark in surf fishing. The quality of the ring and the frame's elasticity ensure popularity.

Surf and casting rings in general. Choice lies between plain wire rings, aluminium oxide inserts, silicon carbide and hardened stainless steel in a cushioned frame. Each ring has its uses, though plain wire has little future.

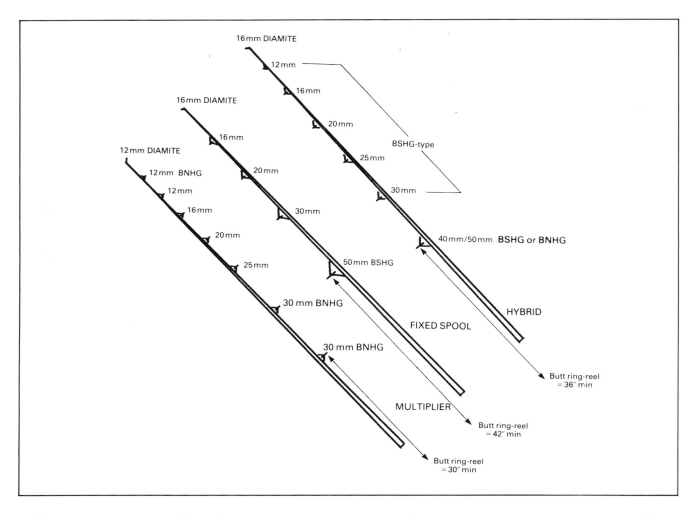

Plain stainless steel and hardchromed steel rings with soldered or spot welded frames offer good performance at low cost. Friction is minimal during the cast but somewhat higher under load, when there is always a chance of line abrasion and burning. Poor quality wire rings fitted to low-key Oriental rods often conceal wisps of loose chrome or patches of rust which cut stretched nylon.

High-quality wire rings, such as the Hopkins and Holloway series, have none of those drawbacks. Their only fault which is endemic in wire rings of all kinds, is fragility. It takes only a knock against the beach to distort a wire ring which will never rebend to perfect shape. Like other travelling anglers I have arrived on the beach to find my rod rings crumpled. Though I like wire rings for casting, I cannot reconcile myself to the risk of lost fishing. I no longer use them on my better fishing rods, though they are useful in testing blanks. They weigh so little that the full power and action of the rod are never masked which is sometimes the case with heavy lined rings.

The Fuji series of lined rings and other brands of the same design are much tougher than wire. You can be fairly sure that the ring will not be crushed beyond value on its way to the surf. There are other snags however: aluminium oxide centres pop out of the plastic cushion rings. Maybe that is no major disaster on a butt or intermediate ring, but if the tip ring bursts, then you are in trouble. The sharp metal frame cuts the leader in mid cast; or even if you are lucky enough to land the cast successfully, the edge of the ring carves out chunks of main line as you wind in. On the whole though, BNHG and BSHG rings are fine for all kinds of surf and distance casting.

Daiwa's Dynaflo rings are a valuable addition to the range of surf and long-distance accessories. The frame is strong and very similar to Fuji. Instead of an aluminium oxide centre, Daiwa use a hardened, low friction stainless steel insert. The inner cushion ring between frame and lining is almost hidden from view and therefore immune to popping. In this respect the Dynaflo is superior to most other rings, and a serious contender for top honours. Service life is the main reservation: Dynaflos lack the track record of other rings, simply because they have not been available for as long. Initial tests suggest they are as tough as necessary except for ultra-heavy fishing which tends to overstress the relatively high frame.

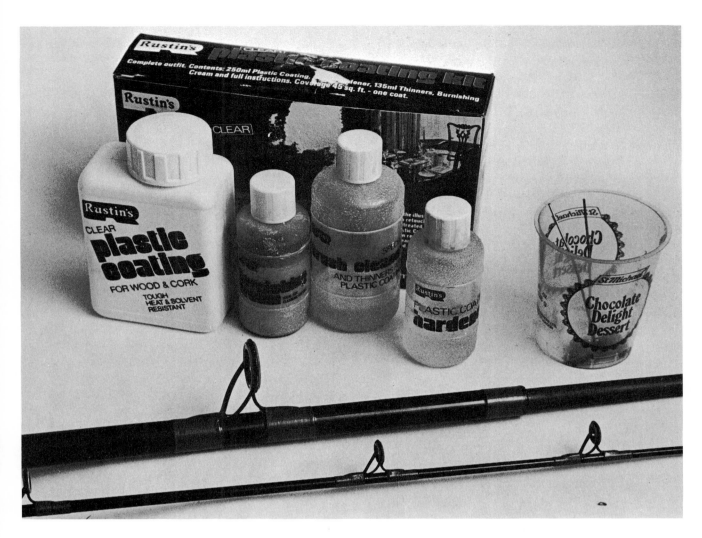

Whippings must be sealed for security. High-build resins are better than varnish. Rustin's Type F plastic coat is a good alternative to proper custom finishes.

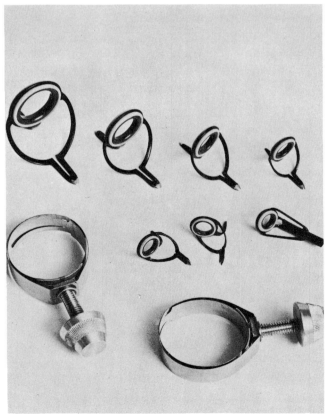

Fuji BNHG rings for multiplier casting.

Fuji offers a silicon carbide centered ring, which they claim cuts line friction and lengthens the cast. Like other surf casters who have tested the rings on a variety of blanks. I am unable to find any real distance advantage in Si C. They are nice to use, however, and are perhaps a little smoother under heavy retrieve pressure, which does highlight the friction coefficient of any material. The rings seems a bit stronger and more reliable too. Decide for yourself if the high cost is justified.

Hopkins and Holloway's Seymo ring for light surfcasting and spinning is the first decent British product for ten years. The frame with two legs moves freely with the blank but still supports the ring under pressure. Ceramic lining fuses to the metal frame without a cushion-ring. In all it is a neat design, worthy of the finest surf blanks. The present model is too low and too small for serious fixed spool casting, but larger versions are in the pipeline. The cost is highly competitive, which is a pleasant change with the price of other brands rising towards sheer blackmail.

Tip rings take a beating from casting, line retrieve and continual bashings on the beach. I am fed up with lined rings that pop open, tungsten carbide which shatters and narrow-edged centres that ruin leader and main line. All my best rods sport Hopkins and Holloway Diamite tips, which are solid almost indestructbile and great value for money. They are the only tip ring that I would care to recommend to keen surf men who cannot afford to make a mistake.

Friction—how can you reduce it?

I have read a lot of technical explanations by ring makers who almost wooed me into ripping apart my surf rods and rebuilding them with the latest Supercasting Rod Ring. Sceptical to the end, I restrain myself and borrow a set to test. I have never found one ring that cast significantly farther than another. There are rings that given half a chance would rip your line to bits. Others are as smooth as silk. None makes much difference to how far you cast, even under tournament conditions. In surf, with bait drag to contend with, you would not see a measurable improvement anyway, whatever the ring did. The microscopic gain in sinker energy due to lower line friction through the rings is far outweighed by the massive loss of distance from a single worm.

Lined rings, and silicon carbide in particular, are smoother under load, and more efficient than wire. You can feel the reduced friction; in this respect the makers are correct—low friction materials offer superior fishing. The mistake they make is to suppose that line flying through rings

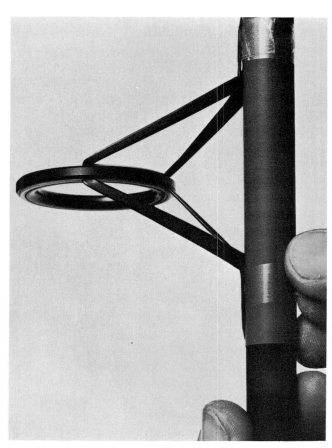

Fuji BSHG rings stand high off the blank for fixed spool work.

Fixed spool attached to aluminium alloy butt by the Spanish method of wrapping with rubber strip cut from an inner tube.

Fuji FPS screw seat. An excellent choice for casting rods . . . but remember to keep the threads clean.

has significant pressure against the lining. It hardly touches, and that being so, varying coefficients of friction make no real difference. It is pressure of line on the edge of the ring, not the area of ring and line that touch, which most determines frictional losses. Maybe there is a difference between ring linings and in the lightest of freshwater fishing, where even the surface tension of water trapped in rings holds back the cast. Casting in the surf is never so complicated and no tournament was ever won nor record set because the caster had access to a magic ring. Size of rings, their position and spacing do make a difference. If rings choke the line, or spacing reduces efficiency of blank, corrective measures produce remarkable increases in performance and control. Those are points to consider when you design and build your own pendulum rod.

HANDLES AND ACCESSORIES

Hand grips. Powerful casting, pendulum or any othe good style, depends on a secure rod grip and correct distance between hands for leverage and speed. The simplest butt construction, still favoured by anglers who value utilitarian rather than decorative surf rods, is a plain handle of glassfibre, aluminium alloy or carbonfibre, either covered with shrink tube or left bare, and fitted with a pair of hosepipe clips which secure the reel. Sometimes there are no handgrips at all. Mostly, for comfort and nonslip handling under pressure, the butt is wrapped with cord, tape, cork strips, plastic foam or leather built up to form separate grips at the butt cap and on both sides of the reel.

The plain parallel butt, lacking even simple handgrips, has the tremendous advantage of flexible reel positioning. Too many mass produced and custom built rods have the reel seat too high or low for precise casting. Even where the spacing is correct for one particular sinker weight, it is just too short or too generous for heavier and lighter tackle. For most surf anglers it really makes little difference. Expert casters searching for those extra few yards must have a reel that clips in exactly the right spots for 4, 5, and 6 ounce sinkers or whatever else they have to cast. They are happy to make do with a 'barebones' look to the rod in return for that range of adjustment.

For general fishing though, you can incorporate variable hand spacing by arranging permanent grips and reel seat so that the lower hand—the left for most casters—works on a grip about three inches longer than strictly necessary. If spacing for 4, 5 and 6 ounce casting is 29, 30 and 32 inches respectively from the centre of the reel seat to the end of the butt grip, you can make the butt 32 inches long, then hold the grip up to 3 inches shorter for the lighter weights. Set up the reel seat to cast the heaviest weight, then choose a butt grip length that matches any smaller sinker you intend to fish on that rod.

55

On most average length pendulum rods matched to 4–6 ounces of lead, a reel seat some 32 inches from the butt cap to the centre of the reel is perfect. Be wary of rods with substantially longer butts. Almost certainly they will not respond to the pendulum cast.

Most modern surf rods use three separate grips: the top pair about six inches long, the butt between 6 and 9 inches. Soft Neoprene, Hypalon and cork are excellent. Hypalon is perhaps the best, but must have walls less than ¼ inch thick. Too thick a wall sponges up hand pressure and wastes much of the casting energy. Aim for a comfortable grip with plenty of security and sensitivity. Watch the diameter as well because much over 1·25 inches across a grip prevents your thumb clamping down on the multiplier spool. The consequences of reel slip at full power are disastrous. If necessary prune the Hypalon with a sharp knife until the grip diameter no longer interferes with reel control. Strip it off altogether if you like, and replace with a strip of cork tape or thin-walled rubber. Tennis racquet handle and bike handlebar grips can be pressed into service if appearances do not worry you.

Reel seats. A pair of stainless steel hoseclips is adequate security for multiplier reels attached to parallel butts without grips. Elsewhere, a Fuji snap-lock clip or conventional screw seat is permanently fitted between the upper pair of handgrips. The snap-lock is bad news in my opinion—forever falling apart, and working efficiently in the first place only if the reel slots perfectly into the base. Many reels are too short for one serrated point on the retaining clip, too long for the next. The reel either slips around in the fitting or strains the mechanism. The device tends to rip apart under pressure anyway—usually when you hook a big fish. However, for all its failings, the snap-lock is suitable for lightweight surf and freshwater rods. Check that your reel fits the seat before building the rod. You will not be the first angler to spend days custom-building a rod to discover, after the glue has set, that your reel is incompatible with the chosen Fuji.

Of the screw fittings available, only Fuji FPS and others of similar materials and construction make sense for casting rods. Once a tubular seat is fixed with adhesive, it is there for life. Even if you cut the seat off in chunks, the rod butt has to be stripped before you can slide on a replacement. Metal seats are either heavy and overpowered for surf fishing, or of lightweight, corrodable aluminium alloy. Stick to stainless steel/carbonfibre Fuji-type for long service life and security. Seats require little maintenance other than washing and an occasional application of graphite powder or silicon spray to the threads. The screw seat also accommodates fixed spool reels comfortably, which is far from the case with snap-locks and hose clips.

Casters in Spain have evolved a neat and cheap fitting for fixed spool reels: they scavenge an old inner tube, which is cut into one inch strips, 18 inches long. These are bound tightly around the rod butt and reel stand to form a waterproof, soft combination of handgrip and reel seat. The end of the strip is tucked under the penultimate coil to hold the whole thing together. Neatly applied, a rubber strip is better than any conventional reel seat and may be instantly shifted to suit hand spacing.

Butt caps. Never cast without a soft rubber cap over the rod butt end. During the final stage of a pendulum cast, the butt drives down towards your lower left ribcage. Should the sinker snap off, the butt stabs hard into chest or stomach. The need for protection is obvious. Never use the metal spear fitted to some surf rods as standard equipment. It is potentially lethal. Cut it off and glue on a rubber cap, which can be homemade or custom-moulded as you wish. A big hollowed out cork is better than nothing.

Multiplier Reels

Multiplier reels—American anglers know them as conventionals and baitcasters—feed line from a revolving spool driven by gears during retrieve and are free-running in mid-cast. For many anglers the conventional reel is never more than a dream. They would love to use one, but are unable to live with continual backlashes and burned thumbs.

If angling were purely an exercise to catch fish, few anglers would bother to learn multiplier casting. The fixed spool is so much easier to master, casts almost as far and winds in line more quickly. But objectivity is not the only aspect to consider. Angling is a mixture of technique and pleasure, mechanics and wishful thinking, competition and relaxation. Reels may achieve the same end results, but they do not feel the same in action. Multipliers are smoother, better balanced to the rod, compact and, above all, precise. In the hands of an expert, the multiplier reel sings. Fixed spools churn like 19th century mangles.

Although most problems of multiplier control are based on faulty technique, the design of a casting reel is important. Many reels cast tolerably well, but only a handful excel in the surf. Freshwater casters should make an effort to pick the best baitcasting reel for their sport—tiny spools are subjected to enormous speeds and pressures. Does the reel you own or aim to buy measure up to the following?

THE ESSENTIAL FEATURES OF THE MULTIPLIER REEL

Strong, light spool
The spool accelerates from zero to over 40,000 revolutions a minute within one tenth of a second when you cast a 5 ounce sinker 200 yards. Even a modest one hundred yard cast spins the reel fast enough to highlight any imbalance and weakness of spool. Ideally, use the lightest spool available. Plastics are acceptable but aluminium alloy is better. Medium-quality reels have sectional alloy spools composed of spindle, flanges and central core, pressed or screwed together. The very best spools are of machine cut, single piece alloy precision bored for the stainless steel spindle. Spool run-out is less than 0·003 inches which prevents thin line trapping itself between spool rim and sideplate. Heavy brass/chrome spools for deep sea fishing are always unacceptable for serious beach casting.

Smallest practical spool capacity
Your reel should be the smallest size compatible with the kind of fishing you do. Every inch of excess line reduces performance and encourages backlash. Maintain the theme by fishing with the lightest line considered safe for the species you hunt. A surf reel designed for 300 yards of 14 lb test is much easier to tune and control than one able to accommodate 300 yards of 30 lb test. The lighter reel probably casts 50 per cent farther too.

ABU 9000C, a large capacity surf reel of high casting and fishing performance.

Excellent bearings

High-performance casting ferrets out poor bearings and destroys them. Floating ball-races are best for long casting and fishing, though they are not totally superior to plain bronze bushes. Much depends on how keen you are to tune the reel. Plain bushes need continual attention and lubrication if they are to stay in peak condition. Ballraces soak up and retain plenty of lubricant, so you can fish and cast for several days without servicing the reel. Both cast extremely well, but the ballrace is smoother under heavy retrieve pressure; on the other hand, plain bearings run more quietly. Highly tuned ballrace reels may scream thoughout the cast.

Tough, rigid frame

There is no substitute for quality in this department. Flimsy reel frames and seats twist under load, destroy alignment of bearings and spool, and overload the gears. Many reels fail to withstand even six months of rugged surf fishing before the frame rots to powder, distorts, or pops away from the reel stand. Screwed, chromed brass frames are excellent although old-fashioned; single-piece machined frames of aluminium alloy are rigid but likely to corrode. The best compromise is a screwed together frame with substantial crossbars as for example, on the Penn Magforce series. Sectional frames have the advantage of adjustment and easy component replacement.

Strong, high ratio gears

Compared to fixed spool reels, multipliers are slow to retrieve line from long distance. As line level falls towards the spool core, even high-speed gears work hard to keep up with a fish or to lift tackle away from the seabed. Gear ratio should be at least 4.25:1. However, the higher the gear ratio, the lower the mechanical advantage of retrieve. Gears may be overstressed if you crank against a heavy fish—smaller tournament reels strip their teeth. Weak spools burst and even explode through the sideplates of the reel. Stainless steel machine cut gears are indispensible for heavy-duty surf fishing. Make sure they are of tough steel—some of the cheaper Oriental steel is soft as cheese. Bronze is an excellent material which soaks up punishment and does not rust.

Be careful with small baitcasters fitted with powerhandles (extend winding handles that boost leverage). They are no faster in retrieve but do encourage direct winching rather than pumping. The result is strained or broken gears and spools. Use them for the comfort they provide, not for additional power.

Useful for light surf and all-round freshwater casting—the new magnetically controlled Daiwa baitcaster.

ABU 6500CT and modified Daiwa Millionaires are favourite tournament reels with a reasonable beach peformance. What you gain in distance you lose in strength and retrieve.

58

Powerful, precise drag system

The trend towards lighter tackle in the surf exaggerates deficiences in drag design and operation. When working 12 lb test at long range, you cannot afford a drag that overheats and either locks solid or fails to grip, or limits the range of adjustments necessary to handle a big fish. Star drags should feel smooth and even as you tighten down on the brake plates. Never buy a reel which runs from free-spool to total lock-up within a single turn of the wheel. It is sure to let you down. Surf fishermen looking for big channel bass, tope, cod or even sharks on light line must not compromise here. Some European and Japanese casting multipliers have notoriously weak drags which burn out on the first big fish that rips 100 yards from the spool. Make sure the reel you choose has the right service back-up: you might need new drag washers every six months if you fish hard and hook lots of heavyweight fighters.

Casting controls

A well designed surf multiplier requires little spool control if correctly loaded and well cast. However, even expert casters rely on centrifugal or magnetic cast controllers to smooth out minor errors and to facilitate reel tuning. The older Penn reels cast extremely well without brakes if you use a plastic spool and thick oil in the bearings. Modern reels with aluminium alloy spools still respond to lubricant control but are better suited to a magnet or brake blocks. Beginners are most at risk unless their reels can be detuned for firm control. Even tournament casters appreciate the confidence inspired by a brake of some kind. It is not cheating to use a casting control . . . it is common sense to take the easy way out.

Corrosion resistance

Modern reels originally designed for freshwater fishing cannot really be expected to last long in the salt. However, even the purpose-built sea reels may fall apart in six months unless you flush out sand and seawater every trip. Aluminium sideplates and spools suffer terribly—usually the inside faces rot to powder. Plastic side plates and well anodised saltwater-grade aluminium frames ward off damage far better than lacquered alloy and cheap stainless steel. Take care to buy a good brand of reel, and be sure to look after it. That means regular maintenance, not a once a year springclean.

THE RIGHT REEL FOR YOU

There are casting reels you fish with, and fishing reels that cast. Choose according to how you fish

Any baitcaster or level-wind reel can be modified for better casting by cutting away the level-wind gears and crossbar. You must replace the front bar with a solid frame brace.

and what you hope to catch. Decide whether pure distance matters most, or if sacrificing 20 yards pays off in faster, rugged handling of big fish in turbulent seas and fast rivers.

Reels for sheer distance

High-performance reels—tournament and ultra-long range fishing—are very easy to tune and control, cast terrific distances in surf and freshwater and, with care, handle average fishing pressures. But at some stage you have to balance sheer power against peak casting performance. The reels listed here fall down, sometimes unacceptably so, when powerful retrieve, drag performance and operational speed are laid on the line. Maintenance is more critical—understandable since these models are plain or modified freshwater baitcasters. The most popular reels are:

ABU 6500GRT
ABU 6500CT
Shimano Speedmaster II FSC
Penn Levelmatic 940
Ryobi T2

Their line capacity with level-wind mechanism removed averages 300 yards of 0.35 mm nylon monofilament or 250 yards of 0.40 mm. In standard form they hold about 15 per cent less. They all feature centrifugal or magnetic brakes, acceptable retrieve speed and adequate drags. Millionaires, Shimano and Penns are strongest in this department. All reels except Penn are wide

Laying on the first 50 yards of line is an important stage in reel tuning. Poor loading causes severe spool vibration.

open to saltwater invasion and subsequent corrosion. Most multiplier spools are machined from a single block of alloy, but a few are still made in sections and are therefore liable to distort or break under heavy loads. However, where casting distance counts heavily towards successful angling, all the reels are highly competitive and there is nothing much to choose between them.

Tough fishing reels

The next group of reels casts very well indeed but never equals the record breaking distances of baitcasters. However, they do offer tremendous bonuses for anglers who fish rough ground, heavy surf, for fast-running tope, stubborn channel bass and massive conger eels. The much higher rate of retrieve lifts tackle over weeds and rocks, whereas baitcasters wind sinker and hook straight to destruction. In real terms loss of range is comparitively marginal—under 10 per cent for the best anglers and of no consequence for the under-150s. Big reels are more difficult to tune, load and handle, however. On the other hand, they are built specifically for seafishing and are thus more resistant to

saltwater corrosion. Generally, drag systems are good enough, gears are tough and frames solid.

ABU 7000, 7000C, 9000C
Penn Squidders and Surfmasters
Newell 220F, 229F
Penn Magpower 970, 980
Daiwa SL20 SH
Mitchell 602AP, 600AP

These reels suit all purses, capacity requirements and levels of sophistication. Some have ballraces, others plain bushes. Squidders and Surfmasters lack casting controls but are easily tuned with oil. ABU reels rely on centrifugal brake blocks, while the Penn Magpower series operate on a revolutionary new magnetic controller. Mitchells are cheap, serviceable reels. ABUs are nicely made but prone to corrosion unless thoroughly cleaned every trip. The frames are adequate, though not as good as Newell or Penn. Newell and Penn 970/980 reels are also very tough mechanically; the Penns are fitted with the Senator 4/0 offshore reel's big-game drag. You certainly cannot do much better than that.

Line capacity varies throughout the range, from 250 yards of 20 lb test on the Newell 220F to the ABU 10000C's 400 yard-plus. In the middle are reels which hold either 200 yards of 20–25 lb test for tough fishing on dirty ground and in heavy surf, or at least 350 yards of 0·40 mm diameter for everyday casting and fishing. Except for the big ABU, every reel on the list will cast close to 200 yards, given the right pair of hands. Shore fishermen can expect an easy 125 yards fishing range— behind the tournament reels perhaps, but still excellent. You see the benefits when a big fish runs hard or heads for rocks: these reels will stop him; the better-casting models may not. The life-span of the bigger reels should be at least ten years, whereas many tournament reels are scrapped after two years' hard work in the surf.

Modified reels

Standard baitcasting multiplier reels are good enough for casting up to 150 yards or so but then the limitations of the level-wind system intrude on the flow, cut distance, and tend to trap the leader knot in the line guide. Most casters find that the top crossbar prevents a firm, deep thumb grip on the spool. It is now standard practice in the surf to cut off the top bar, remove the level wind bar and its internal gears, and to replace the level wind itself with a solid crossbar which strengthens the frame. Normally you do the work yourself or take the reel to a tackle shop or toolmaker with the necessary skills and machinery. A replacement CT cage is sometimes available from ABU, but custom-made conversions are now the more popular (Tony's Tackle, Dave Docwra, etc.).

Removing the level wind also increases line capacity by around 25 per cent. That is why smaller reels cast over 250 yards despite having a quoted maximum capacity of less than 200 yards. Laying on line by hand also produces a neater, tighter load pattern which runs more freely and under better control. The reel also accepts a wider selection of line diameters since level winds usually work best with one or two diameters only.

Distance gains are in the region of 20 per cent with modified small baitcasters and less than 10 per cent on larger models like the ABU 7000. In fact, the 7000 gains so little from modification that very few anglers bother to remachine the cage. The only value is in preventing occasional snapped leaders due to knots catching in the line guide. Spool grip is the major consideration with all sizes of reel. If the spool slips under full power, it pays to get rid of the offending crossbar even if you are not interested in extra fishing range.

Other useful changes to standard production reels include replacement of spools and gears, frames and bearings with custom-made components that are faster running, stronger or less likely to distort under pressure of highly stressed monofilament. Newell specialise in modified parts for Penn reels, although with the introduction of the Penn aluminium alloy spools, higher gear ratios and better drag washers, the need is no longer significant. Newell frames are still an excellent investment if you have small hands and a short thumb. Extra reach created by low-set Newell replacement cages allows easier spool control and better distances.

Mass production tolerances are high enough to ensure your reel is satisfactory for general fishing, but might not guarantee the best possible performance. Check alignment of frame and spool. Make sure the spool is well balanced and evenly machined because you can have high and low spots which induce vibration at high speed. Check that bearings and gears are free from metal swarf and misplaced grease. If the reel will not run fast whatever you do, examine the right hand spindle and its drive sleeve which connects the spool to the gears. Often there is dirt, excess lubricant or too tight a fit between the components. Clean the drive train and if necessary polish it and the spindle. You may gain 20 yards.

Loading a multiplier

Rough running spools, poor distances and too many backlashes are symptoms of a badly loaded spool. Every inch of line on a multiplier is turning fast throughout every cast, regardless of distance. Poor line loading always results in vibration and loss of power. Light and heavy areas on the spool are magnified many times at high speed. Even the knot that attaches the bottom end of the nylon to the spool core must be correctly tied and positioned. A line level just ¼ inch too high makes some reels uncontrollable, while too low a filling slashes distances by 50 yards.

Tie line to the base of the spool with a timber hitch or blood knot. Tournament casters may tape the end with a tiny patch of Sellotape instead, but that is no good in the surf although it does help perfect spool performance. Just tie the smallest, neatest knot you can. I never bother to tuck it into the slot drilled into most spool centres; but there is no reason why one should not do this.

Wind line evenly onto the spool, cotton reel fashion, and under medium tension achieved by passing incoming line between finger and thumb. Load line until you reach the level that best suits your casting. Determine that by trial and error. To start with, fill baitcasters to within ¹⁄₁₆ inch of the flanges. Medium and large reels—Penn 970 and ABU 9000C for example—should be slightly underfilled by ⅛ and ½ inch respectively (with 0·40 mm line). The ABU is much easier to cast when deliberately kept low; but after practising for some time you will know the reel's characteristics well enough to raise the level if necessary. The rule with multipliers of all kinds is to err on the conservative side unless you have full capacity or can really control the beast.

Sometimes a reel fills unevenly for no obvious reason. Strip off the line and start again. Usually that does the trick. If not, try slightly thicker or thinner line, especially valuable on level-wind reels. Should everything fail, check the spool for accuracy. Some cheaper reels are inaccurate enough to destroy your best efforts, and the only answer is to change spools.

Reel tuning systems

Every well-designed beachcasting and freshwater multiplier reel is essentially docile provided that both rod action and casting style are compatible with the reel's operating characteristics. There are some pressures which defeat a multiplier no matter how well it is designed. And, provided you cast reasonably, the converse also is true—a well made reel is not particularly vicious or even sensitive to minor mistakes. Pendulum casters regularly get away with murder because the style itself compensates for a surprising level of incompetence.

Two stages of the cast most affect the multiplier: the initial surge of acceleration immediately after line release, followed by the free flow period onward of halfway through the cast. When you cannot control the multiplier, or want to check the degree of tuning, examine those two periods. Release phase backlashes occur within the first 50 yards, and more often inside 30 yards. Flow period problems begin between 75 and 100 yards out. Sometimes it pays to measure distances to confirm your suspicions.

In both cases you can tame the reel with brake blocks, magnets or even by squirting different viscosity oils into the bearings. Some direct control is always necessary to iron out the initial surge of acceleration and its immediate afermath, flywheeling, which is the tendancy for line flow to vastly outstrip sinker speed. BUT—and this is crucial to success—provided you use a well-designed surf reel, most overruns in release phase are due to bad technique. Nothing you do to the reel—short of overtightening bearing caps and inserting huge brake blocks—can possibly save the cast from a major backlash within the first half-second. If your casts fall into a pattern of RELEASE-SNAP, look to your technique. Provided the reel has at least two medium brake blocks, half-power magnet setting, or 140 grade oil in the bearings, backlash cannot really be due to anything except poor style.

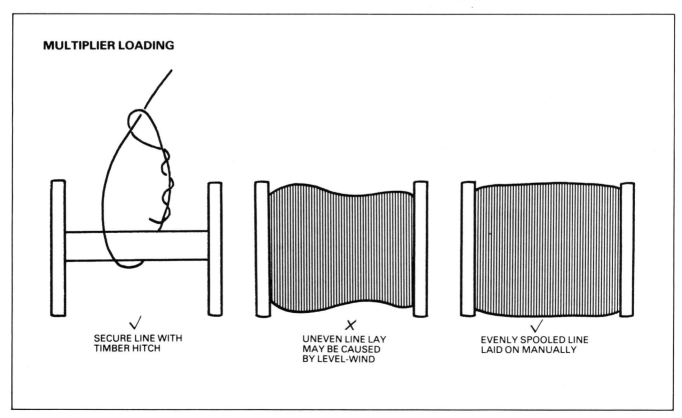

MULTIPLIER LOADING

✓ SECURE LINE WITH TIMBER HITCH

✗ UNEVEN LINE LAY MAY BE CAUSED BY LEVEL-WIND

✓ EVENLY SPOOLED LINE LAID ON MANUALLY

Wind on line evenly and under moderate tension until the spool is moderately filled. Don't cram on every inch of line unless you know the reel runs controllably.

The leader knot could cut your thumb unless you tuck the end of the leader close to one side of the spool.

Adjusting the Penn 970's magnetic cast controller.

The other backlash pattern goes this way: RELEASE-SNAP and the cast gets away smoothly enough; the reel purrs into action, then fluffs up line and overruns. This classic rhythm signals either minor technique error or fractionally insufficient spool control. The sinker flies about 75 yards before the reel pushes off enough slack line to cause backlash. In both instances an increase of block size, a half-turn inward of magnet cap or upgrade in oil viscosity irons out the cast. No matter how well you cast, variations in wind speed, bait drag and sinker weight demand secondary tuning to ensure trouble-free fishing. Heat and cold also influence control settings. Expect any reel to speed up in summer and slow down quite considerably on a winter day.

Assuming your technique is pretty good, sinker, line and rod are balanced, and the reel is the right size and properly filled with light running line and strong leader, tuning is straightforward.

Centrifugal brakes

ABU and Daiwa Millionaires utilise two, three of four blocks according to model. I do not find it necessary to insert more than two blocks on any of them; missing blocks will not affect spool balance. Start with the biggest blocks supplied with the reel.

Adjust the bearing cap to allow a slight but definite end-float on the spool spindle, ignoring the recommended procedure of tightening the cap until sinker falls slowly from rod tip when the spool is released. Although satisfactory for some kinds of light baitcasting, this system of tuning is incompatible with long range pendulum work. The spool MUST float in the bearings.

Begin casting. Aim for nice, comfortable casts at first, then turn up the power. Backlash should be eliminated by the two big blocks. If not, work on your style, because that is where the fault lies. There is no point making the reel go any faster until snatch and ragged power flow are corrected.

Let us assume all goes to plan. Make a note of the maximum distances achieved. Now replace the blocks with two medium size ones. Repeat the casting exercise. Measure the distances and note the reel's response. Is it smooth and trouble-free, or does it fluff up a little in mid-cast? Again, there will be no definite overruns if you are casting well with at least 4 ounces of lead. Ligher sinkers, lures and plugs may cause problems.

Now go down to a pair of small blocks. Check the reel's reaction, and measure distances. Then, if you feel confident to carry on, take out one block. Run through the tests and make notes and measurements. For your last cast, take out the single block. At this stage you will learn one of three lessons: the reel overruns, which proves that

Centrifugal brake systems are simple to tune with varying numbers and sizes of blocks.

Not strictly necessary, but useful if the spool slips under your thumb—the Breakaway Thumbrake device fits all popular reels.

blocks really do work; the reel runs faster but stays under control and gives extra distance, in which case you must be casting extremely well; or the reel stays intact but does not speed up; a sign that something in the reel must be sticking: tight pinion or stale oil, perhaps. However, taking out of the last block is really an academic exercise. Normal results of brake block tests look something like this:

Block settings	Distance	Reaction
2 large blocks	105 yards	No backlash. Reel 'dead'.
2 medium blocks	115 yards	No backlash. Feels faster.
2 small blocks	130 yards	No backlash. Reel 'lively'.
1 small block	140 yards	Occasional backlash.
No blocks	145 yards	Backlash 3 casts out of 4.

The best setting here is 2 small blocks for routine fishing, or one block when the extra 10 yards are important. Weigh chances of backlash against better performance, then decide if the risk is justified. In the long term, work on your style so that single block casting is equally safe. This example is for smaller ABU 6500-type reels. Bigger models normally work safely and well with a pair of medium blocks, two small blocks or one medium. Much depends on tackle weight and line test.

Magnetic brakes
Test the reel in the same way, but this time work from full magnet power to minimum. Chart reel reaction, incidence of backlash and distances. You will soon arrive at the right setting. Remember to set the spindle end-float before starting to cast. Magnets are so easy to set up and so reliable that you may even be able to cast a couple of times then dial in the perfect setting. Apart from being a better control system than centrifugal blocks, magnets also provide stepless settings. Sometimes on other reels one block combination is a fraction too heavy, the next smaller a tiny bit too fast for comfort.

Oil viscosity
Old-style Penn and other simple reels have neither blocks nor magnets to monitor the cast, so, fill the bearings with 90 grade axle oil and make some test casts. If the reel is too fast, grade up to 140 oil or STP additive. If the reel is sluggish, use 20/50 engine oil. Most reels of Surfmaster 100 size loaded with 0·40 mm cast safely with 90 oil. Larger Squidders may require sticky STP. Try to maintain some end float on the spindle since the bearings and the spool will be ruined by overtightening, although a few, like the Mitchells, have special pressure pads which allow a certain amount of safe spindle tension. Traditionalists know that plain multipliers may be controlled by direct thumbing, however, handling a fast reel is quite an art. If all else fails, deliberately underload the reel, beginning with just 150 yards on Surfmaster 100s and 200 yards on the Squidder 140.

Fixed Spool Reels

The fixed spool reel (spinning reel) throws line from a spool set at 90 degrees to the handle axis. Nylon peels unhindered over the spool rim throughout the cast. Backlashes in the conventional sense are impossible. Tournament record casts are within 10 per cent of those set by the multipliers. In principle the reel is very efficient and easy to handle; but despite the potential advantages of fixed spools over multiplier reels, experienced beach fishermen generally still prefer the latter for sheer quality of sport.

On the fixed spool reel, the arrangement of gears and drive mechanism, plus friction from the bale arm roller which guides line onto the spool, add up to a rather unbalanced, clumsy reel. The mechanical efficiency never equals that of a multiplier, where the drive train is direct. Under full load, the fixed spool is an arm-aching beast with gear teeth, bearings and drive shaft subjected to immense pressure and consequently, only the finest reels are worth the investment for heavy-duty surfcasting.

Various sizes of reel cover all kinds of long-range work from ultra-light freshwater spinning to 8 ounce surfcasting. Despite the second-rate 'feel' and their limited winching power, fixed spools do come into their own in certain areas. Which reel should a long distance caster use—fixed spool or multiplier? For total flexibility he needs both. Their individual qualities complement each other.

The fixed spool's strengths

Fishing speed is perhaps the single factor that justifies using a fixed spool reel for long range fishing. Every multiplier, regardless of its gear ratio, is slow to retrieve from long distances. When the spool is even half empty, recovered line per handle revolution falls to a snail's pace. Gear ratio is irrelevant in this situation. A fixed spool reel fishes line quickly regardless of distance because spool working diameter is substantial, even with 200 yards of line out to sea.

Losing contact with hooked fish is common in long range fishing, and doubly embarassing when a fish runs towards you, throwing out yards of slack nylon which you cannot recover. More fish are lost through slack line than for any other reason. In big-money fishing matches, nobody is prepared to miss even one fish—it could just be the winning catch, worth thousands of pounds.

Many matchmen now use fixed spools to be sure that their lines do stay tight. The stronger reels are capable of withstanding fairly hard pressure, so there is no real danger of blowing up the gears by cranking quickly against slack line. Once in contact, you reduce winding speed anyway—full steam ahead with a big surf reel pulls the hook out of lightly pricked fish.

European beaches are overcrowded with anglers casting and losing miles of line, tons of leads and forests of terminal rigs. The more popular beaches—even of originally clean sand—are littered with a spider's web of semi-exposed monofilament and hooks. Slowly retrieved tackle tumbles across the seabed and sticks fast, adding to the mess. The only solution is fast retrieve to lift sinker and rig to mid-water where they plane back unobstructed. Fixed spool reels are ten times more efficient here and many beaches just cannot be fished without them.

Casting into the wind holds no fears for the fixed spool angler. No need to retune the reel, thumb the spool or reduce power. Hit the cast as hard as you like because the reel cannot backlash. (Wind knots are another matter but soon corrected). The only precaution is to avoid a massive belly of loose line which drifts into the tide or catches on a breakwater. High-speed retrieve comes to your aid once more: you can whip back the slack line while it is still hanging in mid-air.

Wind is often associated with cold weather. Together they are a nightmare for multiplier casters. Your thumb is sometimes so cold that it cannot grip the spool and the cast skids of control. Even if it does get away cleanly, wind pressure lifts the flowing coils and backlashes them. Controlling a hooked fish or merely retrieving tackle to rebait is sometimes impossible—your frozen fingers cannot grip the handle and will not guide line back on to the spool. A fixed spool takes the very worst weather in its stride.

Light line fishing is quite possible with a multiplier reel but generally easier with a fixed spool. Fixed spools grow more efficient as line diameter falls and thereby reduces spool rim friction. Multipliers do not show quite the same gains, at least not unless you reduce the size of reel as well, which in practical fishing terms may be impossible due to limited line capacity, slower retrieve and

The rear-set brake screw fitted to the Shakespeare Sigma reels and the ABU Cardinals is faster and more precise than the normal spool adjuster.

mechanical weakness. Even a big fixed spool can be usefully loaded with 10 lb test—and will, anyway, cast better than a smaller one. High sinker velocity creates tuning hazards for multiplier casters. Apart from leader knot flow and line twist, there is nothing to go wrong.

Learning to cast a fixed spool reel is much easier. But it is an advantage that might easily backfire. You can screw a fixed spool reel to a surf rod and cast without backlashes even if you have never been on a surfbeach before. Good news for the beginner, of course, but no blessing for the future.

The reel tolerates poor technique and even encourages it. Many casters brought up on the fixed spool can never change to multipliers because their ingrained casting technique is pitted with mistakes. It is far more difficult to break bad habits than to avoid them in the first place. Ideally, learn on the multiplier, then switch to fixed spool. Casting practice might be more painful for you in the first few weeks, but a good cast from a multiplier at least confirms that your technique is developing in the right direction.

THE RIGHT FIXED SPOOL REEL FOR YOU

PENN Spinfisher 750SS and 850SS
DAM 5001
MITCHELL 498 and 486
ZEBCO QUANTUM SS8
DAIWA DX90

The reels here are all highly respected in surfcasting circles, all share good engineering standards – tough gears and drive shafts, corrosion resistant frames and strong spools. There are some differences mainly reflected in price. Mitchells are functional rather than sophisticated. What they lack in service life is made up with cheap spares and perhaps the best after-sales service of all. Penn fixed spools share the quality of the Company's multiplier reels; the drag is especially smooth provided you look after it. For overall engineering excellence, the DAM takes some beating – is exceptionally smooth under load and shrugs off corrosion except to the anodised spool.

The advanced Quantum SS8 with self-locking cast control is fast, strong and versatile. Its design innovations herald the arrival of a new era in fixed spool performance. The rear-set drag screw complements the smooth and progressive brake places, which are not located in the spool itself. In its way it is as unique as the Alcedo and Sagarra reels: both European, both rather dated in appearance but well made and offering high casting performance. The Alcedo – something of a collector's item (I wish I had one) – can be tuned for perfect line flow with the monofilament diameter you prefer. It's only obvious disadvantage is massive weight, but that is the premium you pay for substantial amounts of stainless steel. Almost every surfcaster in Spain, the Mecca of fixed spool casting, owns a Sagarra for fishing and tournament casting.

67

In contrast with the range of multipliers, this selection of reels does not benefit by individual comparison of casting ability and control. They are virtually identical, and of course none has, or requires, an anti-backlash controller. Pick the reel you like; within reason it will cast and handle fish as well as any other model. Real differences concern price which reflects, among other things, engineering standards, materials specifications and service life. The more you pay, the longer the reel will last. Does it matter, bearing in mind that all should give a minimum of three years hard work? That is for you to judge.

Every reel holds a massive amount of 0·35–0·40 mm line. Total capacity is irrelevant to casting. What counts is how the reel handles the top 250–300 yards, the maximum length likely to be drawn off the reel during a cast. Here there are no fears: listed models cast off that much line without generating excessive friction.

Spool format

Tournament casters argue the value of a large diameter, short spool against that of a narrower but longer line store. Differences arise in unrestricted tournament events where line breaking strain is way below 6 lb test, and spools are loaded into the perfect cone profile theoretically best for long distance casting. A long spool is better, mainly because it is easier to load into a cone. However, in beach and freshwater casting, and even for tournament work with lines around 0·35 mm diameter, the emphasis is better placed on diameter.

Popular saltwater reels are around 3 inches in diameter on the front. (2·75 inches–3·25 inches is the accepted range for top results). The average spool length—0·75 inches—means that 250–300 yards of 0·35 mm nylon take up no more than a 0·5 inch spool depth; if the spool is deliberately overloaded, even 300 yards stripped off still leaves a line level high enough to prevent excessive rim friction.

Minimal spool length brings design advantages in the gear train. The reciprocating mechanism has a short travel and is thus stronger and less likely to distort line profile. The spool can afford to move slowly backwards and forwards to produce a close-set line load. In contrast, the long spool strains gears and encourages ragged line lay. Spools for tournament casting have double bales which separately load the front and back of the coned spool. That is clearly impractical in the surf, and besides, usually does not operate smoothly with lines over 8 lb test.

All standard production reels are improved by modifications to the line profile and bale arm. The line level here is uneven, which reduces effective spool capacity by 150 yards.

Gear ratios

If anything, reels are too fast. Even a 3.5:1 gear ratio working through a 3 inch spool pulls back some 30 inches of line per handle revolution, which far outstrips a multiplier reel, and is sometimes too vicious on a lightly-hooked fish. Coupled to the relatively weak gear structure of the reel, a high gear ratio further reduces mechanical efficiency and promotes rapid wear in components of less than perfect quality. Look for machine-cut gears, not die-castings. Toughened stainless steel and bronze gears and shafts, ball-races and sturdy supporting frame are essentials in fixed spool design. Watch those points rather than worry about the precise gear ratio. Not that you have much choice: except for the special low-speed DAM reels, all fixed spools are geared more or less the same.

Drag systems

Fixed spool drag systems range from primitive to excellent. I am not surprised to see that European-made reels are generally poor, while those aimed at the American market offer more control, power and reliability. A typical European reel—Sagarra or saltwater Mitchell—is either free running or locked. There is not much scope in the mid-range pressure settings, and a strong likelihood of severe juddering or seizure under full load. The DAM is an exception. On the other hand, European anglers do not hook fish that make long, searing runs. Mostly they never give the fish an inch of line.

Reels popular in America and other game-fishing countries rely on good drag systems with powerful but progressive braking, burn-resistant plates and washers, and built-in anti-lock devices. Penns and Shakespeare reels are quite good in this respect; in fact most reasonable quality American and Oriental reels are satisfactory.

The drag mechanism has two purposes in long-range fishing; unfortunately they are antagonistic. You need a fighting clutch with a wide power band and strong resistance to locking up. Hard casting is impossible without a totally locked spool.

Reels with poor drags are usually easily locked for casting, but you suffer if you hook a big fish. The super-quality game drags either will not lock the spool at all, which is exactly the designer's intention, or by so doing they strain screw threads to stripping point. Overtightening destroys a good drag anyway. Once locked, reels like the Penns and Shakespeares never do revert to their previous smoothness and control. In fact, destruction of balance by deliberate overtightening seems a feature of the very best reels.

This is something you will have to come to terms with, either by intentionally ruining a fine brake system or by investing in a reel which does lock without too much trouble. The only alternative is a special modification to the spool skirt as described later, but even that is rough and ready. What anglers really need is a fixed spool reel with a separate locking device. It need not be part of the main drag.

Reel stand security

My general misgivings about Oriental reels centres on weakness of construction rather than on design itself. I cannot come to terms with gears that strip or crumble, bale arms that corrode, or shoddy finish. Most of all, I hate reels that snap off at the reel stand in mid-cast. Cheap castings of low-grade aluminium alloy cannot stand up to a big pendulum cast. There is no way to predict strength and life of a reel stand. Invest in a good make of fixed spool. Should the worst happen, at least you have a reasonable chance of replacement under warranty. Rotor housings seem to share the same fate as the stand; again, cheap castings are the culprit.

Spare spools

Spare spools are neither provided with some reels nor available separately. This is a sad reflection on some manufacturers who presumably do not realise that fishermen mess up their lines and need to change nylon diameters to compensate for varying casting weights and weather conditions. One spool seriously limits the scope of any fixed spool reel, saltwater or fresh, and cannot be tolerated by keen casters. You should ask about spares before you buy the reel.

LINE LOADING AND PROFILING

No fixed spool reel casts efficiently unless fully topped up with line. The level must be no more than 0·125 inches below the spool rim, and ought really to be well up on that figure. The majority of tournament casters and long range beach fishermen deliberately cram on every last yard of line the spool can accept without binding in the rotor head and bale. Top casters start with a 'normally' loaded spool, then wind on the extra 200 yards or more required to produce those massive distances.

Absolute capacity is not necessary for routine fishing. Too much line is fine for tournaments which involve perhaps ten casts all day, after which nylon is stripped off and replaced. A single day's fishing twists line and destroys the original perfect spool profile. Line sloughs off in clumps—either drips off the spool at random or rips off in mid-cast, sometimes taking a few rod rings with it.

If you don't want to cut off the bale arm wire, loop a rubber band between the open bale and the gear case. The reel will cast without snapping shut.

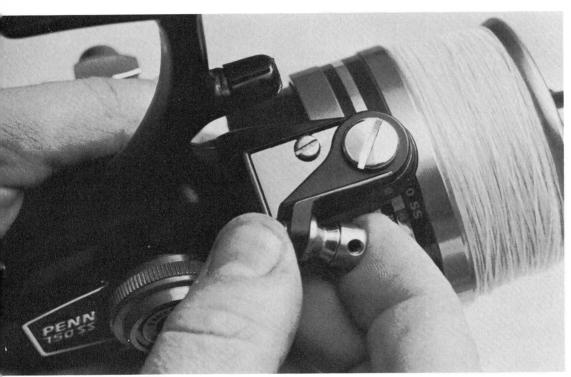

Bale arm removal is simple— usually a matter of cutting off the wire with a handsaw. Even if the reel snaps over during the cast, line will not trap itself.

Re-profiling the lower section of line for better spool control and frictionless casting.

The re-profiled spool filled to capacity. The slight positive cone effect isn't necessary for beachcasting though may add a few yards in tournaments.

Lay the leader knot snugly against the back edge of the spool—it's less likely to foul during the cast.

Remember to lock the spool before casting hard with a powerful surf outfit. Line slipping against a bare finger will cut to the bone.

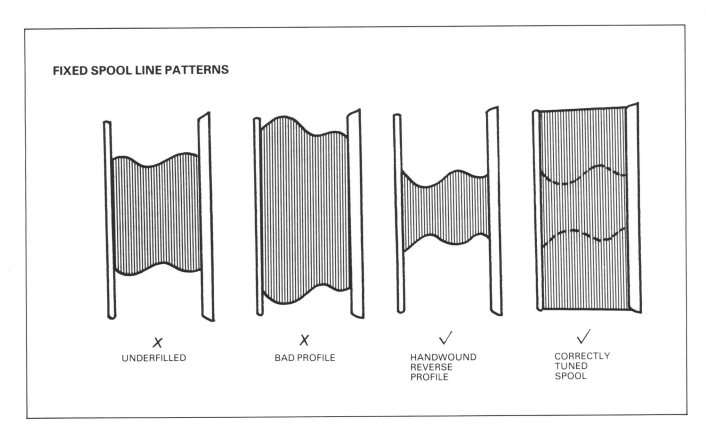

FIXED SPOOL LINE PATTERNS

✗ UNDERFILLED

✗ BAD PROFILE

✓ HANDWOUND REVERSE PROFILE

✓ CORRECTLY TUNED SPOOL

Level loading or perhaps a slight excess is acceptable. As always, avoid underloading the spool—that is where you lose most of your casting power.

Anglers are puzzled about the even line build up on a tournament caster's fixed spool. When they fill their own, line builds up excessively high or low—usually at the back or front face of the spool. Any reel chosen at random from the tackle shop shelf has this nasty habit. So how do leading fishermen produce such neat results? Are reels handpicked, the cream of the manufacturer's stock? Are they custom-made? No, they are simply profiled—a ten minute modification you can do at home without spending any money. You can be sure of casting farther, wasting less line and preventing all but occasional tangles.

Load your reel to the brim with line. See where high and low spots occur. Make a rough sketch of this line profile, then strip off around 275 yards of line. Refer to the sketch. Now, wind on line by hand or by spinning the spool in a lathe. DO NOT use the normal winding mechanism, because this time you are aiming for a profile which reverses the normal pattern of humps and hollows. Using around 50 yards of handwound line, produce a REVERSE profile deep in the spool. The diagrams show you how the system works. Then top up the spool normally. The lower profile cancels out the reel's natural line lay pattern, and should produce an evenly loaded spool with a flat profile or a slight positive cone. You may need to re-run

the experiment a few times to develop perfect lower profile, which is different for every reel. Even reels of the same model throw slightly different profiles.

You will also discover that because the reel now capitalises on the full spool volume, line capacity is raised by about 10 per cent. When you stripped off 275 yards, you will need 300 to replace it. Changing lines is easy: strip off the old line down to the re-profiled, handwound section, then top up the spool lip. Most casters use the lower profile as a permanent arbour. Layers of tape wrapped around the shaped core maintain correct profile and spool capacity.

Re-profiling eliminates humps and hollows and reduces, but seldom corrects, a reel's normal bias toward the back or front of the spool. In minor cases no correction is necessary. Reverse coning—too much line in front—exaggerates tangles, cuts distances and reduces spool capacity.

Either build up or reduce the thickness of the spool base washers, which moves the spool back or forwards relative to the line roller, or rework the bale arm mechanism with shims, (or by filing away the support posts), until the roller angle throws line further forwards or backwards. Some ingenuity and kitchen table surgery are required, since only the DAM 5000 series and Alcedo have adjustable components. The DAM drag/spool support plates is specially slotted for instant cone correction. The Alcedo is more versatile—even the bale arm moves for precise alignment. However, the process is simple enough on any reel, demanding only patience, plus a file, spare washer or two, and maybe a spot of epoxy filler.

BALE ARM MODIFICATION

Full bale arm mechanisms, designed to flip back into operation when the reel handle is rotated after casting, are a nuisance for long range casting and may well ruin your attempts to blast a sinker over 150 yards. The bale is so sensitive to rotor head momentum that it triggers prematurely, drops the roller back over the line in mid-cast and thus kills distance. In extreme cases line snaps. At worst—but surprisingly common on cheap reels— casting force rips the rotor head apart or even snaps the reel stand from the gear case.

Sagarra Tarzan, Mitchell 498 and Penn Spin-fisher 706Z reels dispense with a full bale arm. Line is controlled by a roller on a fixed post. To cast, lift line from behind the roller. Afterwards, guide it back into the pick-up with your finger. Bale closure is eliminated; the chances of line fouling the roller during the cast are small enough to be discounted. Even for fishing lures on the surface, where the full bale arm is generally considered superior, the manual roller pick-up is quite adequate.

A home-made leather finger guard encourages better casting. Without fear of cuts and line burn, you'll be far more confident especially with the heavier sinkers.

DAM 5001 reels are tuned with an adjustable washer which raises and lowers the spool relative to the pick-up roller.

Experienced casters take a hacksaw to the bale wire and sever its connection top and bottom: close to the roller mechanism and tight against the opposite side of the rotor. Some reels anchor the far end of the bale wire with a bolt or screw set directly into the rotor. Most modern reels feature an external counterbalance weight which accepts the bale wire by screw or internal swaging. It does not matter how the wire is detached. More important is that you must replace the counterweight itself. Without extra mass on the rotor, the reel feels lumpy at speed, and eventually knocks outs its bearings.

The German DAM fixed spool reels are fitted with a variable bale arm spring device which raises or decreases bale arm trigger pressure. By resetting the internal tensions you can sometimes prevent bale flip without resorting to surgery. The alternative on other reels is to secure the bale open with a rubber band stretched tightly between bale wire and gear cage. It is a clumsy modification that works very well if you do not want to lose automatic bale action.

Reduction of spool rim friction

The majority of saltwater fixed spool reels are designed excessively broad, slightly too high spool rims. Distance is improved without loss of line control by lathe work—either polishing up or turning down the rim. Reels like the Sagarra Tarzan which have the same diameter rim front and back are much more efficent after being reworked to reduce the front diameter about 0·25 inches. Other reels are less of a problem and should not be cut down by more than 0·10 inches. Do not go mad on the lathe—reduce the diameter slightly, then test the reel. You cannot put metal back.

Spool lock modification

A crude but highly effective modification enables you to lock the spool for hard casts without straining drag plates or even altering brake setting. Only skirted spools respond to this treatment.

Watch how the spool reciprocates relative to the underlying rotor head. Pick a spot well forward on the spool, and drill a 0·25 inch hole through the alloy, so that the hole itself clears the rotor when the spool is fully advanced.

Cut a 2 inch piece of 16SWG or thicker stainless steel wire, and bend it into an even sided 'U' shape. Slightly splay out the last 0·125 inches of each leg to form a hook. Adjust the width of the 'U' until modest finger pressure compresses the clip enough to slide neatly into the spool hole. Release the clip, and it should grip tightly. Now connect the clip to the reel stand with a piece of 50–80 lb test monofilament.

Rotate the spool in the opposite direction to line-lay until the anchor line tightens between inserted clip and reel stand. Check that the spool is firmly restrained and that the anchor line itself neatly aligns with the spool, as the picture shows. Now pull back the bale arm or release line from the manual roller . . . cast as hard as you like. You will find the modification very easy to operate and absolutely reliable. The drag setting is never disturbed for casting; you will not strain plates or forget to reset pressure after each cast.

Casting releases

Supermen and gorillas do not cut their index fingers when casting a saltwater fixed spool reel at full power. The rest of us slice skin or at least rub it away through prolonged friction. A finger cut from an old leather glove secured by a piece of elasticated tape running around your wrist makes life far more comfortable. You will cast more confidently and consequently distances must improve. The leather shield—rubber is just as good—is far superior to various release gadgets on sale. Most are too imprecise at best; at worst they severely abrade line or snap the cast.

LINE TWIST

All fixed spool reels twist line. In theory, cast and retrieve counteract themselves. In practice they do not and eventually the line twists itself into knots. The only difference between reels is how long it takes to do the damage.

Load line as tightly as you can. Keep the tension high as you fish, which is easily achieved by running line between finger and thumb. Combing nylon this way also drives the majority of twists into the top 15 yards of main line, which can then be cut off. Ironing twists from an uncut line is not so simple. Try running off all the line, then drag it through surf or over long grass before respooling—time consuming and none too effective but better than nothing.

Lure fishing soon generates line twist and wind knots, which are aggrevated by soft, saturated nylon. Keep the line tight, and use brands of line which err towards the slightly stiff side when dry. The best line for fixed spool casting in conditions which exaggerate twist—lure fishing mainly—is DuPont's totally waterproof Prime cofilament. It is even better than Stren for preventing wind knots. One thing for sure is that swivels are downright useless for anti-twist fishing and anti-kink vanes are not much better.

SIDE-CASTERS

The Australian Alvey sidecasters are big, tough winches that swivel through right angles to cast fixed spool style. Various models cover the full saltwater and heavy freshwater range, and you can specify a star-drag system if you like.

Though not really suited to short rods with a high-set reel seat, the Alvey is at home on long surf rods cast South African and pendulum style. Distances and fishing control are excellent; the main headaches are sheer weight, poor balance and massive line twist. A valuable reel for rugged work, but unlikely to suit the majority of anglers.

The wire clip modification which anchors the spool without straining the drag system. Any skirted-spool reel may be altered.

Shock Leaders and Reel Lines

SHOCK LEADERS

A shock leader is a few feet of heavy nylon line tied to the main reel line to absorb casting stress. It provides some insurance against losing a big fish in breaking surf—a stage in the fight where you need all the help you can get. A strong shock leader also masks severe errors in casting style and timing: not an ideal property, but at least some protection for tackle and bystanders.

Good leaders certainly aid casting, if only because they permit the reel to carry light running line which would snap were it not shielded from initial shock and abrasion. In practical terms a leader allows long range fishing with 12–18 lb main line regardless of sinker weight. Plenty of line can be stored on a small reel, which is easy to handle and better casting than one which holds 250 yards of 30 lb test—the traditional line load.

Above all, shock leaders boost your confidence. No matter how hard you cast, the line remains intact during the power stroke. The generous safety margin protects terminal tackle and your neighbours on the beach. A leader is the guarantee that your tackle will not snap off and smash into somebody's face. On today's crowded beaches safety alone makes the routine use of shock leaders a moral obligation.

The more way-out casting styles are dangerous even with a shock piece, and you cannot be sure that tackle will hold together during peak power. Super-heavy nylon at least ensures a margin of safety. For most anglers who use ordinary pendulum techniques, though, the risk of skittering a sinker downbeach is considerably reduced by even 40 lb test leaders.

Unfortunately the confidence inspired by a shock leader can wreck your casting in the long term. To understand how, consider what heavy nylon does in mid-cast. *It is a shock absorber which irons out excessive tension between rod and sinker.*

In theory a leader is unecessary. When sinker follows rod correctly though the casting arc, very little strain develolps. You can calculate the forces involved: even on a 200 yard cast with 5 ounces of lead, the perfect style generates nowhere near enough leader tension to snap 40 lb nylon, a modest breaking strain by today's fishing and tournament standards.

Level line tournaments, in which line diameter must be constant from sinker to reel core, spring some surprises for casters who cannot cast without a leader. Four ounce sinkers really are cast over 200 yards on 18 lb line all through. Top competitors seldom snap off. Technique is the key—the cast flows like syrup with absolute smoothness of power. Every ounce of casting effort is precisely channelled into the blank and by sheer experience the caster knows just how near to breaking point he can stress the nylon.

Why not learn to dispense with a leader? Primarily because most casters—even good ones—easily overload normal surf fishing tackle and therefore risk snapping off every cast. Except for short range fishing, increasing line diameter and breaking strain to compensate for power input is not the answer. The thicker the line, the more distance is lost. By retaining the thinnest practical main line and shielding it with a leader, you reach a neat compromise. Even in top-flight tournament casting where styles are close to perfect, leaders boost performance by insulating the caster from the phsychological pressure of potential snap-offs.

Occasional casts inevitably lose control. Peculiar stresses develop when the sinker flies one way while the rod pulls another. Then follows a surge of excess pressure along the leader. The lighter the line, the less room for error. A strong leader mops up pressure and will probably save the cast unless the impact is particularly savage.

The cast either feels normal, or tightens and seems 'solid' and harsh—a sensation difficult to describe but instantly recognisable when accompanied by a burned thumb. The exact result depends on how bad the cast really was.

Real difficulties creep in when the leader disguises permanently bad style. Some men snap 50 lb leaders like cotton, yet they seldom cast more than 120 yards. Total lack of control is the problem here. They cast one way . . . the rod pulls in another plane . . . the sinker flies off just anywhere. Without fluidity of tackle and technique, it does not take much physical effort to snap strong

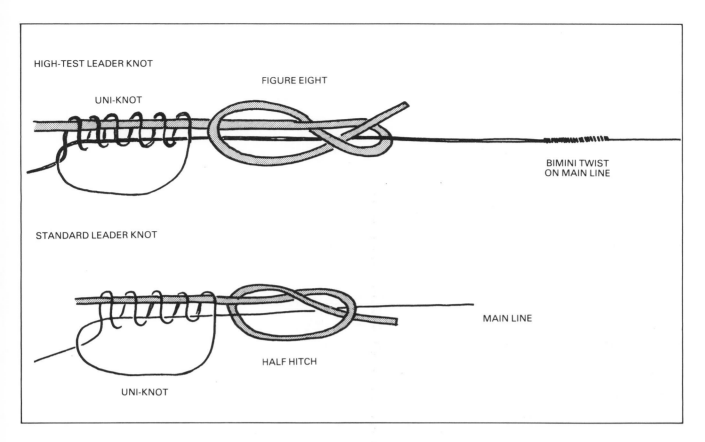

HIGH-TEST LEADER KNOT

FIGURE EIGHT

UNI-KNOT

BIMINI TWIST
ON MAIN LINE

STANDARD LEADER KNOT

HALF HITCH

UNI-KNOT

MAIN LINE

leader. Many fishermen suffer to some extent, and the fixed spool reel aggrevates the situation because it does not overrun in response to a bad cast. Bad casters murder their tackle, confident of avoiding backlash.

Obviously there are practical limits below which occasional snap-offs occur. There are rare casters who really can break heavy leaders even though they cast smoothly—some leading tournament competitors would never be happy with less than 50 lb nylon. But the modern trend towards very heavy leaders is detrimental to average fisherman.

Safe breaking strain depends on casting style, rod action and power, blank length and sinker weight. Extra poundage should be added to compensate for poor knots—we all tie them sometimes—line abrasion and deterioration within the line material itself.

As a rule of thumb, calculate safe leader breaking strain by multiplying sinker weight by ten, and calling the result pounds. Five ounce sinkers cast safely and easily on 50 lb test monofilament; 3 ounces requires a minimum of 30 lb test for absolute security.

Away from crowds, when beaches are deserted or long distances prove unecessary, I cut breaking strain to the lowest figure I know by experience to be manageable. For 125 yards fishing with 4 ounces and a fairly soft pendulum rod, I tie on 30 lb nylon, which never snaps in mid-cast. Run a few tests to establish realistic minimum line tests for the various rigs you cast. Choose a safe area to practise, and progressively reduce leader strength until you find the bottom limit.

Casting 4 ounces on 30 lb leader is a reasonable test of casting smoothness and efficiency. If you consistently break off under 150 yards, something is lacking in power flow or tackle balance. You should be able to reach the target in perfect safety with just 20 lb level line. Very good technicians do it on 15 lb monofilament.

Selecting and attaching leaders

Buy leader nylon in small quantities because some lines deteriorate rapidly. Were you to buy 1000 yards at once—anything up to 10 years supply—most would be seriously weakened or ultra-stiff by the time you half emptied the spool. Much depends on brand, material and how long it has sat on the dealer's shelf. As it is impossible to predetermine nylon's age and keeping qualities, it is wiser to opt for 50–250 yards at a time. That way you reduce losses should line fail on strength or pliability.

Many brands of nylon are naturally harsh and brittle. Others are pitted, crazed, nicked and of irregular diameter. All cast poorly and may snap without warning. On the other hand do not assume that all expensive lines are superior. Some cheap brands are excellent; but in general it does pay to invest a little more for DuPont Prime and

Stren, Berkley Trilene, or even Maxima which though stretchy is still a good leader for general fishing. Of the cheaper brands, Sylcast is reasonable but very stiff in high breaking strain; Triple Fish and Ande are soft and tough. The very best leader? For my money it is Stren.

I am not sure if leader colour has any serious affect on fishing. I have caught fish on blue, green, brown, black, colourless, red and fluorscent gold. I would not rule out variations in catch rate even though there is no evidence to suggest that fish swim away from certain colours. I believe the opposite does occur—a few species are ATTRACTED by the leader. Surface-feeding schools of bluefish sometimes attack fluorescent gold Stren. European flatfish like daps and flounders, well known for their curiosity, bite well on Stren fluorescent blue or gold traces.

Too many anglers unroll a few feet of nylon and tie it to the main line without thinking about leader's correct length. Leaders cut for casting practice should give at least six full turns of heavy line on the spool when the sinker is suspended from the rod tip ready to cast. An extra 24 inches are worth having so that the leader can be retied several times before you lose the six anchoring coils.

Fishing leaders must be at least that long for safety, and might benefit from an extra ten feet so that you have some leeway for pulling a heavy fish through high surf. Never allow the knot to lie outside the rings when the fish beaches itself. One big swell followed by a powerful backwash sweeps the fish out to sea and snaps the main line at the leader knot. The rougher the water, the longer the leader should be.

However, too much leader ruins the cast. The knot MUST be off the reel and through the rings before the spool hits full speed, which is almost instantaneous after sinker release. If you use more than 50 feet of shock leader for really hard casting, expect the knot to wrap itself in the rings.

Cast clearance and line flow are dependent on small, streamlined knots between leader and reel line, but as plenty of fish are lost through weak knots, you cannot afford to compromise on knot strength. There is no alternative to a special leader knot similar to those illustrated. For everyday fishing and casting practice, the simple half-hitch/Uni knot is fine. Serious light line work with heavyweight species demands the more complicated Bimini Hitch/Albright combination. Learn to tie both.

Sinker and trace attachment points are equally important, for they too present a safety hazard. If anything, the sinker knot is even more important than the upper joint between leader and main line. Sinkers snap off in mid cast because the knot was seriously weakened by seabed abrasion. There is no excuse for losing tackle this way. The angler who does so is a menace since all too often sinker, trace and hooks fly down the beach rather than seaward.

There is no substitute for a tough metal link between sinker loop and leader, or for a strong swivel or split ring between leader and trace. Mustad oval split rings are excellent—a direct replacement for swivels in most cases. Stainless steel wire clips work well too. Avoid flimsy link-swivels and safety-pin clips. The best swivels generally available are Berkley and Dexter. At all costs avoid cheap Oriental copies which pull apart under finger pressure, or rot to powder after a dousing of seawater. Someone's life may be at stake here. You cannot afford to take a risk.

Change the sinker/leader knot every dozen casts. Check every knot before each cast, and retie if you have the slightest doubt. Examine split rings and swivels too.

Leader softness
Above all you need a soft leader. Tough, wiry brands will not fly off the spool—fixed spool or multiplier—and they cannot snug down neatly when tied to reel line. Cheap nylon usually has a strong spool memory and springs back into coils when tension eases. The leader knot catches in the level wind or butt rings; main line tangles plague fully loaded fixed spool reels. Leader, trace and baits crumple into a mound of bunched nylon as

Stren, Trilene and Maxima are the best lines to consider for surf and long distance fishing. Stren (and the new Prime cofilament also from Du Pont) is outstanding even in this select trio of lines.

By using thinner lines, you can substantially boost the capacity of surfcasting reels. The ABU 6500CT holds over 300 yards of 0·35 mm (15 lb test) nylon.

soon as the sinker hits the water. You will also discover that springy, glossy brands of nylon tend to burn themselves and scorch your thumb as well.

MAIN LINE

Compared to the cost of rod and reel, transportation, bait and effort involved in learning to surfcast, the most expensive brands of line are dirt cheap. In real terms, expensive brands are usually more economical anyway because they last much longer. Some casters claim to change line every time they fish. The cheap brands they use are burned, abraded and cut after a single day on the beach. According to their logic, it pays to buy cheap line which you can afford to treat in cavalier fashion.

I do not see the sense in that way of thinking. The Stren and Prime lines that fill my reels are so tough and reliable that even 8 lb test lasts up to six months, unless of course, I snap off in mid-cast. One spool of 12 lb Stren has been cast over grass, fished from sand, rocks and shingle for a whole year. It is as close to perfect as you could wish. I am free from continual nagging doubts that go hand in hand with cheap line: is this spoolful safe to use? Is the breaking strain accurate? Is there a weak section to give way when I hook a big fish? Extra money spent on good line is always repaid and it probably amounts to less than one per cent of your annual fishing costs anyway. Maxima and Trilene are useful alternatives to Du Pont line, although not quite so good for saltwater fishing.

Of the cheaper lines, Sylcast, Ande and Bayer Perlon (the soft version) seem fair value despite their limitations. Under no circumstances do they rival the high-grade lines—but they are good enough for learning to cast and for anglers who do not fish particularly hard or often. It makes no sense to load up with Trilene or Stren if you expect an overrun next cast. Lesser nylons encourage you to keep practising. Buy a bulk spool to begin your casting career, master your tackle, then upgrade to pure quality. Use the cheaper line once more when you test out a new rod or reel, or change casting styles. Most keen anglers have favourite 'ordinary' and 'best' brands of fishing line.

Breaking strains and diameters

Confusion still runs riot in casting line selection. Over the years, the largest selling breaking strains of nylon show a steady fall from 20 lb plus, to 18 lb, and now to 12–15 lb test. Information and confidence feed slowly into the angling world—for a long time anglers did not believe you could fish in saltwater with anything under 30 lb breaking strain. Modern tackle and techniques encourage a swing to lightness, but diehards still will not listen. The fact remains that you probably cannot utilise the full strength of even 10 lb line on a powerful surf rod and reel. 12–15 lb test nylon provides a good safety margin: with it you can land massive fish, even in rough water. If you still doubt the resilience of modern lines, tackle up with 15 lb line—even cheap stuff—and test it for yourself. Try to deliberately snap it.

Thinner lines cast farther, improve bite detection, reduce tidal pressure on sinker and rod tip, and provide enough stretch and bounce to cushion rod and line itself from sudden strain. Stretch and its associated spool crushing pressure impose certain restrictions on tackle and how it is used, but with modern reels there is no serious problem. Stretch is largely controlled by line quality. High-grade monofilaments and cofilaments are safe and sensitive without being as rubbery as inferior lines, which can be a menace at long range.

Diameter/breaking strain ratios vary but have little effect on routine casting and fishing. Choose by diameter if you like, and leave breaking strain to look after itself. 0·35–0·40 mm is now the accepted specification for long-range beach fishing with tackle capable of handling heavy fish, rough water and big sinkers. Breaking strain falls between 12 and 22 lb according to brand. 15 lb is about average, and perfectly safe. What you gain with the 'strong' lines may be lost in handling qualities. Many are tough, wiry and susceptible to burns. Knots seem to cut themselves apart.

In specific conditions it pays to use heavier line throughout. Conger eel fishing and codding in rocky ground is short range sport which demands extra power to cope with obstructions and floating weeds. A 25–40 lb line on a large casting multiplier provides easy 100 yard fishing plus crane-like winching power. However, it takes a lot of muscle to achieve and maintain a 20 lb line pressure. Most of the extra power is illusory but the tackle is immune to abrasion and rough handling. Strong line helps winch a ten pound cod up a hundred yards of vertical cliff. Some anglers actually do use a crane fashioned from bicycle wheels.

Sinkers

A surfcasting sinker is a chunk of moulded lead which costs next to nothing compared to the outlay on rods and reels. Yet it is important because it helps control your casting and fishing techniques. Unless the sinker is matched to rod and reel, you are in big trouble during the cast and when the bait is in the water.

A sinker draws power from your muscles during the cast, then expends it to drag tackle and baits through the air. It can generate no more energy than you apply, so its efficiency as a projectile is directly related to your casting ability and strength, which are transferred to the sinker by the blank. Its length, action and stiffness must be carefully chosen—neither soft enough to waste your skill nor so overpowered that the blank cannot bend without brutal treatment.

The released sinker is a tremendous driving force. Mass and speed act together to pull the baits, terminal rig and line skyward. In so doing, the sinker must overcome gravity, air resistance and the mechanical drag of the reel.

Maximum speed of the sinker limits the kind of baits you can fish. The faster the cast, the more bait is torn from the hook. If flight speed is beyond the capacity of the reel, the spool is uncontrollably fast or hopelessly sluggish. Problems escalate with soft baits like crabs and mussels.

On the seabed, the sinker is either an anchor or a means of limiting tackle drift. It must be carefully matched to tidal current, size of bait, fishing range, depth of water and to line diameter. The sinker's resistance as it tumbles over the seabed on retrieve generates line tension. Because stressed nylon monofilament stretches up to a quarter of its original length, line wound back on to the spool imposes a crushing pressure measured in tons per square inch. Sinkers grossly mismatched to line, reel and rod can literally explode the spool and rip out side-plates.

A sinker's three major tasks—absorption of casting power; release of that energy in mid air; seabed control of the baits and terminal rig—must each be considered alone and in relation to the rest of the outfit, to the angler himself, to baits, fishing conditions and even to the expected species of fish.

The most useful sinker is one that offers the best solution in the circumstances. Sometimes it is impossible to choose one weight or shape which perfectly balances all the options. Often a compromise is essential. However, it must be thought out, not guessed at.

Sinker weight

Theorectically, you can cast far enough with any weight of lead. Power generated is related to sinker mass and velocity. The lighter the lead, the faster it flies. Big sinkers accelerate more slowly, but still develop comparable kinetic energy because of their higher mass. More important is momentum—'carrying power'—the product of mass and velocity.

Tournament casters achieve long distances with a variety of sinkers. One or two specific weights provide the highest performance under ideal conditions, but as a rule there is little to choose between 4, 5 and 6 ounce sinkers cast on appropriate diameter lines.

On the beach, the theory does not work out so well. Small sinkers simply cannot manage, particularly into a headwind. They have to fly so much faster to achieve the same momentum as a heavier lead weight that the exra speed is self-defeating. Speed compounds the ill effects of air resistance; control suffers. The faster the rod moves, the more difficult it becomes to time and execute the cast.

A conveniently generous chunk of lead works wonders for long range fishing. Momentum provides the answer: a six ounce sinker travelling at half the speed of three ounces still generates the same carrying power. Bonus points are more leisurely casting and fewer backlashes when you cast into the wind. Once in flight, the sinker is less affected by bait and wind drag. Soft baits stay on the hook.

Comparing heavy and light sinkers is rather like

Conditions	3 ounces	4 ounces	5 ounces	6 ounces	8 ounces
Still air, no baits	160 yds	175 yds	190 yds	185 yds	160 yds
Still air + bait	100 yds	120 yds	135 yds	142 yds	140 yds
Headwind + bait	80 yds	90 yds	105 yds	115 yds	125 yds

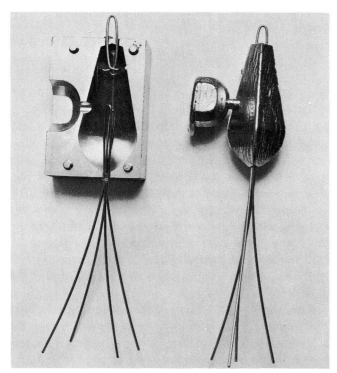

The DCA Aquapedo sinker rigged with fixed nosewires which are bent into grapnels for fishing in fast tides.

measuring cars against trucks. For the same engine capacity, one goes faster, the other carries a bigger load. From the beach, this load capacity is the deciding factor. Additionally, a big sinker holds better in the tide and boosts tackle inertia, perhaps the most important aid to hooking fish at long range. A series of tests carried out over grass pinpoint the strengths and weaknesses of sinker weights. Figures in this table relate to casts made on standard pendulum tackle, 0·40 mm main line and a Penn 970 reel.

The conclusions are self-evident. As far as distance is concerned, choice of sinker weight diminishes in step with drag no matter how it is caused. In practical terms, long range beach fishing demands at least 5 ounces of lead with the standard pendulum rod, reel and line. 3 ounces is fine for short-range fishing in calm weather. 5–6 ounces are excellent for all-round fishing and actually cast a bait farther than 8 ounce sinkers. However, when the wind is blowing hard onshore, the sluggish big weight outclasses the rest. For all-round success in the surf you need a selection of sinkers to accommodate weather, tidal pull and distance.

The results of even limited tests show that 5–6 ounces of lead are close to perfect with ordinary beach tackle, baited or not. Tournament casters in Britain settle for 5·25 ounces or close to it. There is a definite link between 5–6 ounces and the casting ability and strength of the majority of fishermen. Sinkers in this weight band provide an excellent compromise between easy casting and good carrying capacity. They are also best for learning to cast: start with 5 ounces and later experiment with sinkers weighing 5·25, 5·5, 5·75 and 6 ounces.

Quarter-ounce variations produce surprising results. Even without changing rod, reel or line, you will make your longest casts with one specific weight. For most anglers that will be 5·25 or 5·5 ounces, and the distances may be up to 20 yards better than with just ¼-ounce either side.

The same weight is also ideal for general fishing: it casts nicely with a full load of bait, anchors in all but the fastest tides, and penetrates an onshore breeze.

Smaller sinkers

Anglers who are dismayed by the loss of distance caused by exchanging a 5 ounce sinker for, say, 2 ounces usually fail to appreciate that the weight of projectile they cast—lure or sinker—must be balanced to line diameter and rod action. 2 ounces on 0·40 mm line is never much good for getting a big bait out there or for holding in the current.

2 ounces cast on 0·30 mm line (8–10 lb test) is another matter. Distances shoot up and the lower water resistance of the line encourages firm tackle anchorage. Provided bait is relatively small, you can fish at 125 yards. Lures produce much the same response, though low-density plugs never do fly as far as a streamlined bar of steel like the Hopkins lure.

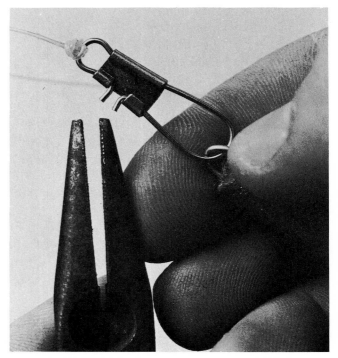

It's ESSENTIAL to buffer the sinker knot against abrasion on the seabed. Tough split rings and secure safety-pin links are safe enough for routine fishing. Guard against cheap clips that tear open under pressure.

Sinker weight/line test combinations for high-performance casting

⅝–1 ounce . . . 4–10 lb test (0·25–0·30 mm diameter)

1–3 ounce . . . 8–12 lb test (0·275–0·35 mm diameter)

Practical fishing distances in reasonably good weather should be around 125 yards with 1 ounce metal lures cast on 8 lb test. 2–3 ounces on 10 lb test will fly 150 yards—perhaps more in perfect conditions with Hopkins lures and others of sound aerodynamic design. Zoned action rods of the correct length and power are absolutely essential, as are small, high-peformance reels like the Penn Spinfisher 650SS and Levelmatic, ABU 5000 series baitcasters, Daiwa Magforce and Shakespeare Sigmas. Do not expect to hit the heights with ordinary surf reels—less than 2 ounces do not provide enough momentum in the cast to make the spool turn fast enough.

Sinker shapes

Only one shape of sinker makes sense for long-range fishing . . . nothing compares to a bomb or torpedo design with a round or square cross-section. Pyramids, bank sinkers, 'Grip' weights and the rest of the traditional and exotic shapes of sinkers are all inferior. It is a waste of time and effort to develop an excellent casting style, then destroy its benefits with an inefficient sinker.

Sinker shape affects the cast in three distinct areas—turn-over, flight and seabed control.

Turn over is the brief but important phase of the cast immediately before line release. The sinker starts by swinging nose down on the pendulum arc. As full power forces the blank into full compression and your arms take over to add the final punch and pull, it flips through 180 degrees to fly nose first into the sky. This turn-over, coming so close to full power and reel release, is inevitably accompanied by severe whiplashing. Inferior sinkers wobble and flirt through the air, lose energy and destroy baits by literally tearing them from the hook.

The phenomenon is much exaggerated with fixed spool reels, which have a much faster and more vicious line release than multipliers. Sometimes the wobble is so severe and prolonged that the rod tip oscillates violently—a frequent cause of trapped leader knots and line tangles. The inertia of a multiplier spool imposes a degree of control on the turning sinker but does not eliminate ragged flight.

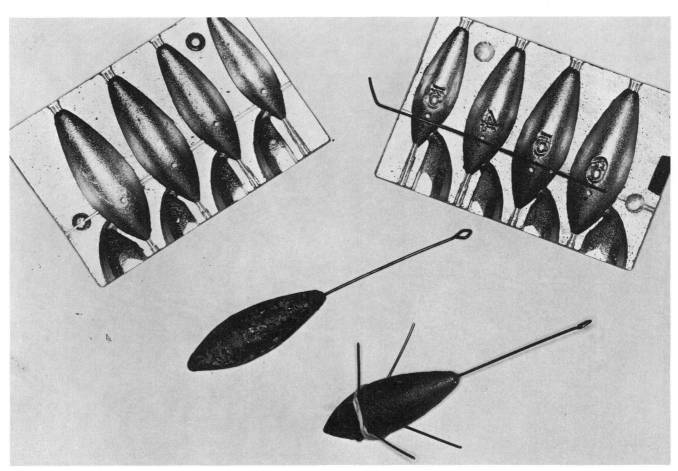

Certainly the best sinker on the beach—the DCA Beachcomb fitted with a long tail wire and optional swivelling grip wires.

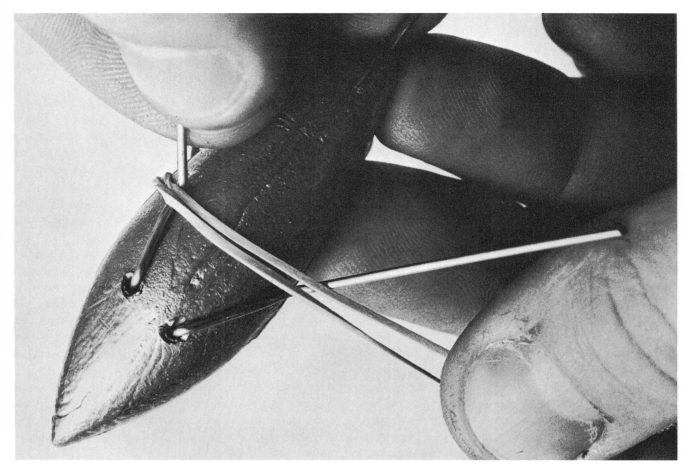

Swivelling grip-wires are more comfortable for fishing because they offer no resistance on retrieve. Make your own sinkers with rubber band security straps. Adjust the pressure so that the wires hold steady until triggered by striking.

In-flight stability helps the sinker cut neatly through the air. You want a 'dead', fully stabilised flight, not one that encourages the sinker to flip from side to side. The faster and lighter the sinker or lure, the more effect shape has on flight path. Cast extremely hard, a leaf-shaped hollow-section lure blade may actually boomerang back on itself to dive, turn 90 degrees left or right, or even take off vertically for the heavens. Heavier lead sinkers towing baits just lose energy, pick up the wind and drop short of the mark. A severe, prolonged wobble originating from the initial turn-over could easily destroy multiplier tuning and cause backlash. Many 'inexplicable' backlashes are directly the result of poor sinker design—check sinker shape if you are plagued by continual casting problems with no obvious solution. The best caster in the world could not control some of the sinkers widely available for surfcasting.

Seabed control. Is the acid test of any sinker efficient enough to get out there in the first place. Once on the seabed, the sinker must either anchor terminal rig and bait, or allow a steady, controlled drift downstream. All kinds of shapes and sizes of sinker were tested during the early days of long-range British surfcasting. Only the grip-wired bomb has survived. 'Watch' leads, pyramids and the rest are totally inferior.

Serious though the design criteria of surf sinkers may appear, the answer is absolutely straightforward. Bombs turn over nicely, fly neatly through the sky, and, wired with swivelling or fixed spikes of stainless steel, hold bottom in the fiercest current. Look no further than the bomb concept for excellent surf fishing.

Short bombs, like the DCA Aquapedo with its characteristic square cross-section, are good all-rounders. The latest Beachbomb sinkers from the same manufacturer are even better in some respects – the lower air drag seems to add a couple of yards to the cast. The 5.29 ounces Aquazoom, also from DCA Moulds (address: The Maltings, East Tyndall Street, Cardiff CF1 5EA, Wales), is the official UKSF tournament sinker. No other company in the world has done more research and development on casting sinker shape. Their range of die-cast aluminium alloy moulds is absolutely unbeatable, and available in all sizes from 2 to 10 ounces, including the 5.25 (150 gramme) competition standard.

85

Adding the grip wires

Plain sinkers are fine for casting practice and still-water fishing. It may be better to drift along the seabed anyway, in which case you can control the rate by adding or subtracting lead. It is a neat way of pinpointing underwater gulleys—the sinker swings around with the tide and drops into the depression; the tide does not have enough force to roll it up the far side. Drumfish and cod anglers use this trick to position their baits to best advantage on beaches which do not dry out enough at low water to expose the foreshore structure.

On the whole, wired sinkers are more versatile. Mould four stainless wires, some 4–6 inches long, into a bomb's nose. Bend them into grapnels, and you will find that the sinker will hold fast in most tidal currents. 5 ounce wired sinkers hold better than 10 ounces of plain lead.

Fixed wires tend to catch in the seabed on retrieve. The Breakaway sinker, either shop-bought or made at home, features swivelling wires moulded close to the sinker's nose and held under tension by a rubber band, or beads trapped in sinker flank depressions by wire tension alone. The sinker casts and fishes extremely well and pulls ashore with minimal resistance. However, once in position, the sinker has to stay put. Moving it triggers the wires and destroys the grip.

For that reason a fixed-wire sinker is useful in conditions which demand that baits be kept on the move. Keen surf men keep both in their tackle boxes.

Long-tailed sinkers

Sinkers with extended tail wires instead of normal short loops have made a big impact on the British market since their introduction from Spain, where they were developed to boost the efficiency of fixed spool casting. Instead of moulding in a normal loop, insert 4–6 inches of stiff wire into the back of the mould. Bend the far end into a strong loop for leader clip attachment.

A long-tailed sinker almost completely stabilises the turn-over phase and proceeds, dart-like, into the sky. Even multiplier casts are smoothed; and smoothness automatically exploits the full power of the cast, resulting in a few extra yards. More important, you lose less distance on a bad cast as the sinker irons out small mistakes. The altered geometry of a grip-wired sinker fitted with a long tail boosts anchorage quite significantly. A 5 ounce long-tail holds in the current as securely as a 6 ounce conventionally-looped bomb. As the message spreads through surfcasting, this Spanish development is sure the become THE sinker preferred by casters all over the world.

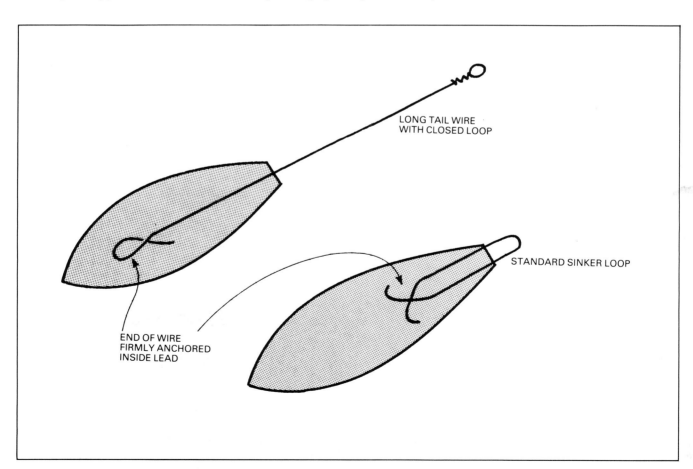

LONG TAIL WIRE WITH CLOSED LOOP

STANDARD SINKER LOOP

END OF WIRE FIRMLY ANCHORED INSIDE LEAD

Terminal Rigs and the Baitsafe Capsule

When you have cut through all the technical and subjective aspects of fishing—sport, competition, relaxation, tackle development and whatever else holds your interest—the entire success of the sport will rely on a fish opening its mouth and swallowing the hook. Bait presentation is the deciding factor, and good bait presentation boils down to casting an attractive offering into the fish's path. Get that wrong, and you are beaten.

Rods, reels, lines and casting style apply equally to natural bait and artificial lure fishing; and to some extent it does not matter whether you fish in freshwater or salt. But at this point—bait presentation—we are looking specifically at natural baits.

Natural baits presented on, or, close to the seabed, stationary in the current or slowly drifting, impose special restrictions. Success is a mixture of dropping the tackle in the right general area, then making the fish swim up to it. Presentation, then, is a combination of casting perfomance and natural bait attraction by sight, taste and smell. The farther you cast, the more dificult it is for traditional tackle to maintain its efficiency. Beyond 125 yards, most old-time rigs simply do not catch fish. Bait rips off in mid-cast. Sinkers drift freely in the tide. Bite detection is impossible, and you cannot strike the hook home anyway. Good fishing results from presenting the right bait at the right time in the right place . . . and having the fish then hook itself. Many anglers spend most of their time on the beach fishing a bare hook: however often they do cast into the best spot, they still will not catch a thing.

The basic rigs—paternoster and running leger

Short traces with the sinker on the bottom cast very well and certainly hook a lot of fish. Choose one, two or three hooks according to species, distance and conditions. For routine fishing in European waters, and especially for bottom-feeding small fishes like flounders, dabs, soles, whiting and eels, a double or triple hooked paternoster is excellent. Cheap to make, simple to fish and adequately sophisticated to hook those species which feed by smell and are not fussy anyway, it is the unviersal terminal tackle for beginners and experts alike.

I tie a bunch of paternosters at home and bundle them, without snoods and hooks, into a plastic bag. On the beach I attach the paternoster to the end of the leader, then arrange hooks according to conditions and the baits that I am about to fish.

The central rib of a paternoster always begins at the upper end with a strong ring or swivel (Mustad, Berkley or Dexter) and ends with a split ring for sinker attachment. Length of the centre rib varies according to number of hooks and expected species. On average, you cannot go far wrong with two or three snoods (a snood is the piece of nylon linking hook to paternoster) spaced 18 inches apart with 18 inches between lower loop and sinker clip, and at least 6 inches gap between upper loop and leader joint.

The central rib is an extension of the leader as well as part of the terminal rig. You cannot expect the sinker to remain safely attached unless the breaking strain of the rib is at least as high as the main leader. An extra 10 per cent breaking strain compensates for the many knots in the trace. Tie Palomar or Uni-knots top and bottom. Ordinary stand-off loops, plain or twisted for stiffness, withstand even long distance casting pressures; however, if you are worried about snap-offs, try using a swivel trapped between two Superglued stoppers for each snood. Extra stiffness and reduction of snood twist are provided by a short piece of plastic tube slid over each loop.

Variations on the two-hook paternoster theme are triple-hook rigs for competition fishing and single-hook, heavy duty rigs for cod and channel bass. Space loops accordingly; adjust the length of the central rib as necessary.

Snood lengths are seldom critical. Short snoods cast more cleanly, help retain baits on the hook and are less likely to tangle. They also jerk the fish up short and make it hook itself. On the other hand, longer snoods encourage some species to bite more freely. Bigger fish, cod especially, need a snood long enough to be sucked deeply into their throats for a firm hookhold. Breaking strain of the snood ought to be the lightest compatible with the expected species. Extra diameter/abrasion resistance is useful for warding off sharp teeth and scaly fins.

Two Hook Paternoster

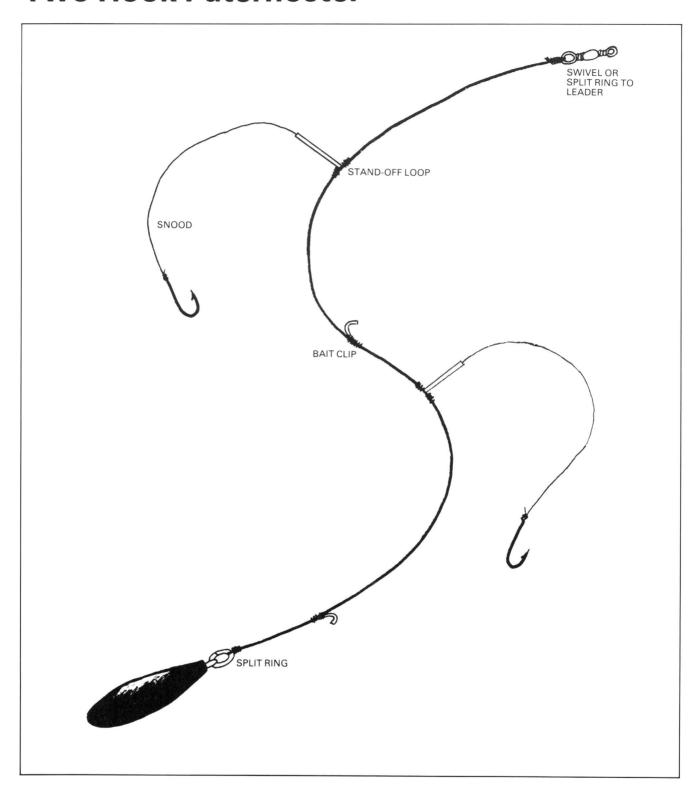

SWIVEL OR
SPLIT RING TO
LEADER

STAND-OFF LOOP

SNOOD

BAIT CLIP

SPLIT RING

PATERNOSTER GUIDE

Species	Overall length	No. of hooks	Snood length	Snood test
COD	48 in.	1–2	9–18 in.	15–30 lb.
FLATFISH	36–60 in.	2–3	6–12 in.	10–15 lb.
WHITING	36–60 in.	2–3	6–9 in.	15–25 lb.
BASS	36–48 in.	1–2	12–18 in.	12–20 lb.

Single-hook paternoster for heavyweight species

Big cod, channel bass and stripers, tope and conger eels can easily ruin a standard paternoster; and of course, you need only one hook on the rig. Modify the ordinary paternoster this way: Shorten the central rib to 24 inches of 40–50 lb test monofilament. Attach upper swivel and lower split ring as before, and tie in a big stand-off loop about 12 inches above the sinker. The snood is 12–24 inches of 25–50 lb monofil (80 lb monofil or 50 lb cable-laid wire for conger) tied or crimped to the loop, which is stiffened with 3 inches of thick-wall plastic tube. Although longer than the loop to sinker dimension, the snood still fishes without tangles.

As an alternative, make a running paternoster (also useful for the smaller species as well if the materials are scaled down). Slide a small, strong swivel directly onto the leader and follow it with a small nylon bead. Then tie the usual swivel or a split ring to the end of the leader. Connect the hook to the split ring with the same 24 inch trace. This time, though, tie in another 24 inch piece of leader-test nylon between the running swivel and the sinker, which must also be connected by split ring, and never directly tied to the nylon. The bait hangs next to the sinker for casting, flies quite well, and creates less tackle resistance when a fish picks up the bait and runs with it.

The standard running leger

For short range fishing in calm or slow moving water, traditional legers may be successful with shy-biting species. Overall, however, they offer no clear advantages and few long-distance casters bother to use them for everyday work. The over-long trace does not pick up cleanly from the pendulum swing, whiplashes bait off the hook, and helicopters the hook around the leader. When clean casts and long distances are essential for good sport, the running leger is just a damn nuisance.

Bait clips—the key to better distances

Bait whiplash on release and in-flight air drag are markedly reduced by restraining hooks and snoods close to the leader. You can add up to 30 yards to maximum fishing distance by clipping down all three snoods of a match-fishing paternoster rather than leaving them to flap in the air currents. Gains are just as significant with a single cod, bass or drumfish rig baited with whole squid, mullet, mackerel or kingsize bunch of worms.

Cut half the bend from a fine-wire long-shanked hook about 5 mm in gape. Slide the leader through the hook eye—it does not matter if you position the hook above or below the stand-off

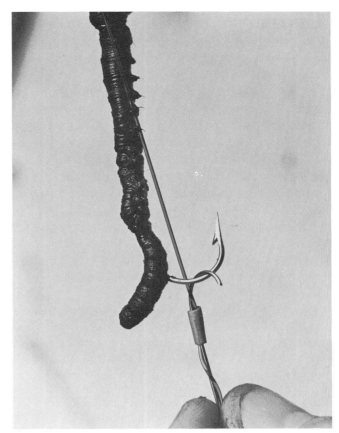

The bait clip ready to cast. The cut-off hook traps the baited trace against the leader until the sinker hits the water.

A Leger Stop (available from freshwater tackle shops) or a nylon stop-knot prevent bait sliding too far up the trace.

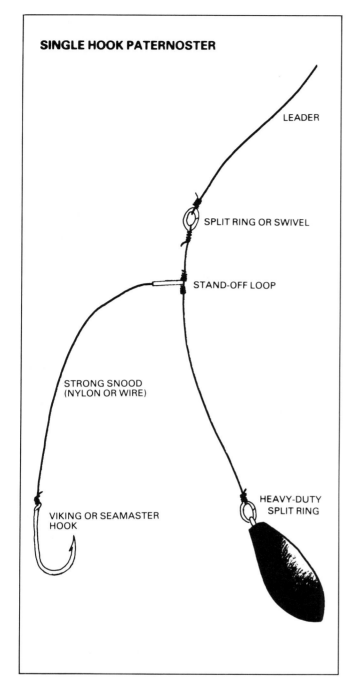

SINGLE HOOK PATERNOSTER

LEADER

SPLIT RING OR SWIVEL

STAND-OFF LOOP

STRONG SNOOD
(NYLON OR WIRE)

VIKING OR SEAMASTER
HOOK

HEAVY-DUTY
SPLIT RING

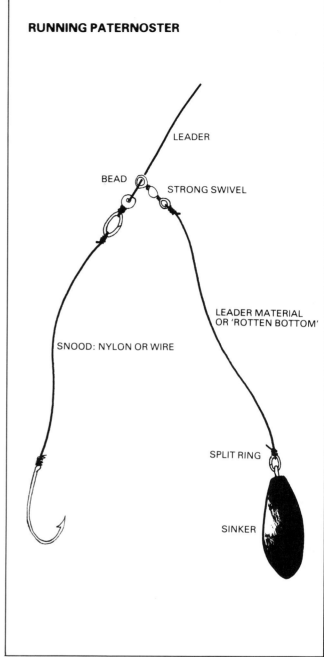

RUNNING PATERNOSTER

LEADER

BEAD

STRONG SWIVEL

LEADER MATERIAL
OR 'ROTTEN BOTTOM'

SNOOD: NYLON OR WIRE

SPLIT RING

SINKER

loop—and whip the shank to the leader with 6 lb test monofilament. Make the whipping fairly tight, so that the hook slides under pressure but does not move at the slightest excuse. Now arrange the cut-off hook so that its bend, and that of the baited hook, loosely but securely interlock. The cut-off hook retains the baited hook throughout the cast, but releases it as soon as the leader slackens, which it invariably does on hitting the sea. The idea is neat and simple and the only important point is to get the tension right initially. Move the cut-off bait clip up or down the leader until its position is exactly right for security in flight and immediate release at the other end. It is a trial and error job.

Small 'L' shaped pieces of brass wire sleeved to the leader with half an inch of plastic tube are equally effective as bait clips. Leger Stops with a bent wire insert work nicely as well. As long as the clip is correctly positioned and fairly open in the bend, it can be made up from all kinds of wires, sleeves, hooks and whippings. Thicker wires seem to provide better release than narrow guage materials.

Some anglers clip the snoods up the trace, others favour an under-loop clip. Small baits on multi-hook paternosters work well either way, but there is some advantage in clipping a single, bulky bait as close as possible behind the sinker. Bait rides in the slipstream.

90

THE BAITSAFE CAPSULE

Suffolk anglers Ted Thwaites and Alan Morrell manufacture and market what probably amounts to the most significant development in surf casting—and freshwater natural bait fishing—this decade. Their Baitsafe casting capsule is a space-age answer to the eternal headaches of bait loss and air drag. In its way, this space shuttle of the surfline takes long-distance surf casting one step nearer perfection. It also holds the key to better fishing for anglers who do not have to cast far or cannot be bothered to learn.

The Baitsafe capsule, available in nominal 4, 5 and 6 ounce models, is a tough, injection moulded plastic box with one open side covered in flight by a hinged door. Cynics reckon it looks like a flying coffin. The front of the box contains the casting weight—a specially shaped chunk of lead permanently bonded to the plastic and immune to casting pressure. The lead is drilled for two pairs of optional grip wires which operate in exactly the same way as the spikes of a bomb sinker.

The back of the plastic shell is hollow. Rig the trace above the Baitsafe, bait the hook, tuck it inside the box and clip on the lid. Bait and sinker are now packaged for hard casting. The shape of the Baitsafe, though rather unsophisticated in appearance, is aerodynamically sound—the cast flies cleanly and far distant.

A special rubber pad cushions the lid in flight. It stays on no matter how hard or far you cast. Immediately on hitting the sea, the lid flies off and releases the bait from the box. Release is triggered by the force of the Baitsafe's impact with water—a pressure of over 20 lb a square inch, more than enough to override the clip mechanism.

A Baitsafe on the seabed grips just as strongly as a sinker of the same weight. In fact it seems to hold even better than a fixed-wire lead. And as soon as you start to retrieve, the capsule takes off like a rocket for the surface. Within 20 yards of leaving the seabed, it is on top and surfing back across the waves. You can imagine how useful that is over rough ground which traps conventional tackle.

All right, so the Baitsafe casts well, holds bottom and stands more chance of surviving rough ground. What else can it do? The totally enclosed bait compartment holds a fair sized bait. Reduced drag adds yards to the cast—at least equalling the results of bait clips. And that is just the beginning.

Any bait inserted into the capsule is totally immune to whiplash and air pressure. You can cast the softest baits imaginable, confident that when the lid flies off out to sea you are fishing a

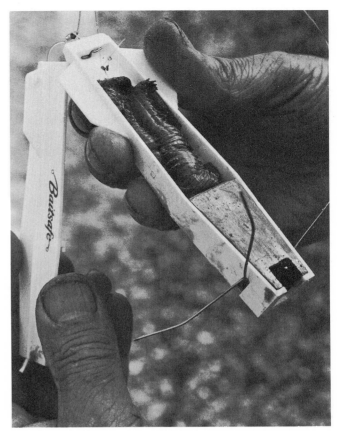

1 The Baitsafe capsule opened for loading. Tuck baited hook and trace inside the plastic case which holds the lead weight as well.

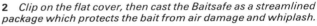

2 Clip on the flat cover, then cast the Baitsafe as a streamlined package which protects the bait from air damage and whiplash.

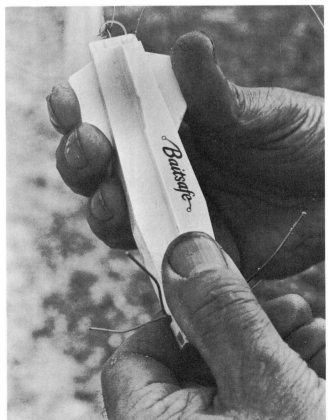

91

perfectly presented bait. Jelly-soft crabs, watery mussel, harbour ragworms or cream cheese for mullet. The Baitsafe excels with them all.

The idea of packaging baits for long distance work has intrigued surf and freshwater anglers for decades. Only now with Ted and Alan's device on the market are anglers free to experiment with soft baits, super-light traces and small hooks, semi-buoyant rigs and groundbaiting (chumming) at long range.

Send an S.A.E. to Intakl Angling, P.O. Box 8, BECCLES, Suffolk, for full details. The device is sold through tackle shops and direct. Do not imagine for one moment that here is one more gimmick to waste a surfman's money. The Baitsafe is a work of importance and sheer genius, a landmark in fishing tackle design.

Hooks for surfcasting

Size of hooks, their design and performance create all kinds of problems for anglers who fish surf and freshwater. Massive hooks, robust wire and specially shaped points and bends are traditionally used for saltwater fishing. Freshwater anglers adopt a more flexible approach and to my mind they teach saltwater anglers some hard lessons. We would catch more fish from surf, estuaries and rockmarks by reducing hook size, of that I am sure.

It may well be forced upon us to investigate better terminal rigs in general and hooks in particular. Falling fish stocks and greater competition between anglers have the same long-term effect in the surf as became clear in freshwater fishing some twenty years ago – fine tackle catches more fish.

The strength of the bigger traditional fishing hooks is largely wasted. What is the value of a 2 ton breaking strain hook on a line that pops at 12 pounds? None at all, save for some protection against the fish's teeth and jaws. And of course a hook must be big enough to accommodate a large bait when necessary. Sheer gape, shank length and point durability ensure we do not reduce the wire diameter and steel temper below reasonable levels. However, there is still plenty of leeway for experiment.

For some years I have progressively reduced the size of my hooks—in wire diameter, barb height and bend. Only shank length remains static— fairly long to assist self-striking by the fish. The lighter I go, the more bites I get. It is true that smaller hooks encourage smaller fish, but you can always throw them back. Small hooks DEFINITELY DO NOT lose your big fish or even deter their biting in the first place. You will almost certainly find yourself catching and landing more

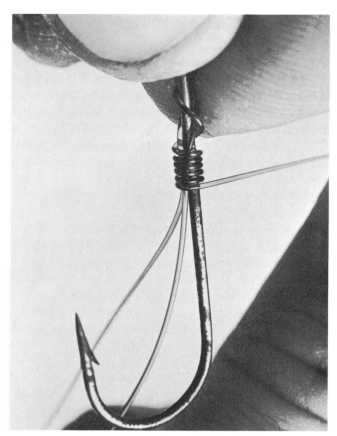

Surface rust and corrosion are almost inevitable. Deeper damage than this should be rejected. This is a medium-guage wire Aberdeen hook for cod fishing.

Small, well tempered hooks are more than a match for heavy fish hooked in the surf.

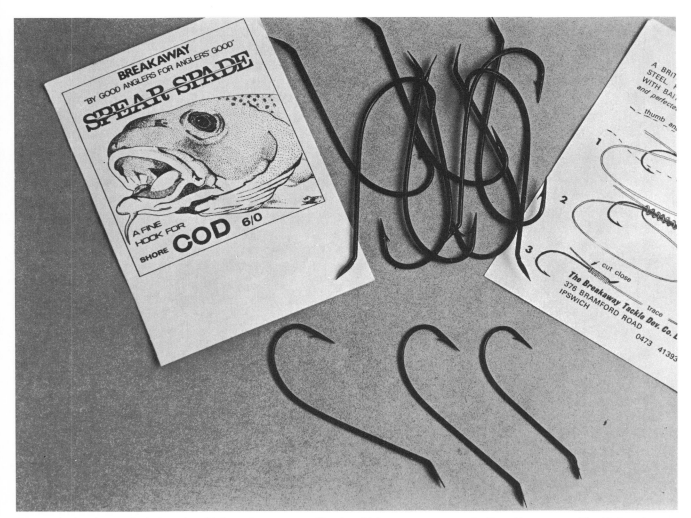

Spearpoint hooks—typical of modern high-performance surf hooks which ensure easy penetration at long range. The high-carbon steel hook is tough and razor sharp.

fish then ever. And you will miss far fewer bites.

For British and European sport, fine wire Aberdeen-type hooks between sizes 4 and 8/0 are the foundation of successful legering with natural baits cast long, medium or short range. Blue-steel Mustad are the sharpest of all; Partridge are tougher. The Breakaway Spearpoint and Spearspade hooks, though not strictly Aberdeen-shaped, are a viable alternative, being extremely tough and sharp, well tempered and small-eyed.

More substantial hooks for big cod and bass, conger and tope range from the Mustad Vikings through to the smaller sizes of Seamaster game hooks. Again, it pays to reduce the hook size to the practical minimum compatible with bait size. Here the Baitsafe helps prevent baits tearing from a small hook. Cast unprotected, a bait should be thoroughly skewered by bend and shank.

Small hooks can be rigged to accept big baits.

The lower inches of the snood or trace replace the missing bend and shank as bait support. You simply thread the baits around the bend, up the shank, over the eye and on to the monofilament. The trouble is that they keep right on sliding and at the end of the cast they are tight against the paternoster stand-off loop.

Prevent this by tying a separate stop-knot on to the snood just above the hook eye. Make it of stiffish nylon—around 12 lb test—and leave the ends protruding by ½ inch so they prevent baits sliding too far. When the knot is suitably positioned, you can cram plenty of bait on to a small hook. As long as the bend and point are exposed, the hook will trap a biting fish just as easily as a larger bend would. Being thinner in the wire, a small hook gets a firm grip and sinks below the barb with no need for heavy striking or high line tension.

Back Casting

Back casting, also called Yarmouth or Norfolk-style, cannot be confused with any other casting technique. Instead of standing head-on to the water and casting with a final punch-pull of the arms, you face away from the water and 'shovel' the rod over your shoulder. It is a rough and ready way to cast, specialised in application but nevertheless too important to ignore. Some fishing cries out for the back-cast.

Though there are seldom occasions when the back-cast is the *only* way to fish, it is still a major force to be reckoned with. Distances are excellent, but the real strength of the back-cast is its easy, slow power stroke which handles very big sinkers when necessary. Soft baits are less likely to burst.

The back-cast technique

First a word of warning. The back-cast is dangerous. Performed well, on an open beach and with a strong shock leader matched to a good rod and reel, the cast is no worse than any other. Unfortunately, it is a style which lends itself to brute power, and the result, inevitably, is that anglers with little or no experience stand in the middle of a crowd and lash into their interpretation of the style. The danger is that the sinker might fly off along the beach rather than out to sea. The message is plain to anyone with an ounce of commonsense: practise on a deserted beach, and keep the power down until you master the swing and pull-through. Then the cast is as safe as any other, although it does demand more space than the normal pendulum. Good back-casters are perfectly safe because they appreciate the limitations of the style, which is totally inappropriate from piers and jetties, on crowded beaches and from rocks.

The back-cast is an extension of the old-time handline fishing style used along the East Coast of England. Nineteenth-century fishermen (and a few of today's traditionalists) learned to increase the range of their handline tackle by levering the coiled line seawards on a casting pole—a six foot stick with a spike on top used to boost the normal arc of throwing. Substitute rod and reel for handline and pole, and you have the elements of the modern back-cast.

Back-casters take up position with their backs to the sea. The sinker hangs on a massive leader drop which is often longer than the normal 13–14·5 foot rod necessary for this technique. A right

1 *Stand back to the sea. Tuck the reel into your right hip and extend your left arm well up the handle. Swing the sinker on a long drop—push it towards, just as in normal pendulum casting . . .*

4 *Guide the rod—still at full power—into an upward arc. Get your full body weight behind the handle. Use your legs too.*

2 . . . then pull the tackle back so that the sinker swings behind your shoulder. When you feel the sinker pause at the top of the arc . . .

3 . . . sweep the handle around and down, building power as quickly as possible.

5 Release at the peak of the lifting action. The sinker flies extremely high with this style. Direction control may be difficult at first.

6 Hold the rod tip high until the sinker and tackle splash into the water.

handed caster would hold the top handle grip of the rod in his left hand. The right hand cradles rod butt cap and low-set reel hard against the right hip bone.

The casts begins with a pendulum swing similar to that of the normal pendulum style and the left hand pushes the sinker away to the limit of body rotation—just as in the pendulum cast. The body guides the long rod to sweep the pendulum in-swing high above and to the rear of the caster's head. Then the main power stroke is a smooth, fast body and left hands sweep which levers the rod around and upwards to release point. Similarity to pitchforking a bale of hay backwards over your shoulder is probably no coincidence—the original handline back-casters were farm labourers well versed in haymaking and harvesting. It is a natural body action, easy to develop and always powerful due to the free application of body weight. Most people can pull harder than they can push.

Tackle for the back-cast
The back-cast is relatively slow and lacks the final arm and shoulder acceleration of standard casting techniques. On the other hand it is extremely powerful, so you can compensate for lack of butt speed by increasing tip length. 13 feet is regarded as short for a back-caster; more experienced anglers prefer at least 13·5 feet for fishing and may go as high as 15 feet for tournament casting. Length of rod is no deterrent to casting, but is a high price to pay in general fishing—heavy, imbalanced, and hard work with a big fish on the end.

The length and weight of the blank make it a non-starter for anglers who fish in surf where the rod cannot be rested. Lure fishing is almost certainly too strenuous with a back-cast rod. The style originated on cod and whiting beaches where you cast out and then wait for fish to detect your bait, so it is not surprising to find that even with modern rods and reels the back-cast has not spread to shore angling in general. The vast majority of back-casters live in Suffolk and Norfolk, or farther up the coast—Newcastle and Hull—where the traditional styles of fishing were also founded on handline and pole.

Critics of back-casting attack its crudeness; from the truly sporting point of view they are probably right. The rod is a monster – 8.5 feet of powerful carbon/glass joined to a carbonfibre or alloy butt about 6 feet long. But they cannot disregard its effectiveness and sheer power.

Very few back-casters bother with a multiplier reel, however there is no reason why you should not use one—except that you will find spool grip and cast control a little more difficult than it is on a normal pendulum outfit. Fixed spool is preferred because it is so much easier to handle—no trouble with spool release, no backlashes of course, and much better balance and power in retrieve. Tucked low down beside your right hip, the reel lies in a most comfortable and natural position. Grip the upper handle with an almost straight arm and then just lean back on the rod to apply full pressure to terminal rig and hooked fish.

Terminal rig, traces and lines are identical to those used in normal casting. You will find it easier to handle big sinkers—6, 7 and 8 ounces are perfectly feasible. (They are just as easy on ordinary pendulum tackle but you do need a far higher level of expertise to avoid burned thumbs and strained rod). In fact, back-casters tend to standardise on heavier than normal terminal rigs which may well prove more effective on East Coast cod grounds.

Advantages of the back-cast
Powerful casting with a slow, relaxed body sweep and no particular emphasis on arm acceleration comes into its own in winter. Thick clothing and frozen fingers are more restrictive in multiplier reel casting with a short pendulum rod than in fixed spool back-casting. Although you may well be able to cast farther in ideal weather with your forward-facing style, the back-cast is a valuable alternative for fishing in conditions which might otherwise persuade you to go home. You may even grow to like it for its own sake as well.

Mostly, however, it is the way to handle big seas, rough weather and low temperatures. Dedicated back-casters may well argue that their style is far more versatile, but the tiny numbers of anglers who fish that way prove that this is not by any means a popular or even interesting way to approach general beach fishing. Like many anglers, I use it as a specific weapon for isolated circumstances; I cannot imagine why anyone would want to use it all the time, unless they fish the same old beaches for the same old species year after year. Nobody could argue that back-casting fails to produce the goods, but there is more to fishing than sheer mechanics. In particular, who would want to lug around such a diabolical chunk of fishing rod for bassing, rock fishing and other situations where a shorter, lighter rod offers better handling and more enjoyable fishing? Angling is a pastime, not a survival exercise.

Winter cod hooked at long range in rough water. Back casting excels with this kind of angling where the rod is fished from a rest. Back casting tackle is too heavy to hold for long.

However, when those big waves drive in on the cod beaches, and wind whips spray and sand straight into your face, back-casting 7 or 8 ounces of lead out there far enough to drop a bunch of worms into a gulley where the fish run is a tremendous advantage, which, in my view, more than justifies building a back-cast rod and learning to use it. Maybe you fish that way ten days a year, but those may be times that cod fishing is at its peak. If ordinary tackle will not toss a bait far enough or will not anchor in the tide long enough to attract a fish, you might lose the opportunity to land a 20 pounder. These days cod have the habit of not coming back to give you a second shot. They are more choosy about moving inshore than ever they were, and if they do show up in big numbers, you can bet the weather and seas will be rough and cold. The best fishing often coincides with storms blowing straight in from the open sea and temperatures below zero.

Night fishing is ten time better . . . but further aggravates ordinary pendulum casting with free-running reel. Sometimes it is impossible to fish that way. Big, slow-flying sinkers are much kinder to soft baits. You will find night fishing with a heavy back-cast outfit brings a greater confidence:

you know within reason that baits hit the seabed rather than explode from the hook in mid-cast. During the day, whichever style you cast, you will see the baits travel all the way or shower into the breakers. If necessary, wind in, rebait and cast again. At night you have to take a chance that all went well—and that is where a back-caster and 7 ounces of lead pay off: when you are striving for maximum range with half a dozen soft lugworms aimed at those big cod. Plenty of night fishermen miss big catches because they fish without baits three casts out of four.

The extra carrying capacity of a big sinker may be useful for matchfishing with the three permitted hooks, each baited differently with a substantial hookload. Back-casters manage very well here. 7 or 8 ounces of lead will carry a peeler crab, two lugworms and, on the third hook, a four inch piece of king ragworm. Distances could be 25 yards more than with a 5 ounce ordinary pendulum outfit which would tend to mash baits, anyway. In addition, extremely long back-cast sinker drops accommodates three snoods over 7 or 8 feet of leader, whereas on a shorter rod you would need to compress the paternoster loops into 6 feet at most.

97

PART II

Why Build Your Own Rod?

Considering the hundreds of different beach fishing rods on the market, you would think that somewhere along the line any angler could find a ready-made rod that suits him—the right length for casting, properly balanced to handle a realistically wide range of sinker weights and line strengths, smooth and easy to cast with either multiplier or fixed spool reel. Serviceable mass-produced beachcasting rods certainly exist, but most lack the special feel and performance that keen fishermen appreciate.

Once the cheap alternative to production tackle, home-built rods now offer significant advantages. In the high pressure world of tournament casting and long-range beach fishing, specialist blanks reign supreme. You will hardly ever see an expert angler using a standard shop-bought surf rod.

It is not done to save money. The best home-made and custom-built rods cost far more than even the most expensive production rods. Dozens of cheaper blanks are available as well, but the current trend is towards high specification and quality. Production rods, once the first choice of discerning fishermen, are now a cheap option, a starting point for beginners and a refuge for anglers less than dedicated to the sport.

Limitations of production rods

Rod manufacturers must tailor their products for the mass market. One or two models of surf rod each selling thousands are more profitable than twenty specialist rods selling a few dozen each. As a result, mass-produced surf rods are designed to a compromise formula, the aim being to make a rod which is all things to all men. While they never quite hit the target, such rods at least offer reasonable performance and value for money.

Most manufactured surf rods are between 10.5 and 12 feet long, balanced to cast 4–6 ounces, and of medium-fast to fast action. Rings are chosen to perform reasonably well with both fixed spool and multiplier reels. It is assumed that the angler uses an overhead or simple pendulum cast with a maximum range of about 125 yards. Handle diameter and reel spacings are chosen with the 'average' man's physique in mind. In Britain, rods are made exclusively for bottom fishing with natural baits. Elsewhere the emphasis is more likely to be on spinning and lure fishing.

Anglers who cast over 150 yards seldom rely on ordinary production surf rods. Blank and handle

Sluggish fibreglass beachcaster with a sloppy butt. A useless rod typical of the mass-produced tackle industry. Rods like this encourage home building.

are too spongy to transmit full power to the sinker. Rod rings strangle the cast or trap fast-running leader knots. Handles feel too fat or too thin, and the reel is in the wrong place for maximum performance. Bite detection, handling and pulling power may all prove inferior for long range fishing, special techniques and light lines.

Smaller rod building companies are flexible enough to cater for the specialist market. It is economical for them to make a dozen rods at a time, or even to build a one-off model to special order. However, the cost is high because rod assembly is labour intensive. Worse still, small companies seldom offer exclusive blanks and accessories—most blanks are freely available through tackle shops. It does not take long to work out that if you buy an identical blank, rings and handle fittings elsewhere, you can make the same rod for perhaps £30 less. The professionally built rod may be more neatly whipped (Americans say wrapped) and better finished, but it won't cast any farther or hook more fish.

Correct hand spread is essential for good casting. Having the reel in exactly the right place is in itself a good enough reason to build you own surf rod.

Performance versus appearance

Rod appearance and cosmetics are far more important to American and European anglers than to the British. The scene is changing quickly; within ten years everyone might be concerned with a rod's appearance. However, at the moment performance is judged far superior to looks. The attitude among British rod builders, amateur and professional, is that while a nicely finished rod is a bonus, few anglers are willing to spend extra time in achieving it. Fewer still are prepared to pay. Custom rod makers in America would be appalled by the lack of interest shown by the pagan British.

On the other hand, the promise of an extra 15 yards casting range or better bite detection triggers an immediate response. Performance counts heavily on British beaches, casting ability especially so. If a rod maker could guarantee that his products outcast the rest, he would capture the market whatever his prices.

The great advantage of making your own rod is that personal choice is easily accommodated. Should you find that a 12.75 foot surf rod with a 33 inch reel spacing gives you an extra 15 yards casting range, you simply buy a blank and butt, cut them to length and glue the reel seat in the right place. If rod cosmetics appeal to you, it costs only time and patience to indulge your creative instincts. With care you can achieve superb results at home without recourse to specialised equipment and tools. When sheer performance is all that interests you, secure the rings on your new super-casting blank with electrician's tape, and be fishing within an hour of leaving the tackle shop. Dozens of expert casters and competition anglers never both to whip or varnish a new rod.

CHOOSING A BLANK

Surfcasting rods come and go as regularly as the tides ebb and flow. New models appear; old rods die out because styles change or the rod itself can no longer rise to the challenge. Fresh materials arrive on the scene, bring with them the promise of better casting and fishing. After a while, your faithful old beachcaster seems to lose casting power and feels sloppy and imprecise. Even if the rod is healthy, it is easy to talk yourself into changing it.

Anglers are showered with advertisements and information about new rods. Tournament casting and fishing competition results may persuade you to look for another, better blank. Be careful. Though claims for a new rod may well be true, they do not always relate to the way you fish and cast.

High-performance casting blanks are a major source of disappointment. Anglers buy them because they think that rods which exceed 250 yards on the competition field will automatically

101

add 30, 40, even 50 yards to their own casts. It seldom works out that way. It is more likely that the new rod is so long, fierce and rigid that you cannot bend it. Even if it does cast a little further (it is most exceptional to find a blank which alone adds even 10 percent to a caster's performance) the extra yards are hardly worth the effort and expense. The rod is so heavy, stiff and insensitive that you miss bites and lose fish.

I have deliberately singled out casting power for criticism simply because it affects so many fishermen. Thousands of anglers buy a rod that is far too powerful. They are physically unable to compress the blank into its correct casting bend, and as a result they find the rod harsh and unpredictable. No rod casts well unless it is fully compressed to locking point during the casting action.

You must be sure that your casting ability measures up to the blank's specification. If it does not, either reject the blank no matter how great its reputation, or learn to cast harder and more efficiently. The latter course demands hard work and reasonable practice. Ultimately it would pay dividends. If this idea appeals to you, it is probably safe to invest in a blank that is initially a little too powerful and demanding. The big mistake is to suppose that even without extra practice you would eventually come to terms with it. Vast numbers of tournament-grade surf rods on the secondhand market are proof enough that many anglers finally give up in despair.

Blank selection is so closely allied to casting and fishing skills that anglers who do not understand the principles of rod action and design are at a serious disadvantage. Talk to other anglers, read advertisements and learn what you can about casting and fishing techniques long before you buy that new blank. Rod and blank selection, casting styles and surf tackle combinations are fully covered in this book's companion volume 'LONG DISTANCE CASTING', published by Crowood Press.

Try before you buy
Regardless of your theoretical knowledge of casting, fishing and rod making, there is no real substitute for trying out a new blank before you buy your own. Specifications may appear excellent on paper; the rod casts record distances; perhaps it enjoyed rave reviews in the angling press. All of these are fair indications of a rod's value and ability, but only on the general level. As a rod builder, you should be far more concerned with how the blank measures up to your *personal* requirements. The only way to find out the truth is to test a blank made up to the length and specification you like.

Manufacturers' demonstrations, tackle shows and tournaments provide an opportunity to test

Tournament tackle regulations help determine blank specification. Many of today's best rods are balanced to 0.35–0.40mm line and 5–5.5 ounce sinkers.

blanks and rods. Club members often discover that someone else in the group already owns the blank in question. It is most unusual to be refused a trial. Casting tournaments and fishing competitions are an excellent opportunity to see the latest rods in action. Somebody will almost certainly lend you his rod for a few casts.

Some enlightened retailers and small manufacturers provide trial rods which can be borrowed for a day or two, usually against a cash deposit. Laying your hands on a test blank is much easier than most anglers suppose. Those who complain about not having trial facilities have rarely bothered to look at all the options.

Don't be a manufacturer's guinea pig

Prototype surf blanks involve little expense and time on the manufacturer's part. When suitable materials and mandrels are already available to him, any competent rod designer can transform an idea into a blank within a few hours. Ideas come from the designer himself and through the angling network—tackle shops, angling public and, most important, tournament casters and well-known anglers sponsored by the company. Every good blank factory enjoys strong support from its field staff.

Casting champion Neil Mackellow unleashes a 250 yard cast. Tournament casters and ultra-long range anglers are happy to trade off casting performance against balance and sensitivity.

Feed-back of information and simplicity of prototype blank construction allow designers to stay in close touch with changes in the angling world. Unfortunately, ease of blank making and a strong desire to come up with something new often backfire, and it is the angler who loses . . . and pays.

Tournament champions and prize winning anglers don't have to buy any of their tackle. Someone in the tackle trade will provide whatever they want free in return for the inevitable publicity. In the case of blanks, these men pick and choose from a stream of prototypes made much to their personal specifications. They try out a new rod, sometimes reject it after a week, sometimes keep it for a year. As a one-off exercise, nobody suffers.

Sometimes it happens this way. A tournament caster dreams up a new design of blank which for some reason gives him an extra five yards advantage. He wins a big event. Suddenly, everyone wants a blank like his. Flooded with demands from tackle shops and anglers, the factory churns out new blanks by the score. There are plenty of anglers who will buy a new blank because it is a status symbol. They get a kick from being the first man in their town to own one. Others think the magic will rub off; this new record breaking blank adds 50 yards to *anyone's* cast, surely?

An occasional blank is successful, excellent in every respect, a thoroughly practical fishing and casting rod. However, by the time the new rod hits the tackle shops, our tournament caster has thrown his away. Perhaps his big cast was really due to perfect weather conditions or to different ballraces in the reel. Having used his dream rod for another week, he now finds it too stiff, too soft, too long. Whatever the reason, he needs another new rod for the next tournament.

Shrewd fishermen delay buying the latest wonder rod until it proves itself worth the investment. Rather than jump on the bandwagon, wait and see how anglers in general accept a product. It takes at least six months for some technical problems to emerge. Blanks split or snap after a few hundred casts. Others are useless for practical fishing. A great many feel so heavy and unwieldy that fishermen reject them as fishing rods regardless of how well the blanks cast. Hold back until you see plenty of anglers happily using the new blanks. Even then, do try one before spending your money. These days a bare blank and butt could cost over £100, far too much to risk on an impulse buy.

There are also financial advantages in waiting. Any blank or rod that catches the angling public's imagination will be copied by other manufacturers. Copyright and patent are almost worthless in fishing rod manufacture. It is easy to take apart a blank, see how it works and make a copy which exactly parallels the original's action and power. Good designers often manage to improve the performance, and they certainly try to reduce the price. In the long run, you could buy a better blank for a lot less money.

Blank quality

Physical dimensions apart, most blanks look similar. It is extremely difficult for the inexperienced to differentiate between good and bad. Glassfibre, carbonfibre (graphite) and composites of the two are available in a wide range of specifications. Fibres and the resins which bind them are difficult to assess outside the laboratory. Looks can actually create a deliberately false impression of blank quality. A good coat of high-gloss finish over a lick of cheap paint makes an inferior product seem highly desirable. Lying alongside it, a vastly superior but unglossed blank looks like a fake, and a very expensive one at that.

Carbonfibre rods are a perfect example. Cheap Far Eastern blanks look nice and cost next to nothing. American and British blank makers cannot compete with them on price alone. The tragedy is that few anglers realise how great are the differences between good and bad. To the man in the street, all carbonfibre is the same. Presented with a cheap import and a nationally-produced blank of similar external appearance, he looks no further than the price tag. Why pay three times as much for Fenwick, Century Composites, Conoflex or Zziplex when you can get a Taiwan rod, made up and ready to fish, for a few pounds or dollars?

Use quality products and you immediately see and feel a difference in balance, performance and sensitivity. Also you can bet that a cheap rod will be dead and buried inside two years. Choice is limited as well. Churning out such vast numbers of rods and blanks, the Far East cannot afford to cater for specialists. The range may include only three or four surfcasting blanks, all around the 11–12 foot mark.

The leading companies manufacture literally hundreds of specialist saltwater blanks. There is an excellent chance of finding precisely the specification you want. The whole idea of building your own rod is to escape the prison of mediocre design, so why trap yourself for the sake of a little extra expense? After you add the

Not all production rods are bad. Old ABU models are quite good. Now obsolete, they are still sought after on the second hand market by custom builders who refurnish the bare blank with modern rings and handles.

cost of rings, fittings and accessories, and the hours spent whipping and varnishing the rod, it simply does not make sense to buy inferior blanks. Stick to the big names unless you have good reason to change.

On the other hand, do not overlook that new blank factory just opened down the road. It could be the answer to your prayers. Wait six months to see how other anglers feel about their product—it is always wise to let somebody else take the preliminary risks. The danger is that the new rods could become so popular that eventually you find yourself on the end of a long waiting list.

Finding a new blank

It is physically impossible for an ordinary tackle shop to stock every model of blank. Expect to shop around for your new rod. In most areas, blank manufacturers limit the number of tackle retailers who sell their products. It is better for trade and ensures faster service and more useful advice. With so many blanks on the market, very few dealers could hope to have a thorough knowledge of them all. You can discover the name and address of your nearest specialist dealer either by checking through the angling magazines and newspapers or by writing or calling the factory itself. Some manufacturers will supply direct in

Casting tournaments and beach matches are the best places to see new rods. If you ask nicely, most anglers are happy to tell you about their tackle, and perhaps they will let you try it.

case of difficulty. The best have either their own showrooms or other demonstration and trial facilities. A blank maker may occasionally be willing to make you a special one-off design. It will much depend on his workload, and everything hinges on whether he has a suitable steel mandrel.

Good blanks withstand a beating year in, year out. Over a very long period—say five years—a high quality blank used carefully and within its limits shows little sign of deterioration. Some blanks soften a little, others tend to grow slightly harsh because resins harden and lose their flexibility. However, deterioration is so slight that you never notice it. As for breaking in half without warning, there is little to worry about unless you are an exceptionally bad caster who continually overloads his blank. Experience shows that if a rod is going to break, it will almost certainly do so within its first year and probably within the initial three months. All of this makes a secondhand blank worth considering .

Fishing magazines and local newspapers are full of small advertisements for secondhand rods and blanks. These are brand new blanks which the owner never got around to building; rods two or

three months old that didn't suit him; and old rods no longer manufactured but still sought after. Prices are invariably a fraction of new. Even secondhand rods from a tackle shop can be quite a bargain. From a keen home-builder's point of view, the state of a blank is all that matters. However well the existing rod is built and fitted out, he will strip off rings and handle, scrape the blank clean and start again.

It can be worth taking a gamble. To start with, you can be sure of a few test casts before you buy the rod. Nobody selling a rod ever turns down such a request. A smooth-casting rod free from obvious damage to the blank is a sound investment. If the rod is in a bad state—except for the blank of course—you may be able to beat the price right down. You can also afford to take a chance on action and power. Should the blank eventually prove unsuitable, just get rid of it. Cunning rod traders make a profit on the deal. A quick check through my back issues of Angler's Mail Swop Shop column reveals that most saltwater rods described as in good, perfect or as-new condition are advertised for around half to two-thirds of list price. And that is before you start haggling.

Rod Building: Blanks

ONE-PIECE BLANKS

In theory a blank without joints should be stronger than one with spigots or ferrules, and it should perform better as well. In practice, any high quality blank correctly cut and jointed is just as strong, casts and fishes equally well, and is far easier to transport and store. Most high-performance rods for casting and fishing are manufactured in sections.

Should your chosen blank be one-piece, do not rush to cut it. There is no overwhelming reason why some blanks should not be cut, but do bear in mind a couple of important points before you start using a hacksaw. Wall thicknesses and diameters are calculated so that unless a cut is made in exactly the right spot—which may not be the centre—a rod is seriously weakened. Even if a blank is safe to cut, you must not glue in any old spigot. Wall thickness, taper, length and the material of the spigot itself must be absolutely correct, otherwise the rod literally tears itself apart.

Cutting and jointing blanks is a highly skilled job. High-performance surf blanks with fast taper and stiff butt are very much at risk. Slower action rods are less susceptible, but in the long run they too may split the outer walls or snap the spigot. There is only one safe answer: before buying the blank, ask the manufacturer if it can be sectioned, and if so at which points. The factory or dealer might supply a special plug for your particular model.

SECTIONAL BLANKS

The vast majority of surf rods are now constructed in two equal-length sections or as long tips and detachable handles. While excellent casting and fishing rods exist in telescopic and multi-section format, modern designers turn the spotlight on the two piece formula which offers a greater scope for performance, lightness and cheaper manufacture. One piece rods are under heavy fire from the tackle trade because they are so difficult to ship and store. It costs as much to send one blank as twenty; express delivery services like UPS and Securicor refuse to handle long packages anyway.

The long-tip/detachable butt formula gains rapid support from blank dealers, retailers and anglers. A handful of well chosen blanks cover all power and length requirements, whereas with equal-length section rods it is necessary to offer a big range of options to cover the market. One long tip plus three or four handle options take the place of a dozen or more conventionally sectioned rods.

Equal-length sections should not be dismissed. At the bottom end of the market are bare blanks and semi-built rods which offer reasonable performance and price. Choice of length, action and power are severely limited, which makes these blanks interesting to anglers looking for the cheapest possible way into beach fishing. At the other extreme, superb carbonfibre blanks cut and jointed in the centre are available for specialist angling and long-range casting. They tend to be few and far between, and prices are high.

Rod length alteration

Rods made in two equal length (or close-to-equal) sections cannot easily be modified. A 12 foot surf blank might withstand trimming back by 6 inches at the butt or 2–3 inches at the tip; but apart from that, you are restricted to the designer's limits. Adding a few inches to the butt is sometimes an acceptable method of lengthening a rod. Apart from loss of balance, the biggest danger is that the relative position of the joint has now shifted towards the tip ring. Joint stress is severely increased and spigot or blank walls may fail. Even if a rod does retain its strength, casting performance drops because the spigot weight reduces rod tip recovery speed.

A long tip is capable of accepting varying lengths of handle. Assuming you pick the correct power and action of blank, overall rod length with the standard 7.5–8.5 foot tips can lie anywhere between 11 and 14.5 feet. Within that range lies adequate scope for pendulum, South African, overhead and back cast styles. It is surprising how versatile some blanks can be.

Conoflex Cod 5's and 6's could be made up into an 11.5 foot pendulum rod to cast 4 ounces, or extended at the butt and trimmed a little at the tip to produce a back-cast rod 14 feet long and powerful enough to cast between 6 and 8 ounces. At the other extreme, the Zziplex Dream Machine, Fenwick Surfstik 5 and other semi-carbon pendulum blanks are better kept around 11.5 feet long for casting 5–5.5 ounces. Just an inch or two cut from the end of the rod would

Two-piece rods offer good casting and fishing along with easy carriage and storage. The only snag is that two-piece rods are available in relatively few lengths, actions and powers.

ruin performance and in some cases make the rod too harsh and vicious to use.

Cutting back the tip of any blank must be approached with caution. The best advice is *not* to cut unless there are overwhelming pressures to do so, or the blank is one which incorporates variable length as a design feature. Some blanks can be progressively cut back to accommodate a wide sinker range. A full length blank balanced to 5 ounces may produce better results with 6 ounces if 3 inches of tip are sliced off. Taking off another 2 inches raises the ideal sinker weight to 8 ounces.

An individual angler's casting power plays its role. Blanks built for 5 ounce casting under normal conditions may respond better to very hard casts with the same weight if an inch or two are cut off the tip. See how other anglers fare after cutting back their rods. Talk to tournament casters as well; they are more likely than anyone to take a hacksaw to the blank. Tip reduction is an area of rod building where it pays to learn by others' experience.

Rod length has enormous bearing on casting distance and control. There seems no practical difference between similar rods cut, say, 11.5 and 11.75 feet long. How could 3 inches alter a pendulum blank's performance? Casters who struggle to achieve 100 yards feel nothing. Moderately good casters who drop their baits around the 130 yard mark might notice a slight difference in handling; perhaps one rod would cast marginally farther.

Beyond 175 yards those 3 inches could add or cut 25 yards from maximum performance; they might require at least a half-ounce change in sinker weight; and they will almost certainly affect reel position, sinker drop and power flow during the cast. Length itself is important, but the altered characteristics of a cut blank also play a part, especially if the 11.5 foot model was produced by cutting 3 inches from the original tip.

Spigots and joints

The position and security of a joint depends on the length and construction of the blank. Slow tapered rods for bass fishing, casting lures and short-to-medium range beach casting are versatile in this respect. Reputable manufacturers offer a range of suitable blanks in the 11–13 foot range, in glassfibre, carbonfibre and composites. Each blank is cut and jointed by overlap or plug spigot. There is no advantage in placing the joint towards the

107

Short aluminium butt and flexible carbonfibre blank—just the right combination for turbot fishing from the rocks.

A rod rest means that you can afford to use quite a heavy, powerful blank with a high casting performance. As a general rule, very powerful casting rods are too unwieldy to hold all day.

butt; the centre or somewhere close by is perfectly all right. Such rods lack all-out casting power but are light, well balanced, sensitive and easy to use. According to design, they are a good choice for all-round and specialist short range work. Spigot and joint failure are unusual in good quality blanks. A full length blank of this type is manageably slim at the butt and therefore requires no special handle provision.

Where casting power heads the list of blank characteristics, rod designers have two roads to travel. The flexible tip/stiff butt, fast action rod can be built either by using a steeply tapered mandrel and thin blank walls, or by reducing the mandrel taper and compensating for the lower diameter (and its associated lack of stiffness) by a substantial increase in glassfibre or carbonfibre thickness. There are plus and minus factors in each design.

Joint placement and construction are very important, yet some rod manufacturers and custom builders ignore them. As a result, many fishermen buy blanks which are fragile and unreliable. Some snap in half on the first powerful cast; at best they have little insurance against abuse or accidental overload.

Measure down 5.5–6 feet from the tip ring of a thin wall/steep taper rod like the Conoflex Cod 5 or 6, and you find that the external diameter is about $\frac{1}{2}$–$\frac{5}{8}$ inch. Walls are thin, giving plenty of room inside the blank for a sturdy spigot. Any blank of this kind is ideal for making up into a rod of two equal length sections. The only cause for concern is the length and wall thickness of the spigot itself. The risk is that the spigot may harm the rod.

The mid-area of a fast-action casting rod is subject to considerable strain. It is also the region of maximum acceleration during the final stage of a big cast. The blank must be strong, but it must bend as well. A rigid spigot tends to lever apart the walls of the blank. Thus, the size of the spigot must be carefully calculated to blend in. All the best rods are designed and built as a unit, and most come from the factory with spigot cut, ground and glued in place.

Thick wall/slim diameter blanks are better left uncut. At the 5.5–6 foot point, walls are substantial and the outside diameter under $\frac{1}{2}$ inch. The central hole, which determines spigot diameter, is too narrow for safety. In this case the blank breaks its spigot. Should a spigot hold together, casting power is severely reduced because the joint flexes more than the surrounding blank and thus forms a soft spot in the action.

With most kinds of surfcasting rods it is neater

to run the blank over a full 8 feet or so and use a detachable butt. Although a few production rods still feature a thick walled blank jointed in the middle by a weak spigot, it is now uncommon to find a specialist blank made in this way. Anglers and manufacturers are wise to the problem . . . too many of the early blanks broke after a dozen casts.

Spigots work extremely well on all long-tip blanks, fast or slow tapered and, unless there is a manufacturing error or faulty material, premature failure is rare. The only precaution is to whip the final 4–6 inches of the blank to prevent splitting. An alternative is to dispense with the spigot and instead use a handle which pushes into the bottom of the tip. Glassfibre, aluminium alloy and carbonfibre butts can be attached this way provided diameters and wall thicknesses are suitable. The overlap area is better ground in the factory, but with care can be produced by hand tools.

The Feralite joint in Fenwick's Surfstik series is particularly neat because upper and lower sections of rod are made on special mandrels which provide for a tapered overlap. By avoiding the need to grind the handle to shape, Fenwick preserve full wall thickness and rods are actually stronger than if they were made in single-piece form.

Where blank diameter is less than that of its chosen handle, you can opt for a reverse spigot. The outside wall of the tip is ground to slide into the butt. Reasonable wall thickness is necessary both sides, and the inside of the butt should be parallel or even reverse tapered. The idea works best with thickwall/slim diameter tips and aluminium alloy butts. As an alternative, glue the butt into the handle. Modern epoxy adhesives are strong enough to take up a reasonable amount of sloppiness between the two sections, so that it is seldom necessary to grind the joint to a precision fit. With thick adhesive and a few yards of string to fill the gap you can bond a 1 inch blank into 1–1.25 inch alloy tube.

Blank design and handle limitations

Fast taper mandrels increase in diameter so quickly that were you to make a blank even 11 feet long, the butt would be too thick to hold. Some of the fastest mandrels used for surf rods are uncomfortably fat by the 8 foot point and would exceed 1.75 inches in diameter at 12 feet. The only practical answer is to cut the blank above the handle, then insert or spigot on a parallel or slow-tapered butt more suited to the average man's hands. Nothing is lost if the rod is made on the long tip/detachable butt theme.

If the rod is jointed in the centre, you still must add a separate butt, though in this case it is standard practice to glue it permanently in position. Properly done, it is a satisfactory but expensive modification. The rod costs more, and it is heavier. Sometimes the extra joint's weight detracts from feel, balance and power.

Fast, powerful blanks built on slower tapers are in theory quite easy to extend to 12 or 13 feet with no need for a separate butt. You can build medium power rods in this way, so why not a high-performance surf blank?

Butt rigidity is the limitation. Handle walls would be so thick that the rod would be heavy and dull to cast. The mass of glass alone would boost handle diameter beyond manageable limits. However, the principle is upheld with carbonfibre blanks because the material is so stiff, even in lower diameter/fairly thin wall construction. Unfortunately such rods are very expensive, but they do represent the state of the art in rod building. Again, regardless of material, the practical alternative is to curtail the main blank at the 7.5–8 foot mark and add on a separate butt.

Blank materials

Glassfibre remains the most popular blank material of all, but is fast losing ground to

Small dabs are all you can expect from some European beaches. Light carbonfibre rods help anglers make the best of a bad job.

109

semi-carbon and carbonfibre. Glassfibre is available in a variety of grades, cloth weaves and resin systems. As far as the angler is concerned, the precise specification matters little. Few if any ordinary glassrods are better than the rest except in taper and wall construction. For powerful casting a sloppy blank of the finest materials is far inferior to a fast-action rod of cheaper specification. On the other hand, a super-fast rod of premium-grade material is useless if your style of fishing demands a slow action blank with plenty of feel and flexibility in the lower half. Judge a blank by length, speed and general construction. Pay more attention to the maker's name than to the formula of his materials; most good designers won't tell you the innermost secrets of their products anyway.

The important exception is 'S' glassfibre, which is a much tougher, faster and more powerful material than ordinary 'E' grade glassfibre. Few manufacturers use it because it is much more difficult to work with. Fenwick and others—nearly all of them American—who have mastered 'S' glassfibre have proved it to be a perfect material for surf rods, especially for those which combine high performance with angling versatility.

Carbonfibre is taking a stranglehold on beach fishing and casting. In time it will dominate the market. Materials used in rod manufacture are a spin-off from the aerospace industry, which is fast moving from glass to carbonfibre. Consequently glassfibre must become scarcer and more expensive while carbonfibre drops in price. Soon the price difference between carbon and glass rods will fall to the point where nobody buys glassfibre rods.

Carbon is much lighter, faster, more precise and more sensitive than other rod materials. Other Space Age products like boron and silicon carbide may eventually challenge its supremecy for sea fishing, but at the moment it reigns supreme. From the designer's point of view the material is still in its infancy. We have long appreciated its theoretical advantages, but early work was plagued by breakages and poor results. Early production blanks and rods created an aversion to carbonfibre that still exists today, despite the massive strides taken since 1980. Today's carbon rods are far superior in every respect. The remaining snags are cost and selection. Carbonfibre rods are only available in a narrow range of lengths, strengths and actions. As more anglers become familiar with the material, carbonfibre will take over on beach and tournament field. If you have never tried a *good* carbonfibre blank, make an effort to do so. It is most unlikely you would ever want to fish again with glassfibre or even semi-carbon.

Rod Building: The Basics

Rod building falls neatly into two stages: basic assembly of the blank and handle, followed by ring whipping and general finishing. Neither requires special tools or great skill, but it still pays to work to a logical plan. With standard blanks this is simply done because ring spacings, handle length and reel seat position are fairly sure to fall into a well known pattern. Specialist rods are not so easy to assess. Wise rod builders know that somewhere along the line every new rod must be tested. If you can arrange to do this before the final whipping, gluing and varnishing, so much the better. There is nothing worse than spoiling a brand new rod by moving the rings or reel seat. No matter how carefully you work, an altered rod will never look as neat as the original.

Most anglers hold the view that rod building should be kept as simple as possible. Handle assembly, spigot whipping, rod rings and varnishing are basic steps in construction, and nowhere along the line should even the raw beginner hit trouble. A first rod never looks perfect, but with care you can be sure it will at least do its work and last a long time. Patience is more valuable than talent.

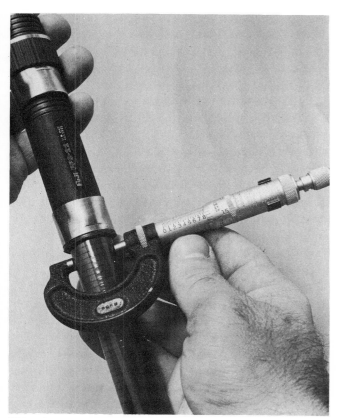

Check the blank diameter and pick the reel seat which most easily marries to it. It is useless to make do—if the reel is in the wrong place, casting suffers.

Your headaches begin when various components do not match up. If you know where the reel seat should fit on the handle, it is easy to measure blank diameter at that point, choose a reel seat of precisely the right size or very close to it, slide it on and apply adhesive. But suppose you did not check the position and diameters beforehand. There is an excellent chance that either the reel seat will sit too high on the handle, or will be so sloppy a fit that glue alone cannot make up the difference.

The logical answer is to change the reel seat. But it seldom works out that way in real life. If the tackle shop were close by, most anglers would indeed exchange the seat; but as more often happens shops are far away (lots of rods and accessories are bought by mail order), and the urge to finish your new rod is just too strong anyway. The rod ends up with its reel in the wrong place, which ruins casting performance, or it is bodged together with packing strips and masses of glue. After a month's hard fishing, the reel seat loosens and skids around the blank as you wind in.

Silly mistakes need not happen; but there are few newcomers to rod building who sail through the early days unscatched. RULE ONE, then, is to make sure that *all* the parts are compatible *before* it is too late to alter the building plan. RULE TWO is equally important. Make sure that all the parts for your new rod are *available*.

Take rod rings for example. The world is littered with millions of rod rings of all shapes, sizes and materials. All a rod builder needs for his new blank is one complete set, tip to butt. Surely no problem? If you need, for instance, 12mm tip, 10mm, 12mm, 16mm, 20mm, 25mm and 30mm intermediates, make sure you have them *all* in hand *before* you start building. Should there be some doubt about the numbers—say you think the rod might need an extra 12mm ring—buy it *now*.

The unwritten law of ring supply guarantees that the one you particularly want is never in stock next week. Try it and see. The same applies to the original set: if the tackle dealer has them all bar one—"but I can get one for you in a couple of days"—watch your step. I bet it does not arrive for three months.

Advanced builders know all about erratic supply and ill-matched accessories. Gradually they accumulate enough spare rings and fittings to overcome most snags. You learn with experience

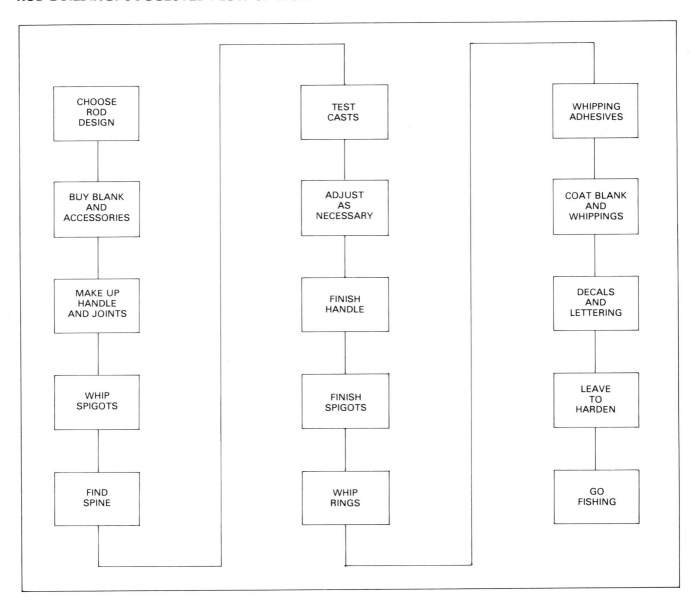

to modify things to fit. Blanks can be built up to take a standard reel seat. Reel seats are sleeved, or in some cases reamed out. Hand grips and butt caps are stretched and shrunk to fit. You can even learn to make special joints and handles. Such versatility takes time and experience. To start with, take the easy way out. Buy the bits, slide them into position, and run through the whipping, gluing and varnishing. Some anglers prefer to buy a semi-built rod with handle and fittings already in place. All you do is whip on the rings and brush on a gloss finish.

Making a start

The flow diagram highlights various stages in making a surf rod. The sequence of events is based on practical experience more than anything. There is no right and wrong way to assemble rods, but

there are ways to save time and disappointment, especially with more complex designs. Most errors are so obvious that you kick yourself afterwards. The classic one is to whip on a butt ring and then discover that you cannot slide on the reel seat and hand grips.

STAGE 1

Find out as much as you can about suitable blanks. Try as many as possible, and ask the tackle shop and manufacturer for technical literature and building suggestions. Pick the blank you like best and check it for obvious surface damage. Unless the rod comes in two sections with a spigot in place, make sure the manufacturer supplies a separate spigot so that you can make up your own butt. Most single-piece blanks arrive complete or are designed to fit inside a parallel butt tube.

Choose whipping thread, rings and handle components. Buy the necessary varnish or two-part epoxy coat, a pack of adhesive (Araldite standard and rapid are both excellent) and a stick of hot-melt glue for the tip ring. Store the kit indoors while you build the rod. Dust ruins a good finish. Condensation and cold are a menace. Glue takes forever to harden. Varnish will not flow. Everything is wringing wet.

The household tool kit provides most of the essentials:
Hacksaw
Craft knife or razor blade
Scissors
Sellotape or Scotch tape
Medium-cut file
Candlewax
Wet-and-dry carborundum paper, medium and fine grades.
Chalk or grease pencil.
Ajax or similar scouring powder
Methylated spirit

STAGE 2: For single-piece blanks without butts

Butt materials available:
Glassfibre
Aluminium alloy tube
Glassfibre/alloy laminate
Carbonfibre/alloy laminate
Glassfibre/carbonfibre laminate
Carbonfibre
Boron/carbonfibre laminate

For any given surf blank there are always several butt options. In general it pays to conform to the designer's recommendations, and to use his chosen jointing method. If a spigot is required, be sure to order it along with the blank so it can be accurately ground and fitted in the factory.

The trend is for manufacturers to supply butts which complement the main blank. Sometimes you have a choice of two or three materials, and there are diameters and stiffnesses to suit preferred rod length. An 8 foot semi-carbon tournament tip made up to 11.5 feet overall would generally be supplied with either a high tensile aluminium alloy butt of 1–1.25 inch diameter or a carbon butt (pure or laminated) of roughly the same dimensions but with a far higher casting performance. The same blank made in 13 foot South African style might feature an aluminium alloy butt between 1.125 and 1.25 inch diameter. Its carbon alternative is slimmer and lighter, far

more powerful and precise . . . and extremely expensive.

According to your purse, casting ability and personal preference, choose whichever option makes sense. The great advantage of single-piece blanks is that should the original butt prove inadequate you can buy another. Two butts—short and long—plus a single tip is an excellent combination for anglers who like to experiment or who choose their casting styles (and therefore their rod lengths) according to season, weather, sinker weight and species of fish. It is quite common to use an 11.5 foot rod for everyday fishing, and to plug in a longer butt (overall rod length say 12.5 feet) for tournaments and extremely long range beach work.

Balanced performance and easy jointing are key factors in butt selection. Take advice before you buy. Most fishermen are content to use the manufacturer's recommended butts. Experimenters and rod building fanatics stray from the easy path. Careful selection based on experience and individual preference may well result in the perfect rod for you. However, consider the disadvantages as well: substantial modifications to butt and tip may be necessary; and full workshop facilities including a lathe and belt sander are often indispensible.

Full power on the tournament court. Ordinary rod handles neither stand the strain nor give the best performance. Alloy and carbonfibre are preferred.

Slim butts with soft grips are essential in surf fishing when the rod is held all day long. Blank weight and balance are important as well.

Which butt material is best?

Given an entirely free choice, most surf fishermen would do better with carbon fibre butts, which are superior in all respects except price. However, more practical advice is to use a butt material at least as good as that of the tip. The world's finest blank attached to a cheap handle would be outclassed by an ordinary tip pepped up by a sophisticated butt.

Some anglers and custom rod builders think the tip is more important than the butt, and they resent paying extra cash for, say, carbonfibre/glassfibre laminate rather than low-grade aluminium alloy. They are wrong. One cast with the better material would convince them. However, it is wrong to dismiss other handle materials without first examining their strengths and weaknesses.

Glassfibre

Parallel wall or slow-tapered glassfibre butts offer reasonable performance with lower-grade surf blanks. There is no point using glass butts with any tip except plain glassfibre. An ordinary 'E' glass butt is no match for an 'S' glass tip.

Glassfibre butts are at their best with medium-fast surf rods and are most often encountered on two equal-piece blanks. Choice of handle does not even arise. On the fast-action single tip design, detachable or glued-in parallel glassfibre butts are a poor choice for high performance casting and fishing. It is virtually impossible to make them stiff enough.

Aluminium alloy tube

Metal tube offers a significant boost in butt stiffness, without imposing too much of a weight handicap. Unfortunately, it is a brutal material which ruins the feel and delicacy of many blanks. Casting distances are much improved, but at some cost in cast control.

Aluminium alloy tube is inelastic compared to glassfibre and carbonfibre. It is a source of rigid leverage and little else. However, it works very well for many casters and fishermen. Assuming that length, diameter and wall thickness of the tube are well chosen, you can enjoy first class casting and pleasant enough general fishing. It is not a material for light surf and lure rods, but certainly comes into its own for heavy sinkers and tournaments.

Alloy is also very cheap. You can afford to buy a longer than normal butt. Test the rod in over-length form, and trim the butt back with a hacksaw, inch by inch, until you arrive at the perfect rod. Very often a rod 3–6 inches longer than normal works better than you would have imagined. Sometimes a shorter than average rod gains distance. It costs little to find out, and should you accidentally over-trim the butt (or wish to lengthen an existing alloy handle) just buy a few inches of smaller diameter tube and push it into the original.

Low cost and easy replacement are useful in the longer term as well. The serious problem with

114

alloy is that butts seldom last more than two years without succumbing to salt corrosion. Sometimes they snap in half without warning, especially if the metal is covered in shrink tube.

There are many grades of aluminium alloy. Best for rod making are HE30 and HT15, drawn seamless tube. These specifications are British Standards which have direct equivalents elsewhere. Engineering text books and aluminium manufacturers supply a conversion chart. HE30 is ordinary high-tensile dural available from non-specialist industrial tubing suppliers and through the tackle trade. It is more than good enough for general rod building.

In ardous conditions HT15 grade alloy is better still. Relatively expensive (though far cheaper than carbonfibre) and harder to find, it is the material of choice for 11.5–11.75 feet pendulum casting rods used with the reel in the upper position for 5–6 ounce sinkers. It may be used for any rod though, and generally you can afford to use one step lower external diameter than necessary with HE30. The best suppliers are airframe and aerospace alloy factors.

Suggested diameter/wall thicknesses for 4–6 ounce surf rods:
Up to 40 in. butt or 11.5 ft. rod, high reel position—*1 in.*/16SWG HT
Up to 40 in. butt or 12 ft. rod, reel high or low—*1.125 in.*/16SWG HE
Pendulum rods, 40 in.—plus butt, reel high or low—*1.125–1.25 in.*/16SWG HE
Back cast rods 13.5 ft.—14.5 ft, reel low—*1.25–1.375 in*/16SWG HE

Composite and laminated butts
A few layers of glassfibre wrapped around aluminium alloy tube one size slimmer than normally standard for the rod, offer protection from permanent bends and introduce a fair degree of control without sacrificing too much speed and leverage. Laminated butts are quite pleasant to fish with, fairly light and unlikely to be eaten away by saltwater. Prices are quite competitive as well. In all, a recommended compromise for medium performance surf rods.

Lamination works well for carbonfibre and alloy. The object is to raise casting power without spending the earth. Three or four wraps of carbonfibre are sufficient to boost casting range by perhaps 5 percent—of little consequence in fishing but useful on the tournament field.

Composites of carbonfibre and glassfibre are marginally better than the above laminate, and represent a useful step closer to pure carbon

without incurring a massive price penalty. The ratio of carbon to glass varies between manufacturers, as do performance, balance and cost. Although hardly lighter than the best alloy laminates—and sometimes significantly heavier—composites do cast farther and, more important, are far smoother than any lower grade of butt material. They are especially good with semi-carbon tips. All lengths, diameters and wall thicknesses are available, mostly direct from the blank factory, spigotted where necessary and matched to a specific blank, rod length and casting style.

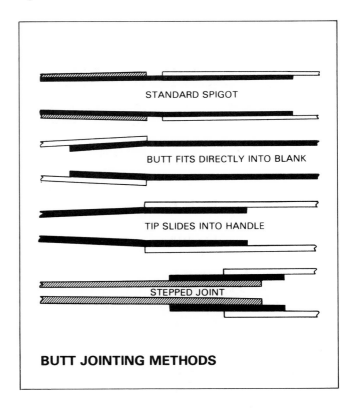

BUTT JOINTING METHODS

Carbonfibre
Carbonfibre is very light, tough, responsive, smooth and lightning fast. The feeling is of an overdrive or turbo-charge boost to the cast. No butt can equal its performance and easy handling. It is expensive; on rods over 12 feet long the butt section costs more than the single-piece tip. These butts are directly responsible for improved tournament records and better fishing. Nobody can afford to make a mistake when buying a carbon handle. Tell the dealer—or better still the blank designer—exactly what kind of rod you need. Buy a matched butt, blanks and spigot. You should know your ideal rod length before ordering, but if in doubt add an extra six inches on to the handle. Nearly all anglers who switch to carbon benefit from a butt slightly longer than they can handle in glassfibre or aluminium alloy.

115

Boron/carbon butts

In theory, boron filaments should improve even a carbonfibre rod butt. The very few handles available are slimmer than pure carbon, extremely stiff and apparently longer-casting. Exactly why, is difficult to say until more work has been done. In my view the very slimness of the handle contributes a marginal boost to the cast. Prices are horrific even though boron content is quite low.

Joints for single tips and separate butts

Long tips and their butts are jointed according to material, comparative diameters and wall thicknesses, and to some extent to individual preference. As with most aspects of blank/handle selection, take advice before you decide, and do try out the rods which appeal to you. There are several methods of attachment, all of them strong and reliable. Some look crude, others are neat but add both weight and cost. Choose either what is available as standard from the blank manufacturer, or carry out your own modifications. One point for American anglers to consider: despite what some rod companies claim, there is absolutely no reason to condemn a plug spigot or indeed the detachable butt format itself. Buy with confidence.

Measure spigot overlap before gluing the components. A half inch gap is about right on most blanks.

Coat the spigot with candle wax to prevent the walls rubbing each other away.

An all-carbonfibre surf blank weighing less than 10 ounces. The rod is jointed in the centre with a carbon plug spigot. The method of jointing is perfectly safe.

116

The options: Spigot, either Feralite or plug
Blank slides over butt
Butt pushes into blank
Permanent joint
Stepped joint

Spigots

At its simplest, fitting entails little more than measuring the male and female ends of the spigot to ensure a tight, comfortable fit, then gluing the lower end into the handle.

Clean the inside of blank and butt. Wipe the spigot. A thin layer of grease and dust alter the overlap quite considerably and severely reduce adhesion of Araldite-type glue. Methylated spirit works well enough, but special epoxy adhesive thinners are available. Ajax powder on a damp cloth soon scrubs away stubborn particles.

Slide the spigot into the blank. Normally it is impossible to insert the wrong end. Push firmly and twist gently so that the walls fit closely but without stress. Mark the spigot depth with a grease pencil or chalk. Alternatively, stick on a circle of masking tape.

Tape collars hold the blank inside the butt while the glue sets. This is the best way to ensure a straight rod.

Stepped aluminium alloy tubing looks better than a direct fit between substantial butt and slim-line carbonfibre blank.

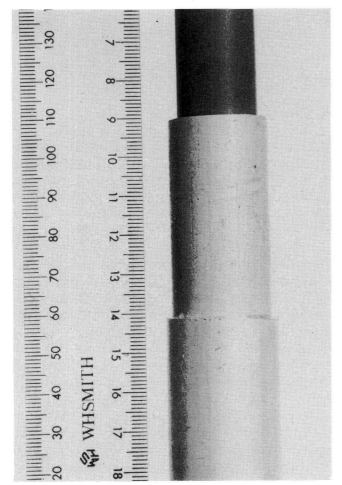

Remove the spigot, then push its other end into the handle. If necessary, rub down the spigot with wet-and-dry paper lubricated with soapy water. A perfect fit is not required. In fact a slightly undersize joint glues up more accurately and securely. You also avoid what is known as hydraulic distortion: soft adhesive in an over-tight joint creates a severe outward radial pressure on the handle walls. In extreme cases the material splits. When you are satisfied with the dry fit, apply glue inside the handle and on the lower section of spigot. Insert the spigot *and remember to leave approximately 0.5 inch between the handle and the blank depth marker*. A gap is essential to accommodate spigot/blank wear.

Where the handle tube diameter is greater than spigot width, build up the gap with string soaked in adhesive or make up a sleeve from segments of a complete ring of suitable glassfibre—from an old blank, for example. String is satisfactory for gaps up to 0.0625 inches. Beyond that, a sleeve of some kind is essential.

117

Usually a spigot automatically sits square and straight in the butt. Where excessive rubbing down or padding out are involved, slight inaccuracy creeps in. Wrap masking tape (Sellotape will do but tends to melt in contact with adhesive) around the lower end of the spigot until it fits perfectly inside the handle. Slide the spigot home. Mark its exact depth—do not forget to allow for the joint overlap—and build that end exactly to diameter with tape. The dry spigot now sits accurately in the handle, supported top and bottom by tape collars. Attach the blank and check the overall rod straightness. If necessary adjust the tapes accordingly. Slight eccentricity might actually produce a straighter rod.

Apply glue inside the handle and between the tape coils. Slide in the spigot and leave it to set. If padding is necessary, follow the same plan as before with string or sleeves, but this time restrict them to the space between tapes. As long as you use tape no wider than 0.25 inch, joint strength and stability are not affected.

Leave adhesive to cure for at least 24 hours. Keep an eye on the joint until Araldite begins to set. Sometimes the spigot creeps in or out of the blank and must be continually adjusted or held steady with tape or clamp. Check that no glue spreads to the male end of the spigot. If it does, wipe it off with thinners. Finally, rub candlewax on the male spigot. Glassfibre and carbonfibre are slightly self abrasive, and the wax protects one wall of the overlap from the other.

Sliding joints
On rods whose butts slide directly into the tip or vice versa, clean the mating parts, check for security and measure the overlap. Between 4 and 6 inches is adequate on any surf rod. If necessary ease the joint with fine grade abrasive paper and soapy water. How do you find the high spots? Slide the joint together and twist gently. Shiny spots on the withdrawn section indicate excess material. Finally, wax the male side.

Glass into glass, glass into carbon, and carbon into glass are all satisfactory. Glass and carbon blanks are safely inserted into parallel aluminium alloy butt tubes. However, in my experience it is bad practice to plug an aluminium butt into a blank unless the joint is glued permanently. A sliding, detachable alloy handle rapidly wears away the inner blank walls and causes sudden catastrophic failure. On the whole, it is perhaps better to glue down all these joints, in effect making a single-piece rod. Unless there are

Ready for a big pendulum cast. This is the ultimate test of joint strength. Avoid taking short cuts as you build the rod.

transportation and storage problems, that is the method I prefer for all my rods.

Stepped joints
In the case of carbonfibre and some semi-carbon, the external diameter of a blank is far slimmer than the required grade of aluminium alloy handle. A powerful tournament tip slightly more than 0.75 inches diameter might require a 1.125 inch butt, which in 16SWG wall is 1 inch internally. A 0.25 gap is too great to fill with tape. Ordinary jointing methods work but the rod looks silly—a tiny blank sprouting from a damn great chunk of metal.

Try this. Find a piece of 1 inch/10SWG HT15 alloy tube about 8 inches long. The inside diameter is just right to accept the blank. Skim the outer wall by hand or on a lathe until the tube slides into the main handle. Leave a 1–1.5 inch overhang to produce an unobtrusive step, which can be completely hidden by a plastic shoulder collar or even by careful whipping.

When you rub down the smaller tube, make sure it does not stick in the main one while you are testing for diameter. Once aluminium grabs hold of itself, it will not shift. Work on a lathe if possible.

118

Rod Building: Testing and Design

When handle and joint assembly are completed, long-tip blanks follow much the same constructional path as sectional and one-piece blanks. The basic unit is ready for rings, hand grips, reel seat. On well-established designs of rod which the angler knows from experience will suit the way he casts and fishes, there is no need for testing until the final coat of varnish has set. In every other case it pays to break the building process into steps which allow periodic testing and fine-tuning. Stages detailed here incorporate such safeguards. On familiar types of rods, or if you are making a rod for another angler and to his specifications, simply skip over the irrelevant parts. On the other hand, testing takes such little time and effort that many highly competent rod builders still prefer to include it.

STAGE 3: Spine and blank alignment

Because of the way blanks are made, every one has a plane of least resistance running from tip to butt. This is not a weakness in the practical sense; it just means that the blank bends a little more easily in one particular direction. The phenomenon is referred to as spine or bias, and while the effect is greater in some blanks than others there are very few with no spine at all.

The vast majority of blanks are also slightly curved, and the curve itself usually takes the same direction as the spine. Even if a blank appears perfectly straight when held vertical, it assumes a slight downward bias when horizontal because the tip is pulled down by its own weight. Many anglers worry about the curve of a blank and automatically reject those with a detectable bias.

A curve is of no consequence provided it is not a sudden departure from the natural plane of the blank. Twists and bends arising suddenly towards the tip, however, are a danger sign, especially if their onset coincides with a bulge, broken cloth pattern, split, depression or patch of loose filaments. On some blanks made from exotic carbon-based materials, a natural bend is the sign of a superior manufacture. Indeed, when a second-rate manufacturer has trouble making acceptably straight blanks, he may increase the resin content or use an inferior chemical mix. 'Wet' cloth soaked in cheap resin, low mandrel taping pressure and minimum curing are all tricks to improve straightness. They also cut performance, add weight and shorten service life.

Rod makers use the spine and curve of a blank to determine alignment points for rings and reel seat. On high-power surf rods used pendulum style, spine direction must be taken into account because in extreme cases an incorrectly aligned blank twists itself apart, loosens the rings and makes the casting action uncharacteristically harsh. It takes but a few seconds to align a blank for spine and straightness, and in the long run you may avoid ruining your rod.

The classic test is to lean the blank against a wall, butt on the floor, and see where it naturally settles. If the spine is pronounced, the blank rolls over until the inside of the spine curve—the weaker side—faces away from the wall. Mark that plane with a grease pencil or chalk. If the spine is hardly apparent, press on the blank and slowly rotate it by hand. At some stage it will suddenly 'drop' under your fingers. This indicates the spine plane. With practice you can dispense with the wall. Just lean the butt on the ground, bend the tip over and spin the blank until you feel the soft spot.

The relationship of spine to rings varies with blank taper, length and power. Spine may be used to produce an absolutely straight rod: rings are suspended from the outside of the curve, and gravity does the rest. Alternatively, rings may sit on the inside bend, which sometimes makes a rod feel smoother to cast. In flycasting and freshwater fishing where blank power and casting weight are small no damage is likely to result whichever system is used.

Every year I come across more and more high-power surf rods which feel strange in action. Many distort the rings, and some have either cracked the blank walls or snapped altogether. In every case, with the rare exception of a genuinely faulty blank, the cause is misalignment of blank spine. The overwhelming majority of blanks are ringed on the outside of the curve or at right angles to the spine plane. Nine rods out of ten were home-built by surf anglers who forgot to line up the rings with the blank.

During the cast, any blank tries to take the line of least resistance—that is towards the inside of the spine. If rings are set on the opposite side, the blank literally twists itself. In the long run the weaker element fails. Either the rings move around the blank, or the blank walls begin to self-destruct.

My standard practice is now to ring a rod on the inside of the spine curve regardless of the slightly exaggerated bend which may occur when the rod is supported horizontal and rings down. Only fixed spool rods are affected; and with most blanks you must look very hard to see any more distortion than there would have been with the rings on the other side of the spine curve.

Multipliers are no problem since you fish them rings upward. In theory, the blank should then twist when a fish bends it but in practice you do not notice any difference. Fighting pressures are never so vicious as those encountered during the cast.

Long tip blanks with detachable butts and equal-length section rods with stiff butts spliced on may not sit quite straight due to slight imperfections in joint construction. Sight along the rod from butt to tip, and see how the imperfection responds to a slight twist of the spigot. A distinct improvement usually occurs at one particular stage of spigot rotation. Make a chalk dot on each side of the spigot as a reference point. Now carry out the spine test with the sections of blank in precise dot alignment with each other. Mark the spine position on both sections of the rod. Use that line to centre the rings and reel seat. The rod may still look a little bent, but it is safe enough to cast. Complete correction is almost impossible anyway.

STAGE 4: The first test

If my new blank is a prototype, I am so keen to test it that the normal building sequence collapses. With the blank jointed and spined, only 5 minutes' work stands between a fisherman and his first cast with the new toy. Tape on the rings and reel, and off you go. But before you cast the rod—and preferably before you even flex it purposefully—REINFORCE EVERY JOINT WITH A TIGHT WHIPPING. If you don't, the blank walls might well split and render the entire rod useless.

When I'm dealing with prototype blanks in the factory, I rely on a dozen turns of Sellotape or packaging tape strapped around the joints to protect them. My theory is that the rod might snap anyway, being a brand new, untried design. I also want to gain some insight into joint safety. In extreme cases I dispense with tape and deliberately try to split the blank. That is hardly a trick to recommend, though it does prove the point that *no matter how well the rod is made, unprotected joints do split under quite modest pressure*.

Sellotape suits me fine, but I would still suggest you use a proper whipping. Whipping thread is not satisfactory unless impregnated with adhesive. Even tightly bound, the blank might weaken. Nylon monofilament fishing line is far superior because it exerts strong radial support on the blank; 12–15 pound test is excellent. Use modest tension and whip at least 3 inches on each side of

Blank designers often use tape to protect trial rods. It is quick but not always safe. Tough Mylar tape is much better than ordinary Sellotape.

120

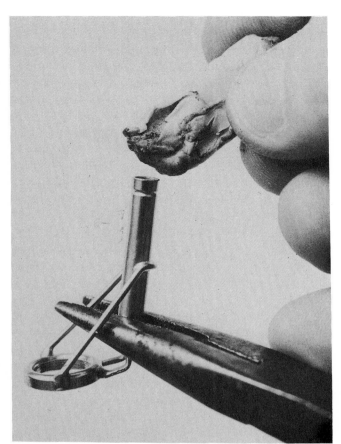

Fix tip rings with hot-melt glue which is easily softened when the ring needs changing. The ring is a Diamite—unquestionably the best choice for hard working surf rods.

every joint, male and female. There is a very slight risk that monofilament could crush thin-walled blanks if the whipping tension becomes excessive. Apart from that, the procedure is safe, quick and easy. Tuck the final turns of line under each other or stick them down with Sellotape.

I fix on my reels with a taped-on Fuji Snaplock, hose clips or strip of rubber whipped over the reel stand. Any method will do provided it holds the reel securely, is instantly adjustable for butt position, and does not crush the blank walls or dig into the surface.

Glue on the tip ring with hot-melt adhesive. Make sure it is exactly in line with the spine—from now on it becomes the reference point for rings and reel seat. Tape on the rings in what seems a reasonable combination and spacing pattern. Sellotape is fine for field testing. Waterproof electrical tape is better if you aim to go fishing rather than just casting. The rod is now quite practical and sound. Two or three of mine never did progress to final building. They have fished and cast beautifully for ten years.

Testing can be as cursory or as exhaustive as you like. If I have experience of the design, a few casts can confirm what I already know about ring spacings, handle length and overall rod length. I

may fiddle around with the rings to check spine angles and see if any minor improvements emerge.

Most fishermen worry about rod testing. They think that without sophisticated equipment and a university qualification, nobody can assess a new rod. Certainly there are some mistakes like not whipping the joints which can ruin a blank. While the very best tournament casters in the world tune their tackle to its limit, even experts manage quite well with less than perfect tackle. A rod two or three inches too short or long will have some effect on performance, but seldom enough to worry one man in a hundred. The best way to test a rod is to try it and see. Fit the thing together, incorporate any useful information gained by experience or gleaned from the angling world, use well-known components . . . and just wave the rod around. Cast it a few times, catch a couple of fish, move the rings up and down, add or subtract a ring, shift the reel seat and feel the various changes in action and power.

There is a lot of nonsense talked about rod design. Fishermen are utterly convinced that within the walls of a rod factory are teams of scientists and technical geniuses who slave over advanced experiments and exotic field test programmes. Rod manufacturers are too clever to dispel the myth, and may even compound it by broadcasting reams of high-flown literature. The poor old fisherman keen to build his own rod feels

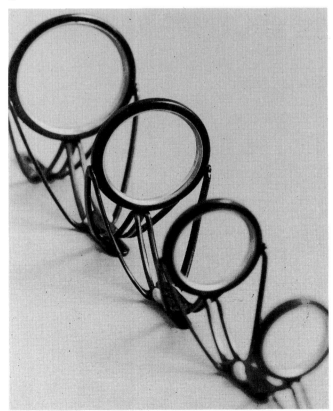

A neat tunnel for the line. All good brands of ring will produce an efficient line flow if spaced correctly. These are Daiwa Dynaflo.

he just cannot compete. 'Why', he says, 'I can't do much more than waggle the damn thing around until it feels right.'

In fact, a lot of rod and blank companies, among them the some of the best known in the world, do most of their experimental work by waving rods around. The long-term fortunes of a company reflect the quality of the man in charge of the waggling—known as a designer, development engineer, or design consultant. If his idea of how a good rod should feel coincides with those of the mass market angler, the company is on to a winner. Technical skill and scientific experiment have their place in rod making but mostly involve the chemical engineers who develop the raw materials and the man who works out the shape and size of the blank. After that, the process of 'designing and scientifically field testing' a new model is very much a seat of the pants exercise.

Knowing the truth about so-called scientific rod designing encourages more anglers to go ahead with projects of their own. As a result, more new designs are born in the home workshops of the world than in every tackle factory and custom shop combined. The only restriction is in blank making, which really is beyond the individual angler. However, with so many thousands of blanks now available, the chances are excellent of finding one pretty close to or even exactly right for you.

Consider the argument in terms of rod rings alone. The vast majority of surfcasting and tournament rods, homebuilt and production, are fitted with rings of very few styles, materials and sizes. Almost regardless of their brand and minor variations in design, the number of rings and their diameters fall into two ranges according to reel type. For example, Fuji BNHG series are universally popular for multiplier casting, and BSHG for fixed spool work. Seven or eight rings between 10mm and 30mm is about average for multipliers. Four or five rings grading down from 40 or 50mm suits 99 percent of fixed spool rods. Dynaflo, Seymo, and a dozen other brands follow much the same theme.

Pessimists assume that rings are so special and important that only a few companies have cracked the code, and that only two or three combinations of ring can possibly apply to surfcasting. Anglers who really believe this are neurotic about making a mistake. Under no circumstances will they risk a few test casts. They want to know exactly which rings to buy and where to whip them on—and they want dimensions down to the nearest millimetre.

Optimists conclude that ring sizes and spacing are quite unimportant as long as you choose a set reasonably compatible with the blank and reel.

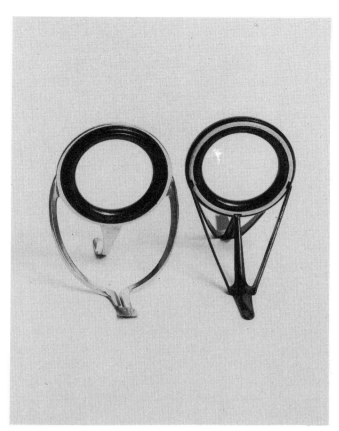

Fuji BNHG and BSHG surfcasting rings. BNHG are used on multiplier rods, BSHG on fixed spool. There is no reason why you cannot change them around.

Fuji lined rings are typical of the modern generation of surfacasting rings. Good casting properties combine with toughness.

A wipe with Ajax scouring cream lifts off dirt and grease. Adhesives and varnish will not stick to a filthy blank.

They argue that, give or take a little, the exact position of the ring is unlikely to destroy casting performance, alter the fishing characteristics of the rod or stress blanks unnecessarily. If this were not so, the fishing industry would need to develop and market thousands more types and sizes of ring. At some stage rods would progress to the point where every blank would have its own special set. The fact that for years nobody has come up with a radically new concept in rings must prove something.

Of course there are differences between rod rings. Changes in pattern do alter the way rods react. The earlier chapters of this book cover ring selection in detail for both fishing and casting rods. While I certainly do not go along with some manufacturers' claims about their products, I have found slightly better results with some designs. Overall, given a choice between the two basic philosophies outlined above, I suscribe to the latter. Unless you are making a very advanced rod, time spent worrying about rings and spacings would be better employed elsewhere. However, it is always worth bearing in mind a few cardinal rules.

1) The butt ring's size and distance from the reel are instrumental in controlling line flow. Minimum figures given in the design profile do much to prevent trapped leader knots, high friction and line tangles with fixed spool reels.

2) Set the rings out on the blank to produce a neat tunnel for the line to travel.

3) Try to avoid rings smaller than 10mm inside diameter. They trap weed and foul leader knots.

4) Use a plain tip ring like the Hopkin's and Holloway Diamite. Rings with inserts are notoriously unreliable, and the tip ring is the only one you cannot afford to lose or damage on the beach.

5) Space rings close enough to spread the load evenly over the rod. It is important to prevent localised stress at any point, and especially near the tip of the blank.

6) On the other hand, avoid whipping on too many rings. Extra weight dulls blank reaction and may reduce performance.

The patterns suggested in this book should be satisfactory for the majority of blanks. Anglers with no experience of rod building will find them useful as a starting point. At worst it will be necessary to shift them just a few inches either way, or perhaps add or take a single ring from the set. Confirmation of the ring pattern is smooth casting, plenty of power in the rod, and evenly spread pressure when the rod is held at full curve against a static line.

TESTING FOR ROD LENGTH is based on trial casts and practical fishing. Of the two, casting is far

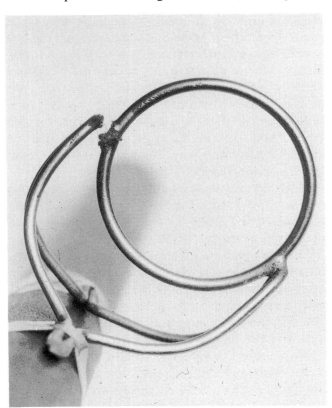

Check wire rings before whipping. Pull gently on the frame brazings. This one looked sound but was completely cracked under the chrome.

123

Spigot reinforcement is essential. Wrap tightly, then glue down and seal the threads.

more important because within reason the length of a rod makes little difference to bite detection, handling and pulling power. Adjustment is usually required only on rods with detachable butts and single-length tips. Most butts are supplied slightly over-long, so you may need to trim back a few inches. You can run quite a few tests without actually cutting the butt. Shift the reel into position and hold the rod a few inches in from the bottom end so that the excess material lies outside your hand spacing. Up to a foot can be accommodated this way. Having found your ideal length, make the cut.

I have already warned about cutting back the tip of a rod. Most rods are better left uncut. Should you feel it necessary to experiment, there is no practical alternative to doing so before rings are finally whipped into place. An inch cut from the tip might destroy the required gap between the tip ring and its neighbour. Sometimes two or three intermediate rings must be moved. Even if tests absorb days of casting and fishing, rely on tape until you are happy with the rod. Trim back inch by inch and make sure you stop in time. The final inch which you didn't know whether to risk is usually the one that wrecks the rod.

Rod building would be easier if every rod did have a set of hard facts and figures to guide its construction. Just accept that nothing is achieved unless you have the confidence to jump in at the deep end. Rod making is a fast-growing offshoot of angling which thrives only because it is a lot easier than it looks. He is a rare fisherman who produces a masterpiece first time; but it is also extremely difficult to make a complete mess.

STAGE 5: Back to square one

Testing a rod inevitably covers the blank with dirt and grease. As soon as you are happy with the tests, measure ring and handle positions, then strip the blank bare, including the joint whippings. Salvage the spine markings and spigot dots, and transfer them to a ring of tape stuck to the blank at some convenient point such as the spigot whipping area or where the reel seat/handgrips will be. Clean the blank with Ajax or methylated spirit, and from now on try to keep it perfect. Once rings and fittings are attached, blanks are almost impossible to treat.

Some blanks are already coated in high-gloss finish and require no more than a wipe down. Blanks with a spiral pattern on the outside and a lustrous finish (actually a layer of resin squeezed from the cloth during manufacture) need no extra protection. Some builders coat them with gloss, most do not bother. All plain blanks need some kind of coat, either varnish or one of the modern two-part epoxy finishes. The decision is whether to coat them now or wait until the rod is finished. For the best possible appearance, do it now. If custom-built looks are of no importance, leave it until the rod is whipped.

High gloss and smooth surface are best achieved by spraying on several coats of thin finish built up layer upon layer. Anglers with access to a spray gun and compressor should have no trouble turning out sparkling blanks. For the rest, dipping is the answer.

To successfully dip-coat a blank you need a length of plastic guttering a little longer than the blank and blocked at both ends to form a tray, a pint of coating and thinners, and a dry room tall enough to permit blanks to hang vertical while drying. First mask off the spigot and seal the ends of blank sections and butt. Pour half an inch of thinned coating into the tray, then drop in the blank and swill it around until every scrap is covered. Pick it up by the tip and hang it upright to dry. Butt downwards is best. Push a tray under the blank to catch the shower of drips. Several thin coats are better than a single dose of syrup.

However you work, make sure the atmosphere is dry, warm and dust-free. Spraying throws off clouds of solvent, some of which are dangerous in confined spaces. Be sure to follow the instructions on the can. Fumes are less of a hazard in dip-coating but soon build up if several rods are treated at once.

I have used all kinds of varnish, high-build specialist rod coats and even paint on surf rod blanks. Yacht varnish and high-build epoxy are best, but without special thinners high-build coat cannot be sprayed or dipped. Be careful with powerful solvents. Many eat into the blank itself. If all else fails, ordinary polyurethane varnish seems as good as anything. Again it depends on whether you have a fetish about appearance, in which case only the expensive products supplied by the custom-building trade will satisfy.

Rod finishing bores me silly. For years I have scoured the market for something you can simply wipe on and polish up. Think of all the time it would save. No dust. No streaks and runs. No waiting for the stuff to harden. Now I've found it: Turtle Wax Formula 3 polymer car wax is what you need, though any equivalent product should be equally good.

Pre-coated and spiral wrap blanks respond beautifully to a few doses of polymer wax. Most of my rods are spiral-wrapped carbonfibre, and these really do shine up after two applications. Besides looking good, the finish is virtually scratch proof. After a bout of heavy fishing, I wash the rods in soapy water and rewax them—blank, whippings and rings. Polymer wax builds into a perfect armour. If anything, rods look better with age, which is more than can be said for those coated in varnish or some of the new specialist rod coatings. Unfortunately, Turtle Wax Formula 3 will not generate a high gloss on plain, sanded blanks. It does, however, build into a smooth, totally protective matt finish.

Rod Building: Handles and Reel Fittings

STAGE 6 — Finishing the butt

Reel seat position is determined by the length and power of the rod, casting style and personal preference. Muscle power, blank stiffness and casting weight are the limiting factors. Adequate leverage is essential; on the other hand, an excessively high reel position reduces tip speed.

Rods in the 11–12 foot range cast pendulum or overhead style usually hit peak performance with a reel set some 28–32 inches from the butt cap. On a general-purpose rod to be used with fixed spools and multiplier reels and 5–6 ounce sinkers, those figures accommodate the vast majority of anglers. If in doubt, bias your decision towards the 32 inch mark. A few inches of excess handle are better than strained muscles and poor casts.

Varying sinker weights demand some leeway in the handle grips anyway: the bigger the weight, the wider the hand spacing should be. A 32 inch butt held 3–4 inches inside the limit provides a 28–29 inch leverage base for casting 5 ounces; the redundant 3–4 inches lying beyond the left hand make no difference to control and balance. When you cast 6 ounces on the rod, shift your left hand to the end of the grip and bring the extra leverage into play.

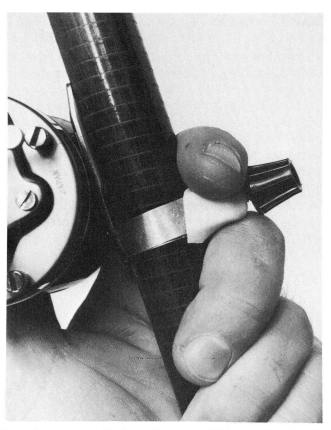

Reel clips are available for butts up to 1.125 inches diameter. If you use the clip as a trigger, wrap soft padding around the steel.

Some minor variations in reel seat position are inevitable if you are particularly long or short in the arm, so it pays to err on the long side rather than splice on an extra butt piece at a later stage. If the butt proves excessively long, trim it back with a hacksaw.

Popular reel seats: Screw winch fitting
                     Hosepipe clips
                     Reel saddle
                     Snaplock
                     Rubber strip

Fuji FPS carbon fibre/stainless steel reel seat.

126

The saddle is a quick, cheap method of holding a reel on a parallel butt.

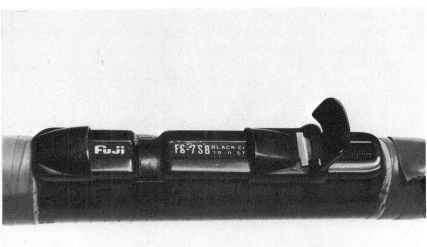

Fuji Snaplock taped to the blank for trial casts. The seat is versatile but none too reliable.

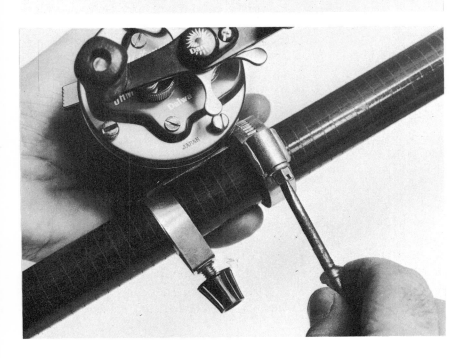

Ordinary hosepipe clips are strong and secure. Trouble is they look horrible and soon corrode.

Screw winch fittings

Tubular seats with sliding collar and locking threads are probably the most secure reel attachment. Modern lightweight fittings like the Fuji FPS stainless steel/plastic seat are reliable, tough and, by virtue of the many sizes in the range, compatible with a vast array of blanks and butts. Any blank with a diameter up to 30mm is a potential candidate for a screw winch fitting; and unless there is an important reason not to fit one, most home-builders are advised to look no farther. Other models besides the Fuji exist, and some of the old-style brass ones are much stronger. However, they are also very heavy and never so versatile. Lightweight aluminium alloy seats are best avoided since the metal crumbles to powder through saltwater corrosion. Choose a seat which matches the diameter of the rod butt, and simply glue it in place with Araldite or another brand of epoxy adhesive.

A limited amount of packing can be incorporated using the same principles described for spigots and butts. Some plastic can be reamed from inside the seat tube, but this is better to avoid if possible. Fuji FPS seats are made in 2mm increments, so there is seldom need to open up a slightly too small model. Which way around should the seat be? Most anglers prefer the threaded side of the tube between reel and butt ring. That way you hold the handgrip not bare threads.

Hosepipe and other clips

Versatility of design is an essential ingredient of rod building. Screw winch fittings are good looking and secure, so they appeal to the practical and aesthetic nature of fishermen. However, the option to move a reel up and down the handle at will is a powerful ally for advanced casters. Fine tuning is impossible with a permanent reel fitting because once the tubular base of the seat is glued down, only a hacksaw or chisel can shift it.

Parallel or slow tapering butts left bare or covered in plastic shrink tube allow free reign for reel adjustment. A stainless steel clip each side of the reel affords an excellent alternative to the traditional seat.

Some tackle manufacturers produce special reel clips with a threaded adjustment knob in sizes to suit butts between 1 and 1.125 inches diameter. As an alternative, screw-slot clips originally meant for hosepipes and automobile cooling systems work just as well, although they do not look as nice and will corrode in time.

Reel saddles

Security saddles supplied with Penn and similar multiplier reels are a viable alternative to a pair of separate clips. Penn saddles are particularly versatile, and if necessary the threaded screws and base can be adapted to fit very large diameter butts. In standard form they suit most butts up to 1.125 inches. Newell clips are very neat and secure but are sometimes too small to clip on aluminium alloy tubes. The small 220F reel is restricted to barely an inch. Some limited adjustment is possible, but full-scale alterations entail machining away the lugs on the base of the reel stand. This is sometimes necessary if you want to attach a small Newell to a large screw reel seat.

Snaplock fittings

Fuji's Snaplock fitting looks like a zip fastener strapped or whipped to the top of the handle. It is also available in tubular form. The fitting works in a similar manner to a traditional screw seat but relies on a clip and corrugated track rather than a sliding collar and thread.

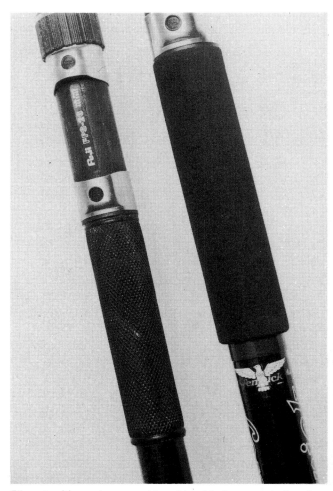

File-cut rubber grips are cold and hard but economical and reliable. Hypalon is expensive and a little more difficult to fit. It is very soft and comfortable, and it looks better.

For lightweight surfcasting and experimental work a Snaplock has much to commend it. Unfortunately, it is unreliable and too weak to handle prolonged casting and fishing pressures in the 6 ounce-plus sinker weight range. Either the whole fitting disintegrates or the security clip skids under load. Loose clips can be repaired but will soon fail again.

In view of their flimsy nature, Fuji Snaplocks are better whipped or taped to the handle. The tubular version can be cut away cleanly, but still leaves an unsightly gap in the blank. Plain Snaplocks combine neatly with a pair of hosepipe clips for use on parallel plain butts, or may be pop-rivetted to aluminium alloy tubes. You should use three rivets, one at each of the normal whipping positions. Some electrolytic damage will inevitably occur, mostly to the rivets themselves.

Rubber strip and sticky tape
Clips and Snaplocks are best used with multiplier reels. Screw seats cannot be moved. So what is the solution for fixed spool casters who want an adjustable reel seat? Try binding the reel stand to the butt with an 18 inch strip of 0.5 inch wide rubber cut from an old tyre. Bind the rubber tightly around the two, and tuck the last 3 or 4 coils around and under each other. Electrician's tape works equally well but is less easily stripped off and re-applied.

Sliding and double seats
A low-set multiplier reel controlled with the left hand makes life much easier on long pendulum and South African-style beach rods. The reel sits about 9 inches from the butt cap. Some anglers find it easy to wind in line and fight a heavy fish. Others wilt under the strain imposed by the reel position.

There are two neat answers. Either use a sliding reel seat—such as clips—or a pair of fixed seats, one high for retrieving, the other glued in casting position. Clips are certainly strong enough for the job, but do require continual opening and closing. There is also an excellent chance that you will drop your reel in the sand. The same drawbacks occur with double Fuji Snaplocks and screw winch fittings, but you soon learn to change the reel position in an instant. If you prefer, use the various fittings in combination. A high-positioned screw seat matches neatly to a pair of stainless steel clips at the bottom of the handle.

A number of special sliding seats have come and gone, and there is currently no specific model available to surf fishermen. However, an ordinary

FPS seat or tubular Snaplock can soon be adapted. The Snaplock is adapted by slitting it from end to end on the reverse face, then attaching it to the rod with a pair of clips. Provided the butt is smooth and almost parallel, devoid of grips and protected from scratching, the system works very well indeed.

An extension butt plugged into the main butt does much the same job as a sliding seat. After the cast, the reel fitting is raised high enough to permit easier retrieve and better leverage. The only drawback is that the rod may be too long and imbalanced for hand-held fishing. It works fine in a rod rest.

Hand grips
Traditional rod builders used cork handles. Tubular sections glued into position, sanded and filled produce a superior rod butt which is warm and comfortable. Of all the materials available, cork looks somehow right for a quality fishing rod.

Good corks are scarce and expensive, especially in the larger sizes. It takes time to assemble and finish the sections, and for best results there is no real alternative to spinning the butt on a lathe. Because surf fishermen generally are more interested in a rod's performance than in its

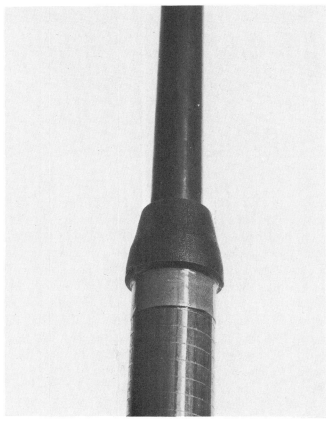

Soft plastic shoulder cap covers the step between a carbonfibre butt and its spigot. You can make your own from rubber or plastic bungs.

129

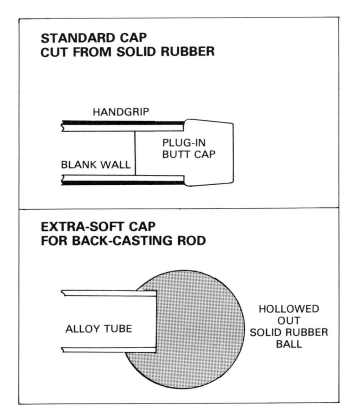

**STANDARD CAP
CUT FROM SOLID RUBBER**

HANDGRIP

BLANK WALL

PLUG-IN
BUTT CAP

**EXTRA-SOFT CAP
FOR BACK-CASTING ROD**

ALLOY TUBE

HOLLOWED
OUT
SOLID RUBBER
BALL

appearance, corks have given ground to synthetic materials. Instead of a single-piece handle running the full length of the butt, we now use three handgrips: one at the butt and one each side of the reel seat.

Hypalon and rubber grips are just as effective as cork. Hypalon is a semi-spongy material, reasonably warm and non-slip under the coldest, wettest hands. It is produced in a wide range of diameters, lengths and wall thicknesses, and as far as possible you should choose grips which require little or no alteration. Hypalon is quite difficult to shape by hand. Very careful cutting with an extremely sharp blade followed by rubbing with coarse wet-and-dry paper lubricated with water creates a reasonably good finish. Specialist professional builders and rod factories use power grinders with profiled wheels which cut an exact handle contour. Even then it is a skilled job to turn out perfect grips.

Hypalon's wall thickness is a potential disadvantage. The sponge cannot tolerate a wall less than 0.125 inches thick. A 1 inch diameter butt encased in Hypalon thus expands by at least 0.25 inches. Handles which are much thicker than 1.25 inches are so difficult to grip that fishermen with small hands are unable to hold down a multiplier spool for hard casting. Many of today's powerful surf blanks sport handles over 1.125 inches thick in bare form, so Hypalon is totally unsuitable unless you have hands like a gorilla's.

Thin-walled plastic and rubber sleeves are much

more accommodating, but are cold, unappealing and often slippery. However they are used on vast numbers of surf rods, home-built and mass produced simply because there is no acceptable alternative.

Choose whichever grip you prefer. Both offer excellent performance, but Hypalon has the edge in appearance and comfort. The ideal grip is one that slides on to the butt and holds its position by elasticity. If the hole in the grip is between 0.125 and 0.25 inches less than the butt diameter, the tube should slide easily into place and require no glue. Rubber and Hypalon slide more easily if you lubricate the inside of the grip and the walls of the butt with plain water. Soapy water never seems to dry out afterwards and the grip skids under your hand during a hard cast. If a sleeve is difficult to apply, shunt it down the butt with a piece of alloy or hard plastic tube.

Tape, cord and shrink tube
Cork composites consist of slivers of cork or ground particles held together in a resin or rubber matrix. Sheets and tapes are available and both may be cut, spiralled around the butt and glued

Butt caps are more than decoration. Sharp ends of carbonfibre and glassfibre are dangerous.

into place. Start and finish of the spiral are best reinforced and protected by whippings or plastic collars, otherwise the tape peels off within a few weeks. Cork composites have most of the advantages of pure cork and are less likely to inflate the butt diameter beyond practical limits. Araldite and Evostik contact adhesive are suitable for bonding cork to alloy, glassfibre and carbonfibre butts.

Rubber, leather and nylon tapes are also used on surfcasting rods. Some are self-adhesive, while others require Araldite or Evostik. Test a small piece of the tape beforehand: some plastics are eaten away by Evostik solvent. As with cork tape, it pays to whip or seal the ends of the spiral. Cord handles are assembled in the same manner. You do not see them around much these days, but some of the old-timers still insist that whipcord is the best handle covering of all.

Plastic shrink tube makes a serviceable butt covering. Many anglers apply it to alloy, glassfibre or carbonfibre butts before adding Hypalon grips or rubber sleeves. Cut the shrink tube 6 inches over-length, slide it on to the butt and warm it over a gas flame or in front of an electric radiant bar. The tube will shrink tightly against the handle, after which you should trim the ends. Spare plastic at the butt cap end can be tucked inside instead of being cut off.

Sometimes it is impossible to make the shrink tube grip the butt. The underlying alloy or blank is cold enough to repel the shrink tube. The plastic seems to tighten down, but it cannot compress through the final millimetre to the blank wall. Warm the butt before sliding on the tube. In rod factories it is common practice to heat the butt rather than the shrink tube. You can do that at home with alloy butts, but I would not recommend it for glass and carbon. Resins used in their construction are susceptible to heat, so you could easily ruin the blank.

Shrink tube lies firm under rubber sleeves and Hypalon grips but will not support a screw winch fitting. Glue that to the bare butt, then slide on two sections of shrink tube, one from each end. Push an inch or so of excess tube over the reel seat, shrink the plastic, then trim back. Some anglers leave a slight overhang permanently over the ends of the reel seat to prevent water creeping between the tube and the underlying butt. This is particularly important with alloy tubes. Six months of hard fishing will allow saltwater to creep inside and rot the butt to powder.

Butt caps and shoulder collars

Butt caps are essential. They look neat, but that is not the main reason to include them on a surf rod. Safety heads the list. An uncapped butt is potentially dangerous if line snaps in mid-cast. Casting force drives the end of the handle into your chest or stomach. Bare alloy, glass and carbon can cut deeply. Glass and carbon may leave behind sharp splinters which are extremely difficult to detect and remove. Back-casters are unlikely to make two casts without a soft, broad cap. During the cast, the butt rides on the hip bone or against your stomach. The first cast hurts so much that you will not be tempted to cast again without adequate protection. There are dozens of kinds of rubber butt caps on sale. Slide one on before you carry out even the initial casting tests on a new blank.

Shoulder collars are either cosmetic or glued in position to stop saltwater running down the upper end of an alloy butt. Either buy one from your tackle dealer or cut your own from a suitable tube of plastic or rubber. I have used cut-down 35mm film containers on several rods. They look quite neat. As a matter of fact, they make nice butt caps as well—a little on the hard side, but long-lasting and safe enough. Araldite holds them in place if the blank is too small for a compression fit.

Rod Building: Rings and Finishing

With the butt completed, ring sizes and spacings established, and spine determined, you are within a few hours of completing a new surf rod. The next stages are so easy that you tend to rush, which makes little difference to the performance and reliability of the rod, but does mar its appearance. Dust, finger prints, lumps and whiskers in the final coating spoil an otherwise perfect rod. Hastily written lettering never looks as good as careful script; and most of us do better with Letraset or a transfer anyway.

Perhaps the biggest failing is to apply more adhesive or coating before the previous layer is fully hardened. Traditional varnishes are notoriously slow to toughen and it is a natural reaction to apply the top coat a little too soon. The result is disaster. For this reason alone you may find modern fast-curing epoxy and polymer coats a much better alternative. Using the very best of them, it is possible to build a rod one day and fish with it the next.

STAGE 7 Whipping on the rings

Whipping is both traditional and effective. In the rush to simplify and hasten rod building, rod manufacturers have tested nylon collars, shrink-tube sleeves and adhesive tapes which in theory should be an improvement on normal thread. Some work fairly well, but none looks as good. Some require special equipment to apply and harden. In time, someone is bound to develop a better alternative, but for now it is the best choice for home-built and custom-made rod building. Surf rod builders should be even more sceptical about so-called 'improved' ring attachment systems. They have more to lose than freshwater and fly fishermen simply because a surfcaster inflicts far more punishment on the rod. Rings are always under attack, and you cannot afford to make any compromises.

Selecting whipping thread

Gudebrod NCP thread is an excellent choice. Available in a wide range of colours, plain and patterned, and in lengths and diameters to suit every kind of rod, Gudebrod is the tackle industry's choice. Very few high-quality rod makers use anything else. The closest rival is Talbot nylon thread available in Britain from a limited number of retail outlets.

Gudebrod NCP is smooth, colour-fast, compatible with most adhesives and rod coatings, and extremely tough. It costs more than inferior brands of thread, but in the long run it is much cheaper. Poor quality materials are covered in loose ends and bristles which become apparent after the first layer of adhesive or varnish. It is then too late to rectify your mistake without stripping off the rings and starting again. Often the blank itself must be cleaned and re-finished. Colours fade or, worse still, discolour when you brush on the finishing coat. Most have to be sealed and doped for security—a stage which can successfully be omitted with Gudebrod and modern synthetic coatings.

As a rule, medium-weight thread is excellent for surf rods. 50 metres is enough for most blanks, although it pays to buy 1 ounce spools instead. Each contains enough to whip two or three surf rods, with plenty left over for repairs later on.

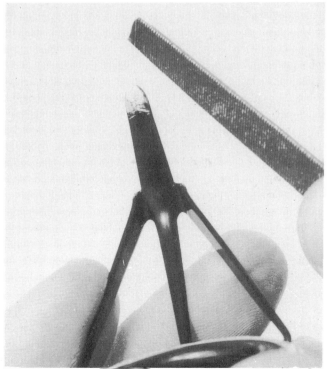

File down the end of the ring feet so that thread climbs easily from the blank.

When you buy thread, bear in mind that reinforcement whippings on spigots and other joints swallow up more than the rings combined; 50 metres is cutting it fine on a 14 foot back cast rod with substantial joint overlaps.

In general, lightweight thread produces a neater finish, although this should be balanced against the slowness of laying on so many coils. Where an absolutely perfect custom-finish is necessary, use thin thread and take great pains to align each coil against each other. Most surf men opt for the medium weight thread, which looks very good but takes less time to apply. The thickest is acceptably tough, very quick to wind on, but always looks coarse. Whipping pressure comes into it as well: thin and thick threads are less controllable than medium-weight Gudebrod, which seems to automatically flow on to produce the correct tension. It also rolls neatly up from the bare blank to the ring foot. Thick thread is likely to produce a nasty gap at the blank/ring junction.

Ring whipping tools

Like thousands of fishermen who make a few rods for their own use, I could get by with a pair of scissors and a roll of Sellotape. Results are perfectly acceptable, and I doubt if anyone could tell exactly how the whipping was produced. The limiting factor is time. While a fisherman is quite content to spend all evening whipping on one set of rings, the semi-professional rod builder cannot afford such luxury. Time means money. He prefers to invest in extra equipment which substantially cuts the labour involved.

A simple whipping frame like the one illustrated is easy to make and operate. The 'V' frame holds a blank steady and allows free rotation; the line holder feeds thread at the correct tension and angle. On my gadget, whipping thread is stored on a multiplier reel. Using the reel's very accurate drag system, I dial in any pressure I need. Other whipping frames, home-made and commercially manufactured, usually rely on a simple tensioning attachment that feeds thread directly from its spool. They work well enough; but by clipping on a reel instead you save time and trouble making a spool holder/tensioner, and you gain sensitivity and control. Just wind the thread on to your ordinary fishing multiplier.

Full-length frames are popular but are far from essential. A frame 12 inches wide supports most blanks with ease. To work right at the blank tip, I

An efficient wrapping frame for surf rods. Thread is carried on the reel spool and fed off under precise drag tension.

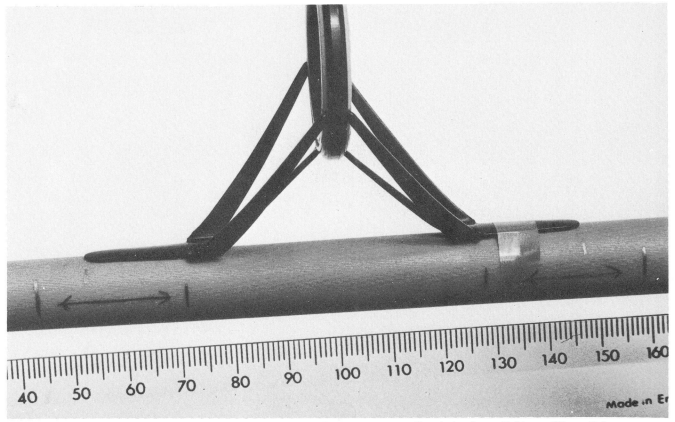

Measure the length of the whipping before you begin. These marks are exaggerated for clarity. A very light pencil line will do.

slide a pile of books or a chunk of wood under the butt for extra balance and control. Anyone can knock together a simple frame from scrap pieces of wood nailed together; or you can make a beautifully finished frame with all the gadgets. Exotic whipping frames are built on the lathe principle with a motorised headstock and speed controller. If speed is essential, the investment is worthwhile. A friend of mine who builds rods commercially reckons that a skilled operator can whip a surf blank, tip to butt including reinforcements, in five minutes on a motorised frame. Mass-produced rods are whipped on much the same principle in two or three minutes, but the standard falls short of that demanded by the custom-rod trade.

A warm, dry and dust free room is essential for varnishing. Thin coats built up one after another are the best. You cannot afford to risk a sudden dust storm—a heated box with air filters offers worthwhile advantages if you build enough rods to justify the outlay. Today's high-build rod coats are best applied to a continuously spinning blank, otherwise the coat sags in one plane. A motorised frame turning three or four times a minute ensures first class results. The home-builders only option is to turn the blank by hand. No trouble with one rod; but you would find half a dozen rods impossible to manage without semi-automated machinery of some kind.

Checking and preparing the rings

Fuji and Dynaflow rod rings, first choice of most discerning anglers, are fairly tough and well made. Chances of their being broken before fitting are slim, but it pays to be sure. Check the frame and its spot-welds, and the security of the linings. Hardchromed wire rings are notoriously weak: until saltwater corrosion highlights the fault with a layer of rust, small cracks in the soldered frame may be almost impossible to spot unless you GENTLY apply pressure to the frame joints. A surprising number of newly-whipped rings do turn out to be faulty.

The ends of ring feet are either ragged, or else the metal is a little too thick for the whipping thread to climb. Every ring should be carefully examined and filed down if necessary. A sharp edge promotes neat whipping but also risks digging into the blank. Some compromise is necessary. Fuji and Dynaflo are nicely shaped in the factory and only the bigger rings require trimming.

Positioning the rings

Ring position has already been determined and tested. Strap one end of the ring foot to the blank, and be sure that the position is correct radially as well—to match the spine curve. Exact alignment in this plane is almost impossible to maintain throughout the whipping process, but do not let the ring slip too far. Sighting down the blank is the best way to check the relationship of the rings to

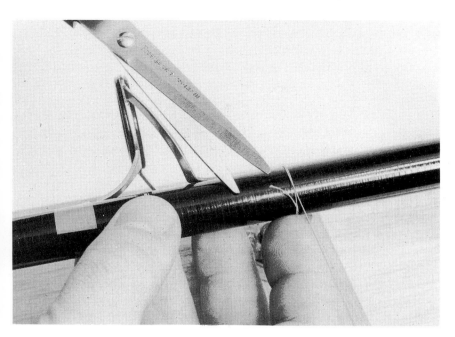

Whipping 1. Wrap the end of the thread around the blank and trap it under the next three or four coils.

Whipping 2. Set the thread tension modestly high, then start to build up the whipping. Lay the thread as neat as possible.

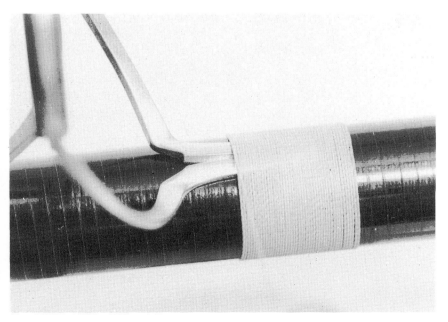

Whipping 3. Work smoothly up the ring foot until the whipping is within a few wraps of its full length.

135

Whipping 4. *Insert a loop of nylon and continue to whip to full length.*

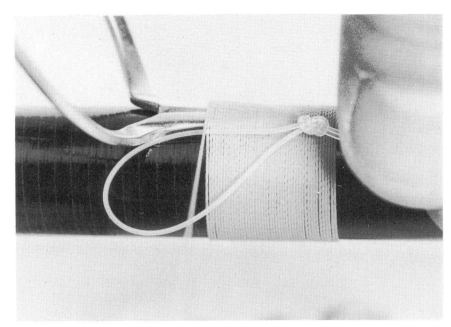

Whipping 5. *Cut the thread, feed the end through the nylon loop, then pull it through.*

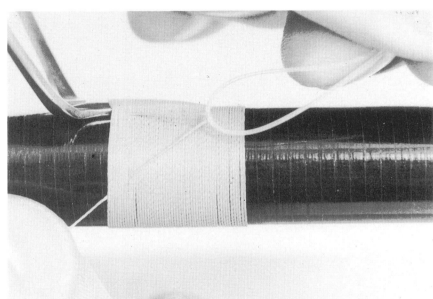

Whipping 6. *Trim the thread, but do not try for a perfect cut at this stage.*

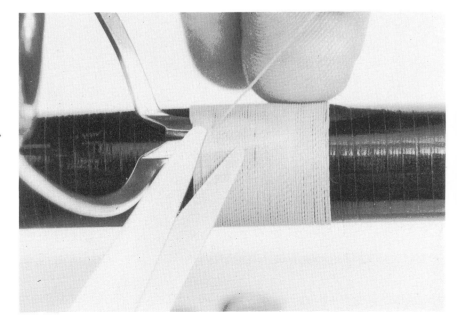

136

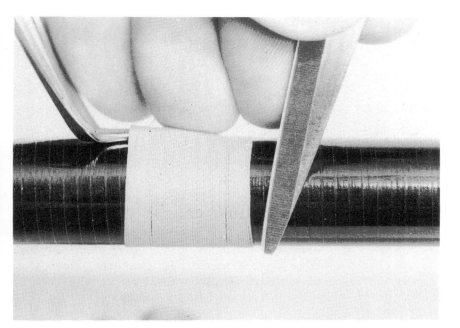

Whipping 7. *Square up the ends of the whipping with a knife blade or scissors.*

Whipping 8. *Smooth the whipping thread to remove gaps. Any smooth metal or hard plastic rod will do. This is the point from an arrow shaft.*

Whipping 9. *Trim the loose end of thread by cutting down between two coils.*

each other, and it helps if you use the tip ring as a baseline. The ring itself should be glued into place and in line with the blank spine. Use hot-melt adhesive, not Araldite. Tip rings usually have to be changed several times during a rod's life.

Use a ruler and soft pencil to mark out the start and finish of each whipping. With experience you can guess the spacings, but it never does any harm to include a pencil line; there is nothing worse than a rod with uneven whippings. No precise formula exists or is necessary to determine whipping length. Design an overlay which matches the ring and blank. As a general rule, the bigger the ring and thicker the blank, the longer the whipping should be.

The patch of Sellotape used to hold a ring is usually removed before the second side of the whipping is applied. However, it is permissible to use a tiny sliver of tape on both sides of the ring to bridge the blank/ring foot step. Whipping thread climbs smoothly up the tape to produce a neat finish.

Marking out the blank is even more important if you prefer to add a tipping of contrasting colour thread to the main whipping. The tipping length itself should be measured. Either make a second pencil line on the blank, or count the number of turns of thread. It is quicker to count and probably more accurate as well.

Length of spigot reinforcements should also be marked out for both safety and neatness. Whipping should extend to or a little beyond spigot depth. On a long joint, you can divide the whipping into several rings. If tippings or patterns are required, carefully mark all the dimensions directly on the blank.

Complex patterns—starbursts, tartan and even signatures—are beyond the scope of this book. For precise details and designs, refer to books on custom building. Some manufacturers produce excellent leaflets. Gudebrod provide full details and comprehensive instructions; Fenwick Woodstream's blank catalogue sometimes features interesting work.

Underwhipping is a layer of thread applied across the ring position before the ring itself is whipped on. It is both decorative and protective. If you like the effect, go ahead. An underwhipping will stop ring feet from digging into a blank, but should not be used to counteract ring twist unless you are sure of the cause. Some rings do loosen and shift around the blank. It is a natural effect of the ring size and height. An underwhipping and a coat of glue between base threads and ring feet are a satisfactory cure.

The risk is that glue and underwhipping are used

to counteract spine misalignment or severe rod torsion from the caster's faulty technique. In both cases a glued-down ring merely transfers the force to the blank, and may ruin it in time. Though underwhips look nice on any custom-finished surf rod, they are technically essential on very few.

Whipping the ring

Two methods are popular in the home-build, custom rod and manufacturing worlds. The easiest way is to tie off each whipping in turn. But when the blank is spun on a frame, motorised or not, a single continuous stream of thread can be wound from tip to butt. Using this technique, a rod can be whipped in a matter of minutes; given good adhesives and coatings, the whippings are just as strong and secure as any other.

Tied-off whippings

The photographs are self-explanatory. Work carefully between the pencil lines to ensure even-length whippings that match the ring size. Use moderate tension, and keep your fingers clean if you feed thread by hand. A piece of 10–15 pound test nylon is just right to pull the last coils of thread under one another. Do not worry about trimming the loose ends at this stage. After one side of each whipping has been done, re-align the rings before finishing the job.

Continuous whippings

Using a proper whipping frame and fully supported blank, start at one end of the blank and whip each spigot reinforcement and ring foot in turn. Unless you use a proper lathe device it is a little easier to begin at the tip and work down. Remember: there are no individual tie-off points other than the very top and bottom of the rod. They are formed by tucking under with the same pull-through nylon loop used in the other technique. Try to maintain even tension on the thread, and work fairly slowly to prevent coils building up on themselves or creeping apart. Although you whip up one ring foot and down the other (usually thought bad practice by the old school of rod builders), rings are held securely and neatly.

There is no reason why continuous-thread whippings cannot be tipped with a contrasting colour applied in individually tied sections or run continuously along the blank. However, it takes considerably experience to do this without disturbing the original layers of thread. How do they do it in rod factories? Usually they don't—tippings are painted on with deeply pigmented dyes. Patterns and fancy whippings have to be applied individually no matter how carefully you work. They are totally incompatible with one-piece machine whipping technique. Try thinking your way through a tartan while the blank spins at 100 revolutions a minute!

Tidying up the whippings
Align side rings with the tip ring. With care, you can wriggle frames into exact position. Should any be fixed too tightly to the blank by thread tension, undo one side of the whipping and then make the necessary adjustment.

white thread retains its sparkle. However, there is no harm in applying a dose of colour preservative if you like. It is far more important to stick the threads to each other and to the blank.

Whipping is incomplete until throughly impregnated with adhesive. Plain varnish is ineffective. Use either glue plus varnish, or a proper finishing adhesive like two-part epoxy—'Hi-Bild' rod finish as it is commercially labelled. Buy a suitable product and use it according to the maker's directions. Some are single-coat, others are built up from an initial thin, highly penetrative coat to a final thick shell.

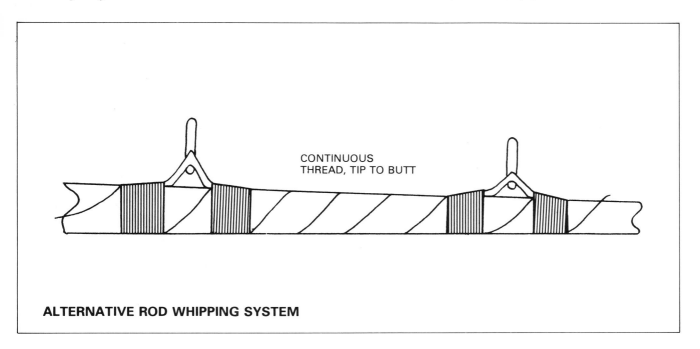

CONTINUOUS THREAD, TIP TO BUTT

ALTERNATIVE ROD WHIPPING SYSTEM

Square off the front and back of each whipping with the edge of a knife blade so that the coils run straight around the blank rather than elliptically. Notice how coils of thread in the main body of whipping are still a little uneven no matter how much care you took. Even them up by rubbing flat with a smooth steel, brass or hard plastic rod about 0.125 inches diameter. Rub from the end of each whipping to its centre; that way you will not open up the threads at the far end of each stroke. Afterwards, trim the loose ends of individually tied-off sections. Rather than use scissors, slide a sharp knife or razor blade between two coils of thread so that the spare end is cut at the base of the whipping, and not on top. Continuous-thread whippings can be straightened and flattened at this stage, but of course you must not trim them yet.

Sealing and gluing
There is really no need to dope-tighten or colour-preserve Gudebrod NCP thread. Given a suitable finish coat—*not* ordinary varnish—even

High-build rod coatings are very expensive in Britain. Most are imported from America, home of custom building. Fanatics prefer to pay the going rate rather than settle for second-rate materials, but if you are more interested in a quick, effective method of finishing your whippings, try a clear epoxy adhesive or even Araldite. I have tested several readily available, cheap brands from Woolworth, Halfords and do-it-yourself shops and found them all acceptable.

Use rapid setting or standard type depending on how long you can afford to wait for the rod to dry. Although the slow-curing mixture finally produces a slightly superior finish, I particularly value the rapid varieties. Rod whippings coated in the morning are hard enough for light duty by afternoon. Application is essentially the same whichever you choose; only the inter-coat drying time differs. Never risk applying a second coat until the first is thoroughly set. Otherwise they tend to fuse together, bubble and finally lift off.

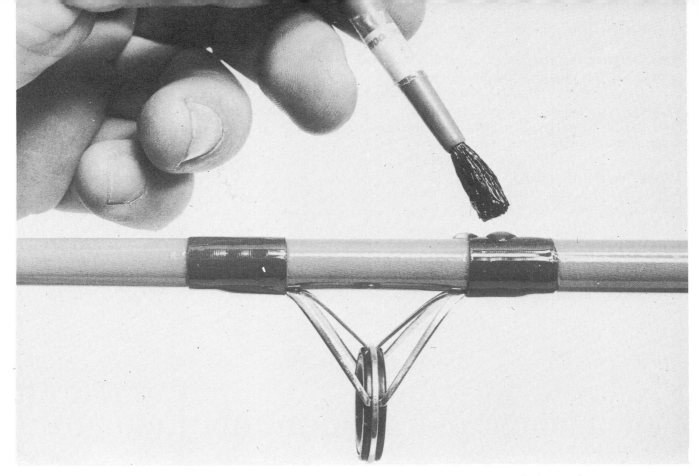

Hi-Bild custom finish is easily applied to whippings and blank. Because it dries slowly, the coating must be kept on the move to prevent drips and lumps. Rotate the rod two or three times a minute.

Araldite coating method

Whippings should be rubbed smooth and trimmed if necessary. Fill a cup with boiling water, and immerse the two tubes of adhesive—hardener and resin. When they are really hot, squeeze out measured amounts into a warm container—I use a 35mm film can—and mix thoroughly but gently to avoid excessive bubbling. The adhesive is runny enough to be brushed on to the thread. Apply a thin coat well rubbed in. Allow it to set hard.

After a couple of hours, mix a second dose of Araldite and brush it on evenly but fairly thick. The first coat should have glued down and sealed the threads, so this time the resin builds a thick layer over the whipping. Support the rod horizontally, and slowly rotate the blank until the Araldite has gelled enough to defy gravity.

Minor air bubbles are destroyed by passing the whipping high over a gas flame whilst slowly turning the blank. Clean brushes and fresh Araldite are reasonably good insurance against lumps and whiskers; you will discover that the coating dries almost transparent. While I would not recommend Araldite as the perfect custom-finish, it is more than adequate for general-purpose surf rods. White thread tends to discolour a little, so it is better to use a fairly dark, well saturated colour instead. Light yellow and blue are about the practical limit.

Most epoxy adhesives work well enough. Some are available with thinners which aids the initial whipping saturation, essential for firm adhesion and smooth foundation. Check before mixing solvents with different brands of glue. Some combinations are effective; others destroy the adhesive properties and cause the resin to bubble and set unevenly.

Varnish and continuous-thread finishes

In my opinion oil-based and polyurethane varnishes are obsolete in rod building. Anglers who still rely on them usually discover that whippings fail to restrain big rings. In fact most surf rods are unstable if the whipping is merely varnished. So even if you insist on the traditional materials, do coat the whippings beforehand with at least one coat of dope or well-thinned epoxy.

There is no alternative to using adhesives on continuously-whipped rods. Brush a coat of Araldite or special rod finish on to the whippings and rub it well in. When the adhesive is absolutely cured—leave it overnight if possible—trim back the ends of each whipping to remove excess thread. Good resin seals the threads to the blank so well that the 'loose' ends of each cut in the thread will not unravel. By trimming the thread very close to and parallel with the body of the whipping, you produce such a neat whipping that without examining the thread under a hand lens nobody can tell which method was used.

Finishing the rest of the rod

Many of the best blanks are pre-coated with gloss finish before they leave the factory. After whippings are coated, a rod is virtually complete. Fastidious anglers will probably run over the whole rod with one last coat of varnish or epoxy-based finish; anglers more interested in casting and fishing will not bother.

Araldite is useless as an overall rod finish. Use varnish or, better still, a specialist two-part coating that builds into a shiny, tough layer around blank and whippings. These one coat high-build resins are easily applied by brush but you *must* keep the rod spinning until the stuff has throughly gelled. If not, the rod literally drips with messy blobs of cured plastic. As most specialist rod finishing products harden relatively slowly—up to 24 hours—it is essential to use a motorised frame.

The saving grace of varnish is that it can be applied very thin, by spraying, dipping or rubbing on with a finger. Several coats spread over ten days eventually produce a mirror-like surface. The trouble is, it soon scratches. At the other extreme, why not coat the blank and whippings with a generous helping of polymer car wax? It takes 2 minutes to protect a rod, and on the right base (see blank preparation section) the results look perfectly all right.

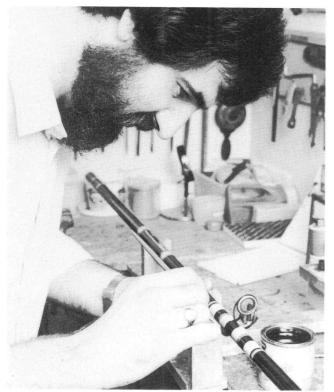

Two-part epoxy rod coatings are excellent for gluing down and finishing the whipping. Araldite adhesive is a quick alternative.

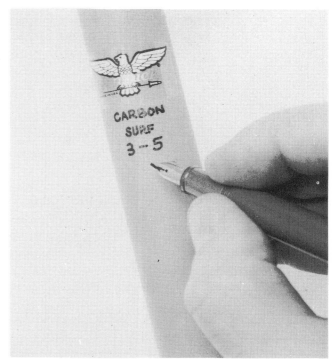

Decals and lettering add that final touch to a new rod. Commercial dry transfers like Letraset are excellent. But with care you can get away with marking ink and pen.

Lettering and transfers

Lettering adds the personal touch to a new rod. Anglers with a steady hand and neat script simply write on the blank with a mapping pen and white ink. (Actually, water-based typewriter correcting fluid is better). The results look most impressive. The rest of us make a rotten job of it. Rub-on commercial lettering like Letraset is so much easier and neater. A variety of type styles and founts are available. Some join up to form italic or copperplate script. The best time to apply lettering is between coats of varnish or before a single high-build layer.

Thin transfers (decals) which you soak in water and float on to the blank are better applied between coats of finish or even on to the bare blank. Thicker self-adhesive decals and stickers should be applied last. Most of them peel off in a few weeks anyway, so it is not worth sealing them in.

Rod bags, tubes and blank plugs

The finest rod can be destroyed by two or three journeys inside or on the top of a car. Just having it stand around at home guarantees dust, scratches and accidental damage. Sew a strong canvas or soft-lined nylon bag for your rod. Better still, make up a tube from plastic drainpipe with wooden end caps. Keep dirt out of the spigots by blocking the open ends with a soft rubber plug. Small details like this preserve your blank for years and prevent cracked rings and loose joints.

Rod Design Profiles

It is impossible to list every available surfcasting blank. These profiles give you an insight into the design of most popular rods for all kinds of fishing and for tournament casting. Armed with this background information, you can go ahead and choose your own specific blank from those stocked by your local dealer or listed in mail order advertisements.

11.5–12.00 FOOT PENDULUM ROD, MULTIPLIER VERSION

Basic construction:

7.75–8.5 foot glassfibre, semi-carbon or carbon tip made up to length with spigot-jointed or permanently attached butt section. Suitable blanks include Conoflex Super Flick Tip, Cod 5 or Cod 6, Zziplex 2500M, GS Match and Vantage.

Bruce & Walker make a special 8 foot tournament-grade carbon tip to order.

Handle materials:

All the above blanks should be matched to the maker's own range of glass-carbon or high carbon handles according to preference and performance level required.

Handle assembly:

Plain with sliding clips or rubber grip/fixed screw seat. Optional double seat for casting with reel low.

Rings:

Fuji BNHG, Daiwa Dynaflo or equivalent. 30 mm butt ring spaced at least 36 inches from reel face. 12–16 mm Hopkins and Holloway Diamite tip ring. Fill the blank with appropriately matched and spaced rings. 25, 20, 16, 16, 12, and 12 mm would suit most blanks.

Reel spacing:

29–32 inches above butt cap for most anglers.
Alternatively, mount the reel about 6 in from the butt cap and control it with your left hand.

Casting weight:

Optimum performance with 5–6 ounces. Ideal for 150 gm tournament work. Also capable of fishing with up to 8 ounce sinkers. Leader weight 40–50 pounds; main line 10–30 pounds.

Fixed spool version:

Same basic construction. Reel spacing 26–29 inches. BSHG rings. 50 mm butt guide at least 40 in from the face of the reel. 16 mm Diamite tip ring.
40, 30, 25 and 20 mm intermediate rings spaced according to blank length and action.

12–13 FOOT SENSITIVE BEACH ROD FOR MAXIMUM SPORT AND GOOD CASTING

Basic construction:
Two-piece full length blank.
Cheap glassfibre versions based on Sportex or Conoflex range of blanks. Mid-quality rod: Conoflex and Zziplex 3–6 ounce semi-carbon range.
Highest quality carbon-based rods such as Zziplex Quattra and Pendleteque series, Conoflex Cobra, Century Long-EZEE.

Handle materials:
Integral with blank except for some Conoflex and Zziplex blanks.

Handle assembly:
Hypalon grips and Fuji FPS carbonfibre/stainless steel screw seat. Optional plain butt with clips.

Rings:
Fuji BNHG, Daiwa Dynaflo or equivalent. 25–30 mm butt ring spaced at least 30 inches from reel face. 12–16 mm Hopkins and Holloway Diamite tip ring. Fill the blank with appropriately matched and spaced rings. (25), 20, 16, 12, 12 and 10 mm would suit most blanks.

Reel spacing:
Reel in high position 26–29 inches from butt cap.
Even the 13 foot rods can be cast without resorting to the low-set reel.

Casting weight:
Optimum performance with 3–5 ounces.
Leader weight 25–40 pounds.
Main line 8–20 pounds.

Fixed spool version:
Same basic construction. Reel spacing is similar 40–50 mm butt guide at least 60 inches from reel. 16 mm tip. 40, 30, 25 and 20 mm intermediate rings spaced according to blank length and action. Lightweight wire rings may be used. BSHG replace BNHG.

13–14.5 FOOT BACK CAST ROD

Blank:
8–8.5 foot very powerful glassfibre or semi-carbon blank with spigot or spliced-in joint. Conoflex, Zziplex, Century and North Western supply suitable blanks.

Handle materials:
1.25–1.375 inch/16SWG HE30 alloy tube.
More exotic laminated and carbon butts used in tournaments are extremely expensive.

Handle assembly:
Rubber taped or shrink-tube covered butt with reel mounted close to the butt cap. Screw seats, Fuji Snaplocks and tape straps hold the reel.

Rings:
Fuji BSHG 50 mm butt ring at least 72 inches from the reel face. Then 40 mm, 30, 25 and 20 BSHG according to rod length and action. 16 mm Diamite tip ring.

Reel spacing:
Low position only. The vast majority of back cast fishermen use only fixed spool reels.

Casting weight:
Optimum performance with 5–8 ounce sinkers.
Leader weight 45–65 pounds.
Main line 12–30 pounds.

12–13.75 FOOT PENDULUM ROD, MULTIPLIER VERSION

Basic construction: 8.0–8.5 foot glassfibre, semi-carbon or carbon tip made up to length with spigot-jointed or permanently attached butt section. Suitable blanks include Conoflex, Century and Zziplex long range fishing and tournament-grade semi-carbon tips with carbon butts.

Handle materials: These rods do best with carbon butts.

Handle assembly: Plain with sliding clips or rubber grip/fixed screw seat. Optional double seat for casting with reel low.
Most anglers would use the low reel position.

Rings: Fuji BNHG, Daiwa Dynaflo or equivalent. 30 mm butt ring spaced at least 40 inches from reel face. 12–16 mm Hopkins and Holloway Diamite tip ring. Fill the blank with appropriately matched and spaced rings. 25, 20, 16, 16, 12, and 12 mm would suit most blanks, but for low reel position extra rings may be necessary.

Reel spacing: Normally cast with reel set 9 inches above the butt cap and controlled by the left hand. Use either double reel seat or extension butt for line retrieve.

Casting weight: Optimum performance with 5–6 ounces. Ideal for 150 gm tournament work. Also capable of fishing with up to 10 ounce sinkers. Leader weight 45–55 pounds; main line 12–35 pounds.

Fixed spool version: Same basic construction. Reel spacing is similar. 50 mm butt ring at least 60 inches from reel. 16 mm tip. 40, 30, 25 and 20 mm intermediate rings spaced according to blank length and action. Fuji BSHG are ideal.

10–10.5 FOOT LONG-RANGE SPINNING ROD

Blank: Almost any carbon-based pike or carp rod with a test curve upwards of 2 pounds.

Handle materials: Integral or supplied with blank.

Handle assembly: Hypalon grips and Fuji FPS carbonfibre/stainless steel screw seat. Optional plain butt with clips.

Rings: Fuji BSHG, Daiwa Dynaflo or equivalent. 40 mm butt, then 30, 25, 20 and 16 mm intermediates tipped by 12 mm Fuji or lightweight Diamite. Space according to blank action and length. The same rings can be used with both fixed spool and multiplier in this case.

Reel spacing: Reel in high position 23–26 inches from butt cap.

Casting weight: Optimum performance with 1–4 ounces.
Leader weight 15–25 pounds.
Main line 8–20 pounds.

Reels: Test Before You Buy

High quality surfcasting reels like Penns, Ambassadeurs, DAMs, Mitchells and Daiwas offer a wide range of line capacities, retrieve speeds and casting performance. Chosen to match your casting technique and the basic demands of your local beaches, any of the popular models should provide long service, excellent casting distances and ample power to control heavy fish and tough conditions. Multipliers and fixed spools, their selection and basic tuning are fully discussed in LONG DISTANCE CASTING.

From the keen shore angler's point of view, reel maintenance and modifications are far more important than initial selection. Very often you have little choice in reels anyway. British tournament casters choose between two multipliers—Daiwa Millionaire and ABU Ambassadeur CT. No other mass-production reel is suitable for specialist work of this kind. Sheer casting power is all that counts; it matters little that the two reels in question are slow retrievers, weak geared and unable to hold more than 150 yards of 20 pound-plus line. Where 250 yard competition work and ultra-long range fishing are involved, there really is no alternative. Except in minor details and name, Millionaire and CT Ambassadeurs are virtually the same anyway.

Choice is similarly restricted in high capacity reels that withstand cranking at full power under heavy load. Channel bass, conger eel and rocky beach anglers looking for easy control, adequate casting range and tough, reliable fishing will almost certainly home in on the Penn Magforce range, ABU Striper, 8000C, 9000C and 10000C Ambassadeurs. What else offers built-in casting control, capacity and speed? Not much apart from the old-style Squidders and Surfmasters. They are plain reels without controls, so you are in trouble if you rely on brake blocks or magnets to smooth the cast. The majority of today's surf and beach fishermen would opt to spend extra cash for a reel that eliminates backlash.

Similar restrictions apply to every branch of surfcasting. When you cut through to the bones of reel selection, you find that despite the vast array of models on sale only a few are worth buying, and of those only one or two match up to your personal preferences. Preferences change of course; new reels arrive on the market every year. Even so, at any given time an experienced surf angler will settle for only a handful of models. You can't wean him away from them, come hell or high water.

In my own case, I would settle for a Daiwa Millionaire 6HM tournament reel, Penn Magforce rugged surf multiplier and a pair of Spinfisher fixed spools—650SS and 850SS to cover light and heavy work. I cannot think of any beach situation where one of those reels could not cope; and as far as I am concerned, no reel of similar specification from another manufacturer would be a viable alternative.

Stick to the respected names, choose the model most suitable for the way you fish and cast. That is the formula for buying a surf reel. Perhaps the most useful extra recommendation is to buy the best reel you can afford. With a lot of fishing tackle, price does not necessarily reflect quality. With reels it is a general rule that the more you pay the better a reel you get. Performance and handling are involved, but the major advantage of highly priced reels is long service life and satisfactory after sales service. Try finding spares for some Oriental reels only a year old; yet Penn will supply spares for even a 20 year-old Squidder. (And there are plenty of ancient Squidders that have never needed a spare part anyway).

Choosing a fine reel is one step towards good casting and fishing. Straight from the box, even the best reels are improved by careful running-in, proper maintenance and tuning. If necessary, you can rework the mechanics of a reel to lift performance and improve the corrosion resistance of its components. Anglers with workshop facilities are free to make quite substantial modifications.

A word of caution though. There is nothing complicated about the innards of a fishing reel, but its parts are often assembled in strict order. Break that routine, and you smash the reel. Read the instructions, study exploded diagrams, and if in doubt stay within the safety net of limited strip-down. Much of the work detailed here requires little more than taking off sideplates and removing the spool and its bearings.

The finest reel of the wrong kind is a total waste of money. Question One: fixed spool or multiplier?

Throw the reel out of gear and flick the spool. It should be smooth and quiet.

Running-in procedure

New reels should always be carefully run-in. Thrashed at full power from new, any good multiplier will respond fairly well and should not die before middle age. However, reels that continue to run sweetly and reliably from youth to senility were almost certainly eased into operation rather than beaten up from day one. Running-in is a simple process of gradually increasing load on the major components: spool bearings and spindle, gears and bushes.

Running-in techniques are aimed squarely at work-hardening the metal surfaces of a reel. Lathe tools and grinders may produce a superb-looking finish on the moving components, but the metal is still relatively rough. Mating surfaces are accurate and smooth enough to feel right as you spin the reel's handle, but microscopically they are far from perfect. Some abrasion occurs when a new spindle turns on its bearings and gears enmesh under pressure.

Perfection is achieved by operating a reel under modest speed and pressure until the mating parts polish each other and work harden. The reel develops that elusive silky feel, casts and fishes much better, and will carry on working for many years. By contrast, a reel thrashed to the limit without running-in will literally tear itself apart. Though mechanical failure takes months to make itself apparent, the reel never does feel quite right.

Rachets are notoriously weak. Bad rachets jump out of the actuating spring when a fish runs.

For obvious reasons, multiplier reels are far more susceptible to mishandling. It is uncommon to see a wide performance variation in fixed spool reels of the same model provided that line height, spool pattern and line diameter are similar. Nothing rotates during the cast; lip friction is highly unlikely to vary between two spools of the same kind. Running-in affects the winding gears only: given careful bedding-in and gradually increased loading, they will outlive the rest of the reel and, just as important, will toughen sufficiently to cope with any sudden excess pressures. Where thrashed gears seize up or strip under the onslaught of a record fish, well run-in components offer that essential margin of insurance. You might never need it, but it is nice to know it exists.

Multiplier tuning is closely linked with running-in. Results vary with makes of reel and spool sizes. Tournament-grade Daiwas and Ambassadeur CTs are particularly vulnerable to premature overload. The difference between a thrashed reel and one progressively work-hardened could be 20 yards. The service life of a spool, gears and bearings might fall between 6 months and 5 years depending on how well you treated the reel in its first month. Differences in casting range are less apparent in the bigger reels, but a well run-in model will last much longer and is less susceptible to sudden shocks.

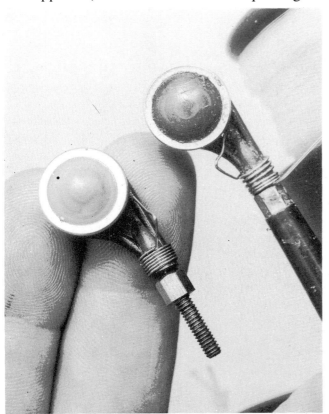

Manual rollers operate beautifully until line accidentally catches the pick-up in mid cast. Always carry a spare.

At some stage your fixed spool reel will need servicing. Some drags are sealed units impossible to repair. Check before you buy—spare spools are very expensive.

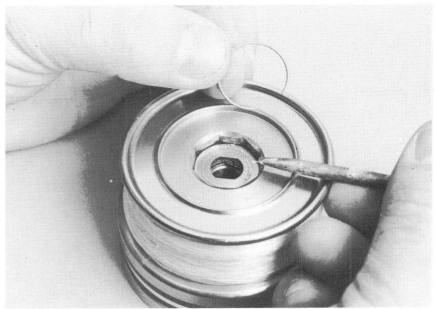

Sloppy rotor bearings are a sign of cheap manufacture. No problems on this Penn 750SS.

Teflon, asbestos and other fibres interleave with steel braking plates. If you take the drag apart, be sure to replace the components in the correct order.

Mass manufacturing techniques ensure a fairly good product at worst; most top-quality reels are as close to perfect as anyone could wish. Inevitably, though, a few rogue models creep off the production line and sneak through the quality control network. It pays to run your own tests before buying a new reel. The dealer might not like the idea of your opening up six boxes to find the best reel of the bunch, but it is your money and enjoyment at risk. I would not dream of buying a new reel on the lucky-dip system of taking the first box from the shelf. If there are a dozen reels on the shelf, check them all to find the best, or until you discover the first one which passes all the tests. Multipliers are more critical than fixed spools, but it still pays to wind a few handles before handing over the cash.

Pre-purchase tests

Imperfect spools, twisted frames and poor spindle alignment are major faults in surfcasting multipliers. Spools and bearings can be replaced—but why should you on a new reel? But there is little or no remedy for misalignment; a twisted reel is junk. New ballraces cannot cure a reel whose bearing cups are in the wrong place. Usually such problems are quite obvious from the appearance of the reel and from the way it runs. Bad gears and bent handles are equally simple to spot.

Above all watch out for a reel which is offered as new but really is not. Mail order customers sometimes return goods after using them for a day or two. Thrashed reels go back into stock. Tackle dealers themselves are not averse to fishing with their display goods.

Test 1

Is the reel new? Look it over for signs of salt and abrasion. Open up the reel. Are gears, spindle and bearings filled with the manufacturer's grease or has that been replaced with oil? Sniff the reel: manufacturers do not use WD40 and similar sprays. Fishermen do, and so do people who want to polish up suspect reels for sale. Check screw heads and nuts and bolts. Are they clean cut or tool-damaged? Are there tell-tale specks of sand inside the reel? Reels become shop-soiled easily enough, but they should not be mangled or show evidence of having been on the beach. If you suspect that a reel has been used but is otherwise perfectly sound, try to negotiate a discount and a guarantee. By the same token, a genuine secondhand reel advertised as such is well worth considering if the price is right.

Test 2

Throw the reel out of gear and spin the spool with your finger. Does the main body of the spool run evenly, or do the core and its flanges wobble?

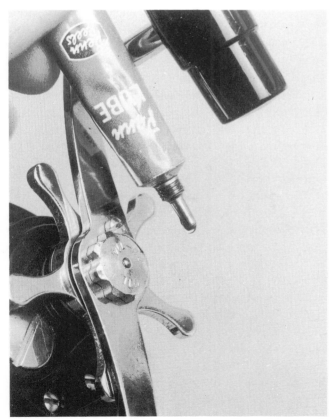
One-way lubricant ports are essential for routine maintenance in the field when you don't want to strip down the mechanism.

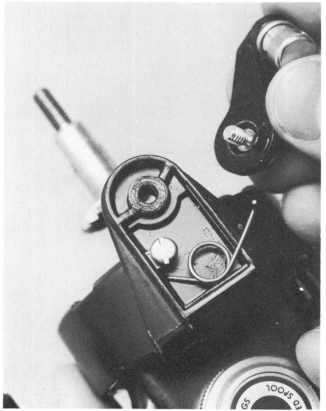
Bale arm return springs have a short, tough life. Does your reel's maker supply spares?

149

Reject an obviously 'lumpy' spool. If the spool itself is satisfactory, check how it fits in the reel frame. Spool flanges and reel sideplates should be concentric or very close to it. A revolving spool should not touch any part of the frame.

All good reel makers insist on a perfect fit which eliminates line trapping between spool and frame. Cheaper companies compensate for lower standards by increasing the gap so that spool and frame remain separated even if the spool flange wanders out of alignment. Though the reel may cast fairly well, it tends to trap line in the flange gap. Anglers often wonder how line manages to find its way into such a narrow slot. When the reel spins, the edges of the spool literally suck loose line into the sideplates by a whirlpool of air.

Test 3

A perfect spool set accurately in its frame is virtually a guarantee of bearing and spindle alignment. Loosen the adjustable bearing cap until the spindle develops a slight end-float. Spin the reel and feel how smoothly it runs. Speed is less important than silkiness. Be acutely critical of mechanical harshness transmitted through the reel body. Listen for grating and rubbing sounds. Reject any reel that fails this test.

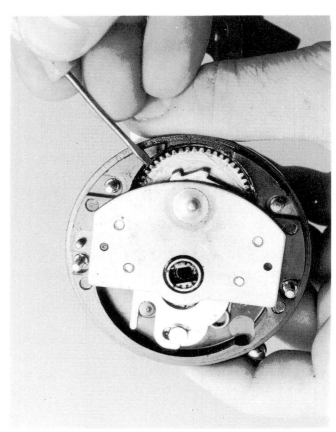

Strong gears and simple design are most valuable in the long run. Some complex reels fall apart in a few months.

Nearly all reels have an Achilles heel. The Sagarra range is superb in every respect but one: the line-lay gears are weak. However, spares are cheap, so you can afford to carry replacements.

Spools should run quite quickly. However, a new reel is usually filled with cloying grease which masks the free-running qualities of bearings and spindle. Very light spools lack the momentum to spin fast unless filled with line; and no reel ever runs at full speed until correctly run in. So long as there is no obvious mechanical fault in the reel, speed should not concern you. In fact the reverse is usually the case: most reels are inherently too free-running and must be governed down for casting even on the tournament court. If you like, clean off excess bearing grease and re-check the running speed.

The exception is where a reel sounds quiet and feels smooth but is so slow that the spool hardly rotates in response to a heavy flick. The bearings and frame may well be out of alignment. Loosen the sideplate security screws about half a turn. Does the reel now spin faster? If so, alignment is definitely suspect. Remember to back off the bearing cap tension before you run the test, otherwise results are meaningless. It also helps to clean out packing grease, another cause of false readings in small reels. In extreme cases, frame and sideplates will look warped; but it takes only a fraction of an inch distortion to destroy a multiplier's performance. There are plenty more reels available, so why take the risk?

Test 4

Check the operation of gears, drag, handle, rachet and any other features which may affect life and performance: reel stand security, chrome-plating, no cracks in plastic components, no dents and corrosion in metal plates and covers. Basically, if it looks right and operates smoothly, the reel is almost certainly acceptable. Fixed spool tests really extend no further than this. Beware of flimsy bale arm wires and frozen line rollers. Check the quality of rotating aluminium castings that support the bale assembly. A sloppy fit and side-play indicate poor design. There is every chance that the drive spindle also runs unevenly and loosely in its bearings. If so, main gears will overload and wear out. In extreme cases teeth jump out of mesh under load.

Test 5

This is not a test of quality or mechanical soundness. In its way, though, it is more important than the other tests combined. Is the reel suitable for your style of fishing? Tuning and running-in cannot transform one type of reel into another. Tournament casting and lightweight fishing multipliers never offer the same rugged fighting power as a purpose-built heavy surfcasting reel. A 300 yard/25 pound test model built for dragging 50 pound channel bass and conger by the snout will not cast 250 yards unless you happen to be Superman. On a more mundane note, it is no good buying a multiplier reel of any kind unless you are prepared to devote time and practice to mastering it. You need a big fixed spool reel instead.

Thousands of newcomers and ill-advised fishermen walk out of the shop with a beautiful reel which is totally inappropriate for their way of fishing. Some dealers help, but too many of them do not really give a damn what you buy. The rule is never to part with a penny unless you are absolutely certain the reel is exactly what you need to fish the surf. If you don't know, ask around and try to borrow a selection of reels to test. At the end of the day, it is your decision and your money. Mistakes can easily cost £50–£75.

Reels: Running In and Maintenance

Expert fishermen argue about the best way to run in a new reel. Some consider that you should strip down and relubricate a new reel before loading it with line. Others, myself included, prefer to start the bedding-in process beforehand. In the old days, it certainly was better to check the mechanism, regrease gears and lubricate spindles. Most reels were full of metal swarf; the lubricants were chosen simply to protect the reel during transit and storage. Often it amounted to no more than a skim of thick grease over the gear wheels. Bearings and spool spindles were almost dry.

Modern reels are adequately pre-lubricated and free from heavy swarf. Sometimes gears and drive components are lubricated for life and thus better left alone. The gear case on a fixed spool reel is stuffed with grease and, barring accidents, should not require attention for at least a year. Why make extra work for yourself?

Look inside the reel: make sure there are no chunks of scrap metal floating in the grease. As a precaution, add a drop of thick oil to the spindle ends and bearing cups. Check that the blocks are in position (centrifugal braking systems only) and adjust the spool tension to give perceptible end-float on the spindle. Load the reel and go fishing.

It is unrealistic to expect a brand new, tight reel to run at full speed. Be prepared for moderate casting performance, and do not try to force the pace. Deliberately reduce casting power, set the drag to modest pressure, and wind in steadily. After fishing, wash the outside of the reel free of salt and grit. Open it up and add a dab of grease or oil where necessary. Next time you fish, gently increase the casting pressure. Work on the theory that it takes at least 100 casts to polish bearing and spindle surfaces. During this period, which may take a couple of days or 3 months, depending on how often you cast, keep the reel clean but do not worry about tuning it for speed. Live with modest casting performance a little longer. In the long run patience pays big dividends.

After 100 casts in the 100–125 yard bracket, most reels are bedded down well enough to accept a reasonable increase in casting force. Before that can be achieved, you must tune the mechanism to flow more easily. At the same time, re-lubricate the main gears as well; 100 casts later, most reels should be work-hardened and ready for maximum power.

Strip-down and lubrication

Strictly speaking it is rarely necessary to strip a reel beyond its main components: frame, sideplates and spool. However, I prefer to make a thorough job at this stage, then I do not have to worry about another complete stripdown for at least 3 months. Work carefully and refer to the maker's diagrams. Lay the parts in sequence on a sheet of clean

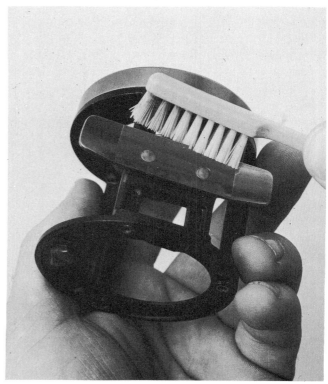

Scrubbing with hot water and an old toothbrush is the only way to get rid of encrusted salt and grit.

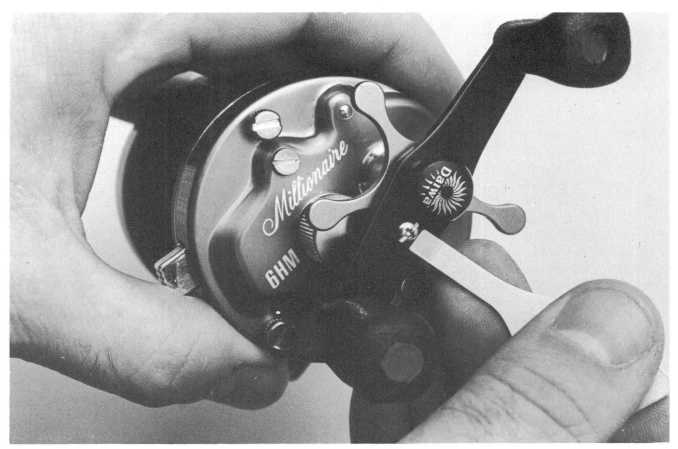

Strip down 1. *Take off the screw that holds the handle nut locking plate.*

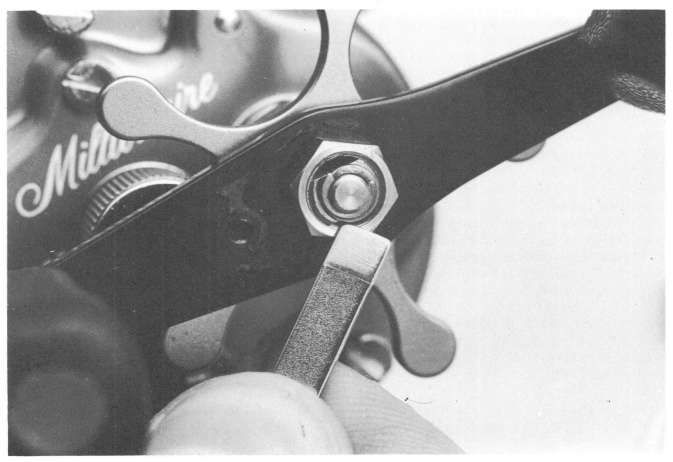

Strip down 2. *Push off the circlip on the end of the main drive shaft.*

absorbent paper. Most work can be done with the multi-purpose wrench/screwdriver supplied with the reel. Daiwa and Penn tools are versatile enough to strip a reel to the bone. Lubricants are wide open to personal preference. I like Teflon or Molydenum grease for gears, waterproof grease for the handle and SAE 20/50 or thin machine oil for spindle and bearings. One spot of lubricant in the right place is more effective than a handful splashed in the general area. A well set-up reel looks almost dry inside.

Strip-down and lubrication are essentially the same in routine maintenance as they are for running-in and tuning. Thorough cleansing is essential before routine oiling and greasing; day-to-day maintenance demands no more than taking out the spool to expose major internal units and bearings. Adjust the following schedule accordingly. It is the grand banquet—and usually a snack will do. Much of the work is based on the Daiwa Millionaire and the Penn 970, which are representative of the majority of good reels on the market.

STAGE 1: Clean the exterior of the reel.
Gently wipe away sand and salt. Flow hot water over sideplates and frame, and scour off stubborn particles with an old toothbrush. Squirting a powerful spray of water on to a reel merely forces dirt and salt inside. Tape, tie or rubber band the free end of the line to the spool, shake off excess water, and leave the reel to dry out for an hour in an airing cupboard.

STAGE 2: Take off the sideplate.
Modern Penns, most Ambassadeur and Daiwa reels feature quick take-apart screws on the right-hand sideplate cover. Loosen the screws—which are a captive-fit so you do not lose them—and pull off the sideplate. Gently remove the spool. Be careful not to drop the centrifugal brake blocks. A few reels like the Ambassadeur 9000C take apart from the left-hand side. Newell 220 and 229 reels are better stripped from the left because then the left-hand ballrace is less likely to drop out and fall in the dust. Older Penn reels are either stripped from the right-hand side by taking out the sideplate and frame screws (usually 6) or by loosening a single locking screw before undoing the bayonet fitting.

STAGE 3: Clean and check the spool.
Wipe spool flanges and spindle ends. Examine the spool for cracks and the spindle for rough edges and signs of excessive wear. Check the brake blocks—they often split—and clean their support

bar. As a matter of routine, there is little more to be done. Once a year, strip off all the line and examine the inside faces of the spool for pressure damage and corrosion. Handle spools carefully. Dropping them to the floor may crack flanges or distort spindles.

STAGE 4: Remove the spindle bearings.
Guard your bearings jealously. One speck of sand or a drop of saltwater may destroy them. On modern reels the ballraces are supported by removable caps on the sideplates. Unscrew the caps by hand or carefully with a screwdriver. Most reel manufacturers apart from Penn allow the ballrace to float in its cap; packing shims are used for adjustment and alignment. Be careful not to drop a ballrace or to lose track of shim combinations. Be particularly careful about the pressure plate that controls spool tension. Penn use a sealed cap/bearing unit with an internal spring plate. It is more difficult to clean and lubricate but is neater and a great deal tougher.

After the initial run-in period and periodically thereafter—every 3 months—it is wise to flush out and relubricate. Lubricants do break down after a time, either by burning up or absorbing saltwater, and cannot be expected to safeguard bearings forever. Day-to-day topping up is always necessary to maintain lubricant levels and to smooth the cast. On older reels without blocks and magnets, lubricant viscosity is all that stands between you and a monumental backlash.

Solvents are generally unnecessary, but in extreme cases you could use petrol or Gunk. Soak bearings in a jar of solvent, or squirt them with a medical syringe. Normally, flush out the old oil with a stream of fresh lubricant.

If a ballrace is detachable from its cap, try this simple alternative. Drop the bearings into a dessert spoon, cover them with fresh oil, and *gently* heat the spoon over a gas or radiant ring. Old oil melts out; fresh oil percolates inside. The same technique re-impregnates solvent treated bearings—but do not try it before the petrol has fully evaporated.

Saturate the ballraces, then drain off excess lubricant. Reassemble the caps and shims, then store the assembly well out of the way. There is no point putting caps back inside a reel which is still full of muck and old grease.

Solvents are essential for checking the state of old bearings. Wash out every scrap of lubricant so that the ballrace runs in metal-to-metal contact. It should still spin smoothly and quietly. Bearings that grate or clatter should be replaced.

Given adequate bedding-in time and reasonable

Strip down 3. *Unscrew the main handle nut.*

Strip down 4. *Unwind the star drag and take out the two screws holding the sideplate cover to the inner plate.*

155

Strip down 5. *Lift off the plate. Clean the mechanism as necessary. Look for broken gear teeth and other signs of excessive wear.*

Strip down 6. *The spindle pinion is responsible for poor casting. Check the sleeve for tightness. Clean out old grease.*

156

care, a set of ballraces should last as long as the rest of the reel. Most failures are due either to abuse or to the wrong lubricants. Some anglers intent on the last ounce of speed squirt in WD40 and watery Teflon or silicon-based additives. They are not intended for this kind of work; the bearings rip themselves apart. Spares are available at high cost from the reel manufacturer. A specialist bearing supplier may, however, stock a suitable replacement, which could be of a higher quality—and half the price.

STAGE 5: Strip down the left hand plate.
The left-hand plate is usually secured by 4–6 slotted screws. Take them right out and make a note of their lengths and positions. Screws threaded into the main frame crossbars are usually longer than the pair attached to the reel stand. They are not interchangeable.

Pull off the side plate. Wash out plain plastic covers in hot soapy water. Bearing cup sleeves and rachet assembly on simple reels like the Penn Squidder are made from brass or stainless steel. Water does them no harm. Afterwards apply a smear of grease or thick oil to the sliding surfaces.

Pressed or machined metal sideplates can be flushed with soapy water, Gunk petrol or paraffin.

Dry them, then wipe the entire surfaces with waterproof grease, silicon jelly or wax-based coating like Waxoyl, a motor vehicle spray-on underseal. Only a *smear* is used. Keep it away from level wind drive wheels, bearings and rachets. It is a fiddly job to coat every corner of the sideplate's interior but there is no other method of slowing down corrosion. Alloy sideplates are wide open to saltwater attack. Usually they rot from the inside outwards.

Finally, examine the level-wind drive gear and lubricate its support axle with a spot of thin oil. On big ABUs, clean out the brake block mechanism and check the blocks. The Penn magnetic controller threaded into the left-hand plate needs no maintenance, though it does no harm to run a film of oil over the magnet's face.

STAGE 6: Frame maintenance.
Most frames are of unit construction. Penns are screwed together; ABUs are pressed and brazed Daiwas are die-cast in aluminium. They are all quite good—provided the frame and sideplates are squarely aligned with the spool. Corrosion is a major problem, so frames must be washed after every trip. Afterwards, squirt on WD40 to drive out moisture; inject a little waterproof grease into

Strip down 7. The anti-reverse mechanism tends to slip out of alignment when the reel comes apart. Make sure it is clipped back before you assemble the reel.

157

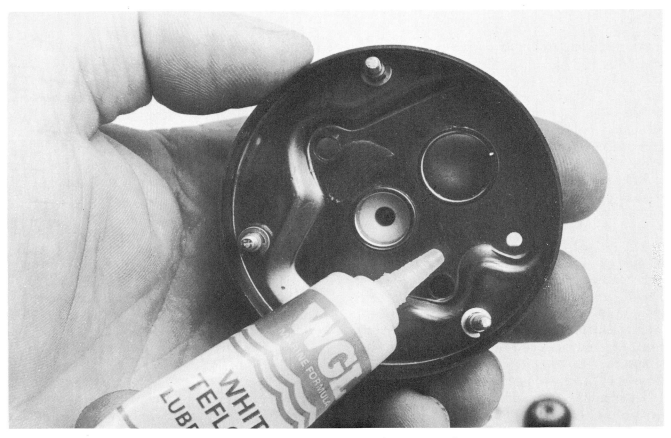

Strip down 8. *Coat the sideplate with waterproof grease to counteract saltwater corrosion.*

Strip down 9. *The left hand sideplate. Check the rachet system and lubricate the level wind drive cog. The plate itself must be coated to prevent corrosion.*

the screw holes. Preventative maintenance is your only hope.

STAGE 7: Stripping down the drive unit.

This is the frightening part. Fishermen live in mortal dread of stripping down the right-hand side of their multipliers. Penns are deceptive. They look so easy to strip, and they do slide apart easily. Now try getting the thing back together. If you know the trick of rotating the brass 'D' shaped internal plate, go ahead. Otherwise, leave it to the experts. A Penn is so tough inside and so easily lubricated that full strip-down is unnecessary unless a component is broken. Why tempt fate?

Most other reels are easier to work on. The same broad technique handles them all. First, make sure the gear lever is in its engaged position. Lay the sideplate inside face down on a clean towel. Towelling is a soft but steady base to work from, and any bits that fly out of the reel are trapped. There is nothing worse than grubbing around on the kitchen floor for a missing spring. Nine times out of ten you never find it.

1) Remove the grub screw that secures the handle drive nut. Sometimes the screw butts directly against the nut faces, more often it operates on an anchor plate surrounding the nut. Take off the handle nut as well.

2) The tip of the exposed drive shaft sports a screw or nut and a circlip. Detach both—and make sure the circlip does not fly into orbit. Now lift off the handle.

3) Unscrew the star drag wheel and lift it off. Note the position and exact order of spring washers which may be above and/or below the star wheel. If a plain collar follows the star wheel, take that off as well. Sometimes it stays deep down on the shaft, in which case leave it alone.

4) Remove the screws that attach the cover-plate. Lift off the cover to expose the internal workings of the reel. Most drive mechanisms are of unit construction, so nothing will spring off. However, it pays to keep the reel face down on the

Strip down 10. *Wipe the inner faces of the reel to remove sand and salt. A stray grain of sand will mark the spool and ruin performance.*

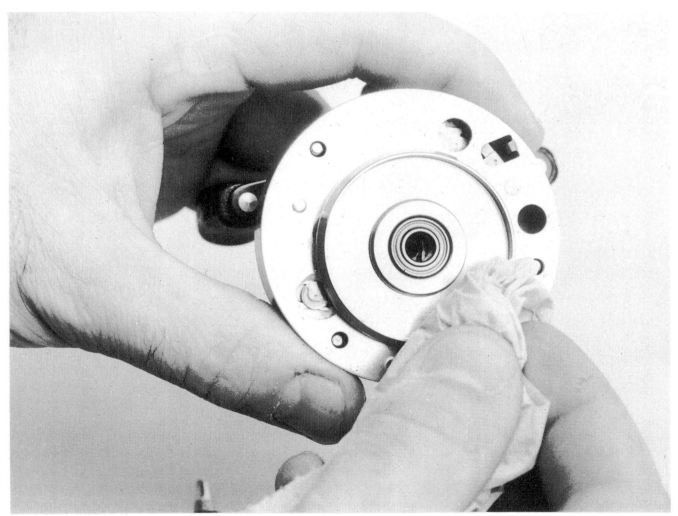

Strip down 11. *Open the level wind guide cover and check the thread follower for wear.*

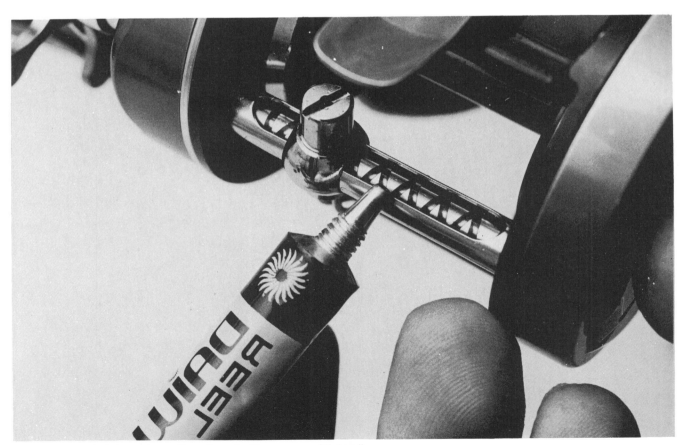

Strip down 12. *Lubricate the endless thread with a smear of light oil.*

Strip down 13. *Oil the ballraces with thin lubricant.*

towel. The worst problem is that drag washers and main drive gear lift up when you take off the coverplate. If they come away altogether, refer to the instruction book for replacement details. Otherwise, press the whole unit back down its shaft. Unless drag washers are burned out or a gear is broken, leave well alone. Watch out for the anti-reverse dog and washer at the base of the shaft. If it drops out of engagement the reel will either seize up or rotate in both directions.

5) Gently clean out the old lubricant—using solvents if necessary—and relubricate sparingly with grease. Keep grease away from the inside of the sliding pinion that drives the spool spindle. Make absolutely certain that no mineral grease or solvent strays into the drag assembly.

6) Clean out the inside face of the cover and coat it in grease or Waxoyl. Though less exposed than the other sideplate, the drive side cover is prey to saltwater corrosion and must be protected.

Its anodised layer is not sufficiently tough.

7) Rebuild the right-hand side of the reel by reversing the strip-down procedure. No force is required. If the components fail to seat perfectly, it is because you have gone wrong. Watch out for the anti-reverse dog, the gear lever and that drive shaft circlip. It goes back *after* the handle is in place. A bit left over? Probably the spring washer from between the star drag and handle.

8) In the event of some mechanical failure inside the reel, take out the broken component and order a new one either by sending back the old piece or, better still, by looking up the part number in the catalogue. Do not try to describe the part. Handles, spools and bearings are easy enough; washers, drag plates and gears are another matter. It is even more confusing when a reel is available in standard and high-speed versions or if two reels are quite similar—like the ABU 9000C and its cousin the ABU 12.

Reels: Tuning and Modification Aids

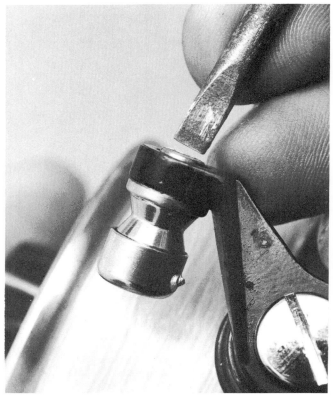

Bale arm removal is an essential step in fixed spool tuning. It throws a great strain on the line roller. Check security and if necessary lock the support threads with Loctite.

Basic maintenance and lubrication, correct line load and built-in cast controllers ensure adequate reel performance. Even in standard form a modern surfcasting multiplier or fixed spool reel more than equals the average man's casting and fishing skills. Tuning and modification are unnecessary in the strictly practical sense.

Surfcasting is a fascinating subject which extends far beyond bread and butter techniques of casting baits and winding in fish. Tackle itself provides endless scope for self expression and technical advancement. Even if you cannot cast hard enough to push a reel to its limits, it is still interesting to experiment; because no reel is ever perfect, there is ample opportunity to improve its strength, service life and performance. Some modifications demand special equipment and workshop skills. Most rely on bolt-on accessories and simple alterations well within the realms of the household tool kit. A piece of oil-soaked abrasive paper wrapped around a matchstick might be the key to an extra 10 yards on your cast.

Replacement spools

The present generation of multiplier spools are either pressed from sections of aluminium alloy or machine cut from a solid block. A single-piece spool is inevitably stronger and more precise, but even the pressed version is sweeter running and more reliable than older types of plastic spool. Plastic spools explode under severe nylon line pressure; very few run without some wobble and vibration. Back in the early days of British tournament casting we sorted through perhaps fifty plastic spools to find just two that ran perfectly.

Aware of the inherent problems of Penn plastic spools, Carl Newell of California manufactures a range of replacement spools in die-cast alloy. Strong, precise and far more reliable than Penn's original spool, they enhance the performance of Surfmaster and Squidder surf reels. The only drawback is that Newell spools are made in sections. Under extreme pressure they too can open up.

High-quality drags are designed not to lock up. Some threads are soon stripped by excess pressure. Use an external spool locking system instead.

Penn themselves awoke to the Achilles heel in their popular casting reels. Squidders and Surfmasters of all sizes are now available with a single piece aluminium alloy spool as standard. Modified reels carry an 'L' suffix—146L and 140L in the case of Squidders. Spare spools are freely available, and may be fitted into older Penns. Though a little heavier than the plastic casting spool, new alloy spools are fairly tame if you squirt thick lubricant into the bearings. Try STP oil additive. As well as running smoothly and accurately, these new 'L' spools are almost indestructible. Corrosion apart, there is little to go wrong. Line capacity is a slight improvement on the plastic spool, and there is no need for soft backing.

Owners of ABU Ambassadeur 6000C and 6500C series reels are acutely aware of the limited resilience of the standard spool which easily distorts under load and may explode. Spools from the DAM Champion 800B reel are very close to a perfect fit in some Ambassadeurs. Because of variations in manufacturing tolerances, you cannot guarantee an acceptable match, but it is worth testing the idea. The DAM spool is extremely well made, tough and sweet-running—vastly superior to the standard ABU product.

A few anglers make their own spools from solid

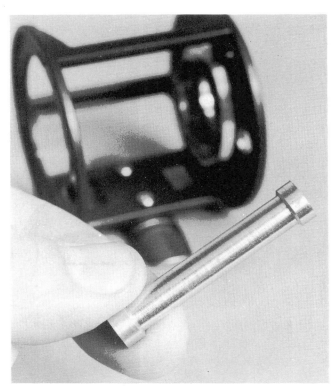

Unless the reel is used for very light fishing, level wind removal must be followed by cage replacement. A simple brass crossbar screwed across the level wind position holds the reel rigid and true.

aluminium alloy. For the man with lathe experience it is easy work. The spindle is more of a problem than the main body of the spool, and it usually pays to build a new spool around a spindle cut from an old production model.

At the other extreme, a few anglers regard ABU 8000C and 9000C spools as slightly too heavy and slow for the reel. They drill a pattern of holes in the flanges, thus reducing weight without seriously weakening the spool. It is slow, painstaking work unless you have access to a lathe or drill press fitted with a dividing attachment which accurately reproduces the hole patterns. One hole in the wrong spot will destroy spool balance.

Replacement handles

Manufacturers of smaller tournament-grade reels originally aimed their products at the freshwater baitcasting market. Small handles are perfectly suited to that kind of work, where pressures are low and distances seldom exceed 50 yards. Cranking 250 yards of line across the seabed with a tiny handle is sheer murder. Special power handles are available for most popular reels. They work quite well but introduce a problem of their own. The extra leverage encourages direct cranking in circumstances where pumping is much easier on the reel. In extreme cases handle pressure and excessive line tension overload the reel. The gears are the weak spot, and their teeth

Newell seat and crossbars improve the performance of old-style Penn reels. New Penns now incorporate stronger frames and one-piece alloy spools.

Bale arm triggering pressure is adjustable on reels like this DAM5000. The high setting may be sufficient to prevent mid-cast bale closure; if so, you don't have to cut off the wire.

A stepped washer helps improve line coning on fixed spool reels. Either use washers or, in the case of the DAM saltwater reels, dial in the appropriate setting.

shear off or jump out of mesh. On the whole, though, a power handle makes more sense than the tiny wrist-snapper fitted as standard.

New reel frames

Newell produce a series of frame modifications which overcome the inherent weakness of old Penn crossbars. Newell bars and reel stands are a most valuable accessory for older reels. Unfortunately they corrode like mad. Modification of modern Penns is unnecessary because the company has switched to a different frame design which is at least as good as Newell and, in the usual Penn tradition, virtually immune to saltwater attack.

Replacement and modified cages are an essential aspect of tournament casting. Small ABU and Daiwa reels dominate the casting scene, but must first be modified to remove the level wind mechanism. Level winds reduce line capacity and cut distance. They also prevent maximum power input: the top crossbar gets in the way of your thumb, so that a firm grip on the spool is impossible.

ABU make a special plain frame for the 6000 and 6500 series reels. Called the CT cage, it is available through tackle shops or direct from the company's spares outlet. Fitting is a 5 minute job involving just a screwdriver. Existing spools fit the CT cage.

However, there is no reason why a level-wind cage cannot be modified. Take off the level wind bar and guide, plus the drive gear in the left-hand side plate. Cut off the top crossbar for thumb clearance, and insert a solid stiffening rod where the level wind guide came out. A suitable bar can be machined from stainless steel or brass, and is screwed securely across the frame. The same technique applies to Daiwa and other level-wind reels for which a CT cage is not commercially available. Some tackle shops sell converted reels or offer to modify the angler's own reel. Kits and conversions tend to be expensive for what little is involved, but they do save time, particularly if the alternative is to look for a friendly lathe operator who can machine the necessary stiffening piece.

Gears and drive pinions

Newell replacement gears are available for many Penn reels. They may have some worthwhile application in the offshore game fishing reels, but certainly appear to offer little advantage for surfcasting. It is not so much that Penn are particularly weak and Newell significantly stronger. The Newell gear probably is a little tougher, but in the long run it is the design limitation of small multipliers that sets the pace.

Gear wheel diameter and tooth size limit the potential strength of any surf reel. The higher the gear ratio, the less the margin of safety. In other words, no matter how hard one tries, small multiplier gears turn out to be quite weak; to some extent material and tempering count for little. The only answer is to run in the reel and use it with reasonable care—in practical terms, pump the rod rather than crank the handle.

Drive pinions are also notoriously fragile, but their main fault is excessive drag on the spool spindle. The pinion retracts into the sideplate to free the spool for casting. Fine . . . but it does not prevent the pinion from rotating with the spindle or from acting as a brake drum. A pinion must not be so tight that it fouls the spindle: merely touching it rips yards from the cast. Check pinion and spindle for friction. Excessive drag is easily felt. In some cases you must strip down the reel, take out the pinion, reassemble the frame and sideplates, then spin the reel. If the pinion is even fractionally tight, the spool will now freewheel for much longer. The solution is simple. Polish out the pinion hole. Proper reamers and laps ensure a perfect cure, but you can come very close with abrasive paper wrapped around a matchstick.

Polishing the innards may make the reel run better. Friction between spool spindle and drive pinion is a common cause of poor results.

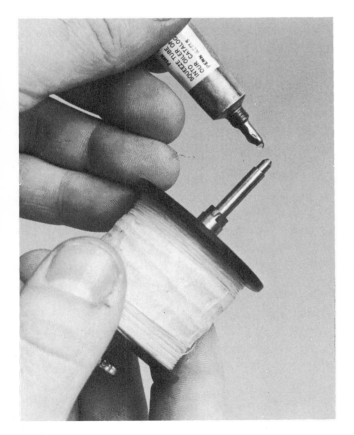

Experiment with a range of oils to find those that best suit your reel and the way you cast.

The spiral spring behind the Penn 970's control magnet can be removed to give extra control. Good casters benefit from the new low setting which may add 20 yards to the cast.

165

Use the finest grade of wet-and-dry paper soaked in thin oil. Work carefully and with featherweight pressure. Polish up the hole so that it enlarges by a few thousandths of an inch only. Clean it out, check the fit, then burnish with a strand of cloth soaked in metal polish. At a guess I would say that at least half our surfcasting reels are affected by pinion friction to some degree—say 5–10 yards on a 175 yard cast.

Drags

The drag (clutch, brake or whatever you care to call it) it is a menace. Not one mass-produced beach reel, fixed spool or multiplier, excels in this department. Penn's Magpower reel is fitted with a Senator-based drag which has been around long enough to prove reasonably reliable. Daiwa drags are quite good to start with, but tend to fade to insignificance after a time. Some accessory manufacturers—including Newell—offer replacement packs for popular multipliers and fixed spools. Most are acceptable; but I think their superiority is largely an illusion. They seem better than they really are simply because anything must be an improvement on the chewed up, heat blackened discs you took out. You might just as well use the reel manufacturer's own spares.

Fixed spool drags are more critical. On multipliers it is usually possible to compensate for poor drag washers by backing off on the tension, so that the drag operates smoothly, then add extra pressure by thumbing the spool. Much depends on the size and speed of fish; but on the whole it is a practical proposition. Not so with a fixed spool. Thumbing is imprecise and difficult. Backwinding—paying out line by turning the reel backwards—is strictly for lightweight tackle and puny species. The average tope or channel bass would rip your knuckles off.

Unfortunately, really good braking systems make a fixed spool reel almost impossible to cast hard. The drag washers prevent the spool from locking up. However, it is unsafe to cast without locking the reel. If the spool rotates under full casting power, line cuts your finger. Fishermen tend to screw down the drag until it does lock, then they leave it there. When they hook a big fish and slacken the drag, the washers are fused together, which means the brake is either fully on or off.

Never abuse a fine drag system. It is far better to modify the reel so that the spool may be locked without resorting to the drag nut. Drill a hole in the spool and use a wire locking clip anchored to the reel frame, as detailed in the photographs. Aesthetically it is a mess; in practice it locks the reel firmly and extends drag life and reliability.

Taking out level wind mechanisms sometimes leaves gaping holes in the reel frame. Rubber inserts prevent saltwater invasion and protect the delicate internal mechanisms.

Species of fish like the false albacore are more easily hooked on light tackle and small lures; 6–10 pound line would be about right for working lures along the surfline. Albacores hit hard and run like torpedoes, and their initial attack highlights a serious fault in fixed spool reel design. The drag cannot accelerate quickly enough to prevent a sudden build up of pressure that may snap the line.

Setting the drag to minimum pressure helps enormously, and there is some advantage in 'slippery' washers which literally skid one on another. Some surf fishermen squirt WD40-type lubricant into the drag washers so that they do slide rapidly into action when the fish first hits. Unwanted lubricant is soon thrown out or burned up.

Cast controls

A good many fishermen modify and tune their multiplier reels to prevent or minimise backlash. As long as brakes are not used to compensate for atrocious casting technique, there is no harm in running a few experiments. Looking at it from the other direction, really good casters can tune a reel to gain speed even at the expense of control. All things are possible as long as you recognise the limitations of the reel's basic design. All multipliers are potentially uncontrollable, and the more you extend their performance the less room there is for error. Backlash may not be a significant factor. If a tournament champion can wring an extra 10 yards from the cast at the expense of, say, a one in three chance of backlash, he is happy enough. On the other hand, an inexperienced angler might jump at the chance of 5 good casts out of 6 even if the tuning process does swallow 15 percent of his casting power.

Small, light spools are easier to cast than a heavy one crammed with 250 yards or more of thick nylon. It helps to use the smallest reel you can get away with. Excessive weight and diameter decrease the initial acceleration of the spool from rest, then exaggerate the flywheel effect which causes line over-spill.

All spools are capable of running fast enough to backlash. Some are inherently more docile than others, so design and construction do play a part in safe casting. Line level and diameter are also involved: within reason, the less line and the thicker it is, the faster the spool empties and the less chance there is of a backlash. Good casting style and rod design do much to eliminate ragged power flow—and roughness alone is responsible for the majority of backlashes. In all, design and

tackle matching contribute the lion's share to multiplier control. Tuning whether by oil viscosity or with inbuilt controllers is really a fine adjustment. Approach it from that angle for the best results.

OILS ultimately determine the maximum speed of a reel in response to any given casting power. The thicker the oil, the slower the spool responds. Oil's effect increases in step with spool speed and casting power. The braking effect of SAE 90 or 140 grade gear oil—very thick and restrictive—is greater during a 150 yard cast than at 50 yards. Water-thin machine oil has virtually no braking effect at any speed. The vast majority of surf reels are uncontrollable if thus lubricated.

The best technique is to start with thick oil—SAE 90 is excellent—then step down in small stages until you discover the oil which exactly matches your style and casting power. Bait drag, air temperature and wind affect the results; thick oil is useful in summer, lighter grades compensate for icy weather. A useful progression of oils is 10/50 engine oil, SAE30, SAE90 and finally syrupy STP when all else fails. Ultra-fussy casters fill in the gaps with home-made dilutions. SAE90 added to an equal part of SAE30 provides an

Spool end float is extremely important. No reel casts well that is restricted by a tight bearing cap.

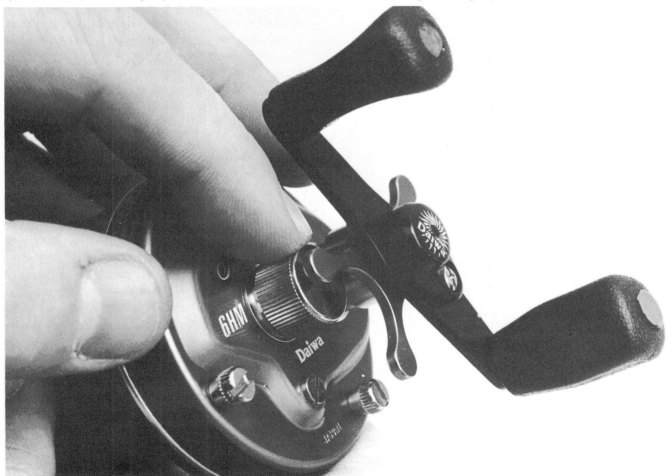

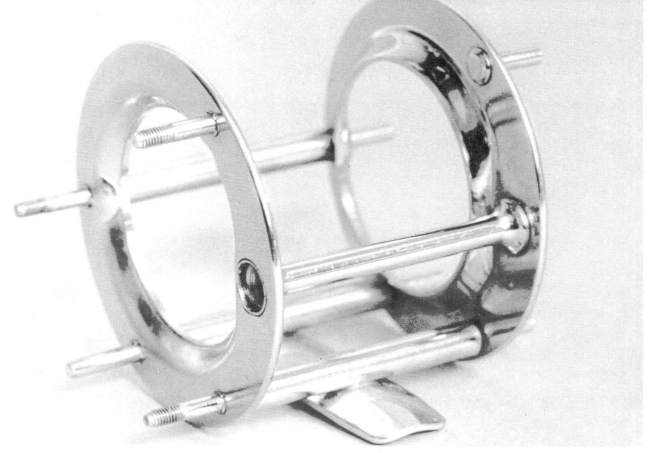

The ABU Ambassadeur CT cage fits most 6000 and 6500 series reels. A plain crossbar replaces the level wind. "CT" reels are favourites in the tournament world.

intermediate stage between the two straight oils.

Oil viscosity is used mainly to control reels without special braking systems. If a reel has a centrifugal brake or magnet, use thin oil in the bearings, then dial in the right amount of control with block size or magnet position. A change of oils may provide a mid-way point between one size of block and the next, but on the whole it is used as a lubricant pure and simple.

BRAKE BLOCKS are best chosen on the trial and error principle. There are few worthwhile tuning modifications available. You could try using plastic blocks instead of fibre. Plastic blocks are more slippery and might produce a braking force unobtainable with fibre. Sharpening the blocks to reduce contact has no effect, since it is the weight of the block and its coefficient of friction that determine the outcome, not its area in contact with the brake drum.

Cutting blocks in half is perfectly acceptable. You will reduce the braking force that way, though with a slight risk of splitting the material. It is better to grind fibre blocks, although plastic can be successfully hacksawed. It is unnecessary to use the same number and sizes of block on each arm of the brake spindle; spools do not fly out of balance.

Modern Ambassadeur baitcasting reels use an 'improved' brake block system which most competent anglers find detrimental. Plastic blocks

are clipped on to a special bar positioned across the spool end, but unlike the old bars which were parallel, these are built up at the ends to prevent blocks sliding too far and falling off. The drawback is that you cannot use tiny blocks—and one small block is the ideal tuning weight for tournament-grade casting. The only solution—tedious but often essential—is to drill out the bar and insert a parallel one which marries up to the older fibre blocks. Old style spools will not interchange with modern ABU designs unless the spindle ends are reworked.

MAGNETIC CONTROLS are set with a few turns of the screwdriver. For routine fishing no modifications are necessary. Simply dial in the braking power necessary to control the cast and overcome headwinds.

Penn's magnetic brake is specially chosen to accommodate the widest cross section of surf anglers who fish in all kinds of conditions with tackle ranging from light lures to 12 ounce sinkers and a half mullet bait. Penn trades off reel speed in return for safe casting for the majority. Even at its lowest setting the magnet has quite an effect on the spool, more so on the smaller 970 reel. However, a small modification or two adds a new surge of power to the cast.

Take off the left-hand sideplate and screw the magnet inwards until it falls out of its threads. Catch the retaining spring which pops out.

168

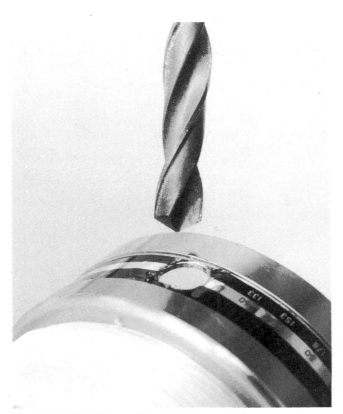

Spool lock 1. *Drill a small hole in the spool rim.*

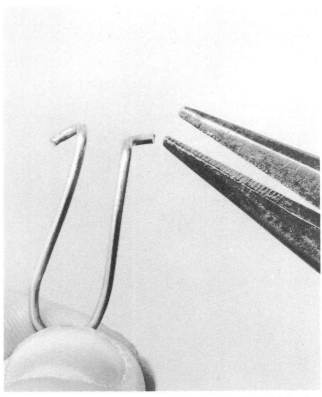

Spool lock 2. *Use stainless steel wire to make a "U" with hooks.*

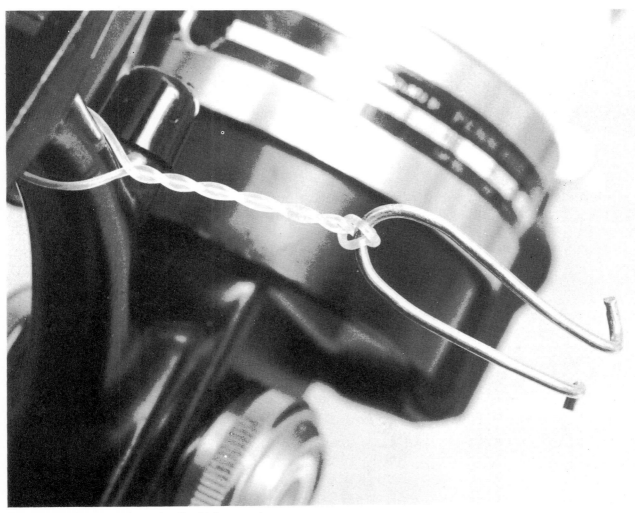

Spool lock 3. *Secure to the reel stalk with heavy nylon.*

Spool lock 4. *Before casting, lock the spool to the reel frame with the hook. Now there is no need to tighten the drag screw.*

Replace the magnet but not the spring, then rebuild the reel. Wound fully *out*, the magnet now gains the extra 1.75 turns of thread previously occupied by the spring. The braking effect is substantially reduced. Most competent casters can easily accommodate the extra speed and could gain up to 20 yards. For the ultimate state of tune, machine down the inner flange of the housing so that the magnet can be set even further out from the spool. This way it is possible to make the reel run uncontrollably fast. Should the magnet housing prove unstable once the retaining spring is out, press a strip of tape across the screw slot and reel sideplate.

Machining a fixed-spool rim

Front lips of fixed spool reels are responsible for a great deal of line friction during the cast. Some spools can be improved by machining away the excess metal until only a thin lip remains. This is polished to a mirror finish. There is no need to re-profile spool lips for general fishing, but a tournament caster usually gains a few extra yards. Just 5 yards could make the difference between winning and joining the also-rans. The only point

to watch is that in mounting the spool in a lathe you must ensure that the rim turns accurately, otherwise the new front lip loses concentricity with the bale rotor and the back of the spool.

New spools and permanent arbors

LONG DISTANCE CASTING gives full details on spool profiling for maximum casting range with fixed spools. Compensating arbors are usually hand-wound from old nylon line, but once you have determined the shape of the arbor it is better to make one from machined plastic or aluminium alloy cut into mating halves which are glued around the spool core.

A logical extension of the theory is to make a completely new spool, much shallower than standard. The bottom half of a normal spool is occupied by backing—wasted space and a definite contribution to bad line loading. A custom-made spool reduces waste and promotes better performance, particularly if the spool base is cut into an arbor profile.

Roller and bale arm replacement

Bale arm wires and line rollers are a nuisance, the

Like most reels, the Sagarra Tarzan suffers from excessive lip friction. Machining the lip then polishing it reduces friction and lengthens the cast.

great weakness of every fixed spool reel. Cutting off a bale wire and re-setting the arm roller angle help reduce snap-offs in mid cast and produce a positive cone of line on the spool. Apart from that, or resetting the spool base washers as an alternative means of coning the line, there is little to be done with a fixed spool unless you are particularly ingenious. One excellent accessory has recently come on to the market. George Shingleton of Hull, England makes a folding replacement for the Mitchell 498/499's manual roller pick-up. Instead of getting in the way during a cast, the new roller folds back and locks the rotor against the reel stand. Casts are smoother and trouble-free, and the spool remains in a fully extended position, which in theory at least is ideal for maximum performance.

Make Your Own Sinkers

Backlashes, wear and tear on the line, rocks and weeds buried in the seabed ensure that no sinker lasts for ever. Life expectancy is probably no more than two or three fishing trips. Plenty of beaches are a graveyard for terminal tackle, and you might lose a sinker every other cast.

Losing tackle is part of the game. From a cash point of view it makes sense to minimise the risk, and the best solution is to invest in a set of moulds. Home-made 5 ounce sinkers costs a few pence even if you have to buy the lead; commercially produced sinkers are around ten times more expensive and often not as good.

Casual fishermen probably would not recover the outlay on a set of two or three moulds. If you use half a dozen sinkers a year, buy them. Twelve or twenty sinkers cost as much as a pair of moulds and a few yards of wire, so if you use more than that in a season, do-it-yourself definitely repays the investment.

Home moulding encourages better fishing. If sinkers cost 50 pence each, you will not want to cast them into rocks where the recovery rate is less than 50/50. Faced with that prospect, a beach angler would almost certainly move to cleaner ground . . . and often lose contact with his fish. Cod and bass love rocks and weed, and successful fishing means taking a calculated gamble. You are more likely to do that if replacement costs are low.

Shop-bought terminal rig, snooded hooks and sinker could easily cost £1 a throw, half of it on lead. Assuming you lose 6 sets of tackle a day—by no means excessive—the £3 worth of lost sinkers is equivalent to a boxful of home-made sinkers. Doing it yourself (make your own weights, tie snoods, cut down on swivels) slashes outlay to a few pence. Losing 10 rigs a day is of no consequence. Think how many more fish you would catch compared to the angler who is terrified of sacrificing his precious stock of 3 sinkers.

Moulding is the only way to be sure of the exact weight and shape of sinker best suited to your style of casting and fishing. Tackle shops tend to steer a middle course. They stock, say, 4, 5, 6 and 8 ounce weights, either plain bombs or Breakaways. American dealers prefer pyramids and bank sinkers. What if you need a 5.25, 5.5, 7, or 10 ounce weight? A long-tailed sinker instead of a squat bomb? You won't find one; it is as simple as that. The tackle trade is generally miles behind beach trends and developments. Thousands of British anglers use tournament-grade 150 gram sinkers. Not one shopkeeper in a hundred has even heard of them.

A note of caution

Sinker moulding is dangerous without strict safety rules. Very few serious accidents occur, but inexperienced fishermen burn their fingers or scare themselves silly. All but a handful of mishaps are the direct result of ignorance. It does not require genius to melt and mould scrap lead, but it is absolutely essential to follow a code of practice. The golden rule is NEVER POUR MOLTEN LEAD INTO A COLD, DAMP MOULD.

Hot lead instantly vapourises water. Steam expands . . . and literally explodes from the mould, blasting out a shower of metal. If you are looking down on the mould, the discharge hits you in the face and eyes. At best hot metal pours over your hands and clothing.

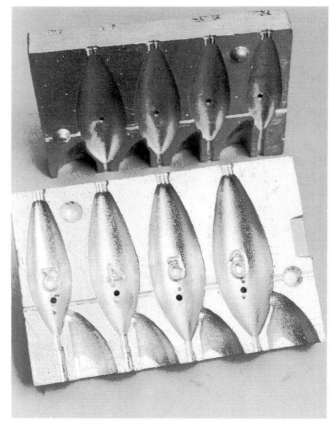

DCA's Beachbomb 4 in 1 mould is perhaps the finest investment for sinker making. Easy to use, accurate and safe, the four cavity mould produces conventional and long-tail sinkers.

Simple rules for handling molten lead:

1) Pre-heat the mould to warm it up and drive out dampness before you pour the first sinker.

2) Heat lead to well above melting point. Hot lead is easier to pour and runs cleanly into the depths of a mould. Semi-melted lead solidifies in the pouring hole and splashes on to the floor.

3) Make sure that the melting pot and boiler are secure. It is no fun tipping 10 pounds of molten lead over your toes. Moulds should be clamped if necessary, and laid on a flat surface. A tray of *dry* sand is an excellent base.

4) Use insulated gloves. Handle a very hot mould with pliers or clamps. Wear safety goggles and look away from the mould as the lead pours in.

5) NEVER COOL A MOULD IN WATER. This is the cardinal sin responsible for most serious accidents. Immersion inevitably results in a wet mould cavity. Pour molten lead inside that and you are in big trouble.

6) Pre-cut scrap chunks, make up wire loops beforehand and work to a pattern. A simple production sequence is faster and safer than flitting from one job to another.

7) Don't set the world on fire.

8) Lead poisoning. Metallic lead is unlikely to cause any problems. Bearing in mind the limited time spent in lead moulding and the low toxicity of clean scrap metal, an amateur who makes a few dozen sinkers now and again is perfectly safe provided he works in a well ventilated atmosphere.

Most lead poisoning is caused by fumes from lead-based chemicals like paint and organic compounds. There is more risk in burning off old lead paint than in melting scrap metal. Take care if your scrap is painted or corroded. Work in the open and avoid breathing the smoke. However, the risks are minimal—less than the intake of lead from petrol engine exhausts. But if you go on to make sinkers for friends and the local tackle shop, think about proper ventilation and regular health checks.

Moulds

Dozens of moulds are available from tackle shops and by mail order. Pyramids, grip leads and old-fashioned bombs in the 2–8 ounce range still grab a share of the market, but over the past 3 or 4 years new surf designs have infiltrated the home workshop. Aerodynamically superior bombs dominate tournament casting and top level beach fishing. Of the many moulds available, the DCA range are unquestionably best in both design and quality.

The Aquapedo bomb is short and fat, square in cross section and available in a 3–8 ounce range of 1 ounce increments. The sinker can be made up as a plain bomb, nose-wired sinker or collapsible wire version. Use either a short tail loop or a 3–4 inch single attachment wire. Aquapedoes are single cavity, die-cast moulds with a superb finish. The sections of mould are an absolutely immaculate fit, and no afterwork is necessary other than to trim off at the pouring gate. A snip with tin cutters produces the perfect sinker.

Beachbomb and Aquazoom sinkers are medium and long body sinkers respectively. The Beachbomb is shaped like an elongated tear drop, neatly pointed back and front, and with a centre of gravity just forward of the halfway point. The cross section is round. Aquazooms are longer, slimmer, and polygonal in cross section. Like Aquapedoes they may be assembled in plain and wired form with short loops or long tails. Beachbombs are particularly good for conversion into Spanish-style long tailed casting sinkers.

The range of sizes expands in step with modern thinking. The 3–10 ounce range is adequately covered, and there is a special 150 gram version of both sinkers. The Aquazoom 150 gram has been chosen as our official tournament casting sinker. Moulds are produced with double and multiple cavities. The 3, 4, 5, 6 ounce 4 in 1 Beachbomb unit is excellent—good value for money, easy to use, accurate and covers every basic requirement of beach fishing.

Glynn and Michael Williams of DCA moulds are sometimes willing to make up special designs and sizes to order. However, as the standard range continues to expand this service is largely unnecessary. If you cannot find a DCA mould to suit, your must be very fussy indeed. Most good tackle shops stock them. In case of difficulty—and for export sales—contact DCA Moulds, 41 Lon Isa, Rhiwbina, Cardiff, CF4 6EE, WALES, Great Britain. Telephone 0222 65340. Prices range from around £4 for a single cavity mould to £8 for a 4 in 1 Beachbomb outfit.

Other moulds exist of course. Some manufacturers offer a reasonable product at respectable prices, so do not despair if you cannot find a genuine DCA mould. The difference between the majority of mould makers and the Williams team is that Glynn and Michael regard sinkers as technical products worthy of deep research and high quality engineering, not as chunks of boiled scrap lead.

Lead

Fifteen pounds of scrap lead should last most beach fishermen a year or more. That much can usually be scrounged from somewhere: demolition sites, ripped out plumbing, ancient drainpipes. If all else fails, buy clean scrap from your local metal dealer. Even at full price it is far cheaper than ready-made sinkers.

Lead varies in weight and texture. Pure lead is heavy but soft. Scrap wheel balance weights are harder but weigh less. Mix them together if you like. Using several different batches of scrap metal in a nominal 5 ounce mould, the sinkers turn out between 4.75 and 5.25 ounces—accurate enough for most purposes.

Clean sheet lead is easiest to work with. Raw scrap is dirty, painted, corroded, in pipe form or in crunched blocks. Scrape off the worst muck and carve the lead into manageable pieces with an old axe, metal shears or by hammer and cold chisel. Aim for a piece of lead which can be lowered straight into the melting pot.

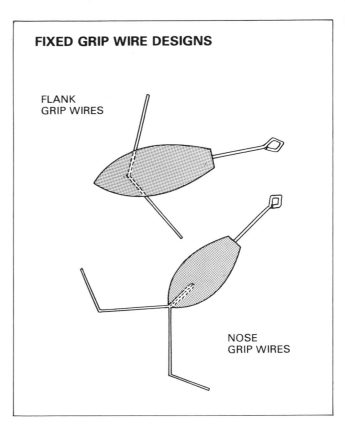

FIXED GRIP WIRE DESIGNS

FLANK GRIP WIRES

NOSE GRIP WIRES

The mould set up for lead pouring. The halves are securely clamped and rested on blocks of wood which allow clearance for the long tail wire. Angled brass wires form tunnels in the lead for sinker wire attachment.

Wires

Stainless steel, galvanised and brass wire loops link the sinker to its trace. All three are satisfactory but stainless steel is best in the long run. Loops must seat deeply inside the lead for security. Cut off 3 inches of wire, bend it into a 'U' the same width as the mould channels, then fold over the last 0.25 inch of each free end. Even small tags of metal will handle 8–10 ounce weights without slipping out in mid-cast. Long tail wires must be made from stainless steel wire. Cut 5–6 inch pieces of wire, fold the last 0.5 inch of one end into a 'U' and insert it about an inch into the mould cavity.

Grip wires are best cut from springy stainless steel wire. Failing that, piano wire will do despite the rust. Brass and galvanised steel are usually too soft to bother with; thicker wire works well enough, but creates so much air resistance that casts are noticeably reduced. For nose wires, cut a pair of 7–8 inch wires, fold them in half and insert the hinged ends about 0.5 inches into the mould. Fixed flank wires are cut to the same length but bent into right-angles for mounting in the mould holes.

Wire specifications:

Tackle dealers sell wire by the yard or metre. Metal stockists prefer to sell by weight—usually one kilogramme minimum order. There is no precise diameter and grade of wire best suited to sinker production but do choose fairly springy wire that is easy to cut and bend.

Purpose	S.W.G.	Diameter	U.S. equivalent (Brown and Sharpe)
Heavy	14	0.080″/2.03mm	No. 12
General	16	0.064″/1.625mm	No. 14
Light	18	0.048″/1.219 mm	No. 16

General purpose wire suits 4–8 ounce sinkers with grips up to 4 inches long and short or long tail loops.

Heavy wire encourages firm anchorage in very fast tides. Wires can be extended to 6–8 inches if necessary. Extra strength is some insurance against snapping off 8–12 ounce sinkers cast very hard, and is mandatory for 14–16 ounces of lead.

Light wire is of limited usefulness in surf fishing. Sinkers up to 3 ounces are safely cast on 18SWG loops. For the long tail design, stick to 16SWG wire when hard casting cannot be avoided.

Pre-formed loops

DAC Moulds produce a range of brass and galvanised steel tail loops which slot into the mould. Unlike ordinary loops, Aqualoops can be inserted after the mould is closed and clamped. Instead of having metal tags at the end of the 'U' piece, Aqualoops are corrugated for most of their length. The arrangement seems flimsy but it works extremely well. 8 ounces of lead cast at full power are perfectly secure. However, lead must be poured red hot otherwise it does not run into close enough contact with the wire to infiltrate the corrugations.

Tools and equipment

Asbestos gloves
Blowtorch to melt lead and pre-heat the mould
Container to hold molten lead
Pouring ladle
Wire cutters and pliers
Sand tray
Clamps
Old knife to trim sinkers
Rubber bands for collapsible sinkers (optional)
Fire bricks to reflect and conserve blowtorch heat
Secure stand for lead pot and ladle

Over the years my sinker moulding equipment and technique have evolved into a streamlined production system. Once it took an hour to set up the heater and melt the first batch of lead. Now I make a dozen weights in 30 minutes.

The traditional way of handling lead is to melt it in an iron pot heated by a gas ring or brazier.

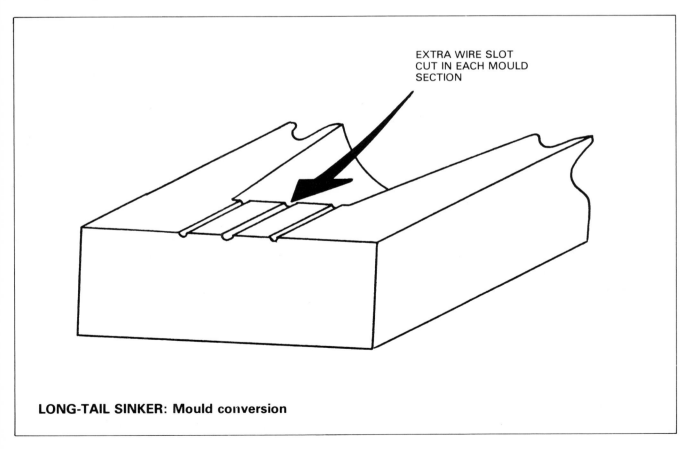

EXTRA WIRE SLOT CUT IN EACH MOULD SECTION

LONG-TAIL SINKER: Mould conversion

handle the hot mould with insulated gloves or pliers. The 5 ounce sinker shown here is ready for trimming. Note the brass wire used to pre-drill the sinker body.

Work with 5–10 pounds of lead at once, and skim off dross which rises to the surface. Heat the ladle, fill it from the melting pot, then pour the sinker. Nothing wrong in doing it that way, except that it swallows up too much time and heat. Besides you need a proper gas ring which securely supports the lead pot, a separate ladle, and a lot of fuel to first break down that great chunk of lead and then keep it molten. It takes as much heat to maintain molten metal as it does to melt it in the first place.

I now use a powerful propane blowtorch (butane is just as good) aimed directly on to a lead ladle. The ladle is either hand held over the flame or steadied in a cradle of fire bricks surrounding the burner nozzle. Instead of melting several pounds of lead, I use enough for, say, 4 sinkers at once. Using a pair of double-cavity moulds or a set of individuals, I can set up the moulds and wires, melt lead and pour the whole lot in one go. Molten metal runs out from under the dross, so there is seldom any reason to skim the surface beforehand.

Any safe method is acceptable, and with experience you soon develop your own particular way of working. Full-scale production does require a lot of thought and plenty of equipment, but at the other extreme plenty of anglers knock out

enough sinkers for their own use by melting lead in an old saucepan on the kitchen range. Gas cookers and electric radiant rings make short work of scrap lead.

Systematic working reduces waste, speeds production and is safer. The method detailed here is by no means the only one, and perhaps not even the best. However, it is both easy and safe—prime considerations for a beginner.

1) Work outside or in your garage. Use the floor rather than a bench. That way, spilled lead splashes less. Plain concrete is best. Avoid combustible dust and wood shavings!

2) Set up your mould with wires in place, halves firmly clamped together and the whole thing set firmly on a sand tray or supported on bricks. (Sometimes the mould must be held high because there are wires dangling below.)

3) Arrange 4 or 5 fire bricks in an open square: 2 for the base, 3 for the sides. Turn on the blowtorch and rest its nozzle on the brick floor with the flame directed into the box. Drop a chunk of lead into the ladle and melt it. Either hold the

ladle or make up a simple iron stand for it. I hold mine because I find it easier to work that way. I use insulated gloves all the time though; some people find them a nuisance.

4) When the lead is nicely melted, pick up the blowtorch and cook the mould for a minute to drive out moisture and to ensure that lead does not harden in the pouring hole. By this time the lead in the ladle has cooled a little but it takes only a minute's more heating to bring it back to optimum working temperature.

5) Pour lead steadily into the mould until it overflows into the pouring hole. If you are working with more than one mould, fill them in turn. Warm the ladle between pourings. The hotter the lead, the smoother and shinier the sinker will turn out.

6) Rest your ladle somewhere safe—it should now be empty or almost so—and turn off the gas. Lead sets within 30 seconds, so it is already time to split the mould. Remove clamps and open the mould halves with gloved fingers (carefully!) or with pliers.

If necessary, first remove the anchor wire guide pins from their holes. These are brass wires one size thicker than stainless wire used for grips. Slide them into the access holes in the mould, pour the lead, then pull them out to produce a pair of neat tunnels through the sinker body.

7) Knock the sinker from its mould and leave it to cool. At this stage it is safe to drop just the sinker into water. NEVER SOAK THE MOULD. Finally, insert new tail loops and wires, close the mould and clamp it. Melt more lead for the next batch of sinkers. It is no longer necessary to preheat the moulds. By the second pouring most moulds are throughly hot; after moulding 3 or 4 sinkers they are too hot to handle even with gloves.

AFTERWORK

Plain sinkers

Trim off excess lead and clean out the tail wire loop. Check loop security. There is no need to pull

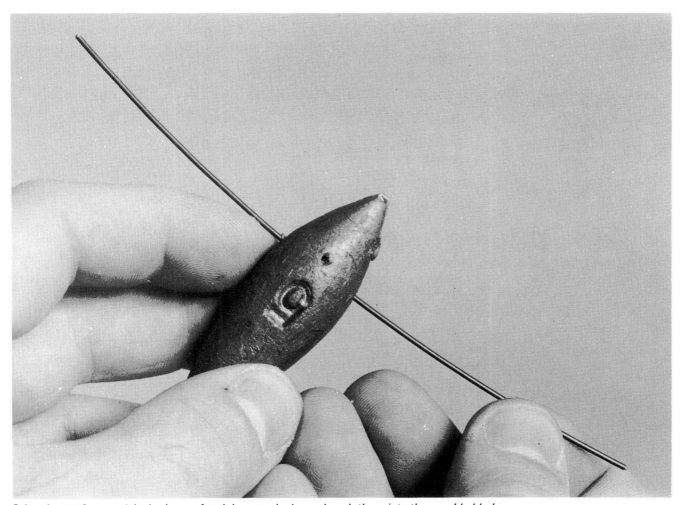

Grip wires 1. Cut two 9 inch pieces of stainless steel wire and push them into the moulded holes.

Grip wires 2. *Centre the wires in their holes, then bend the ends over.*

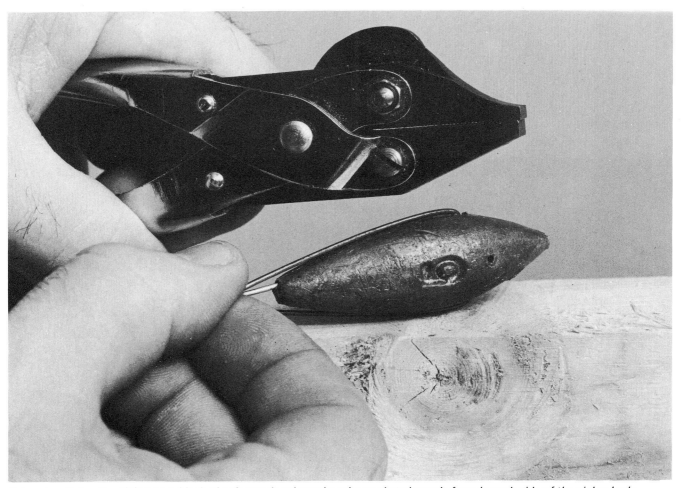

Grip wires 3. *Lay the sinker on a block of soft wood and tap the wire so that channels form in each side of the sinker body.*

Grip wires 4. *Allow an inch of wire to lay along the sinker flank. Bend the rest outwards by 45 degrees.*

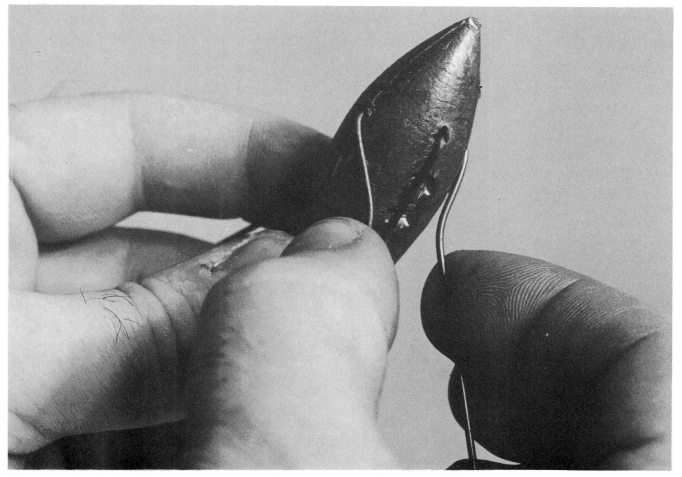

Grip wires 5. *Bend the wires inward so that they slot tightly into the sinker body channels. Wire tension determines the line pressure at which the wires flip from the seabed.*

179

hard. Unless the wire loops has shifted in the mould and now pokes out of the lead body, it will be safely attached. Aqualoops should be tested by pulling on the tail with pliers—use about 50 pounds pressure. This test confirms that molten lead has set in close contact with the serrated wire. The final test is to weigh the sinker. Unnecessary for general fishing, it is a valuable step for tournament casters. There is no point practising with a 5 ounce sinker if 5.25 ounces are standard for the event.

Grip-wired sinkers

No extra work is involved if wires are permanently fixed inside a lead body. Nose and flank wires should be cleaned of lead flashing and stray blobs. Sometimes excess lead must be pared away before the mould halves will separate. Store the sinkers with nose wires left straight and flank wires folded against the body. Just before use, bend the wires into grapnel pattern. Wire angle depends on the seabed and tide flow. Hard tides and sand/grit require steeply raked wires. Soft mud or a gentle flow are better handled with reduced gripping power, so spread the wires well away from the lead. For even more grip in adverse conditions, form a shallow hook in the last inch of each grapnel finger.

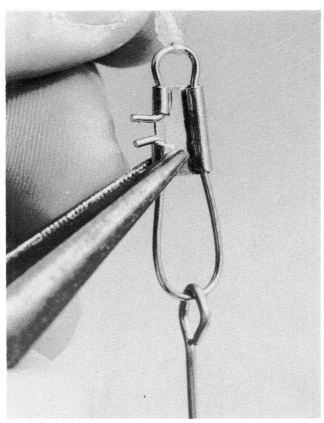

Conventional clips and split rings are perfectly safe provided the design is right. Safety pin clips like this tend to open under pressure. Nip the tag of metal to lock the wire in place. Note the open diamond loop in the tail wire.

Collapsible or breakaway wires are threaded through holes moulded into the sinker, bent into shape and held in position by rubber bands or wire tension. Wire tension is a better system because there are no bands to snap. The picture sequence shows exactly how to make a Breakaway, perhaps the most versatile sinker ever developed for surf fishing.

Mould modifications

DCA moulds are available pre-drilled for grip wires either in the nose, fixed in the flank or swivelling. Other moulds are easily drilled to take either anchor wires or brass guide pins. Drill the holes one size larger than anchor wire diameter. For accurate hole alignment across the halves of the mould, mark the drilling positions before hand, and bore each half of the mould separately from inside the cavity.

Some moulds are predrilled for conventional and single-tail wires. Others are slotted for the loop only. Three or four strokes of a sharp hacksaw in each half of the mould produce a neat central tail hole into which you insert a single wire. Long tail wires have many advantages over the short loop. They cast smoothly and perhaps a little farther than the regular design; seabed anchorage is at least 30 percent higher.

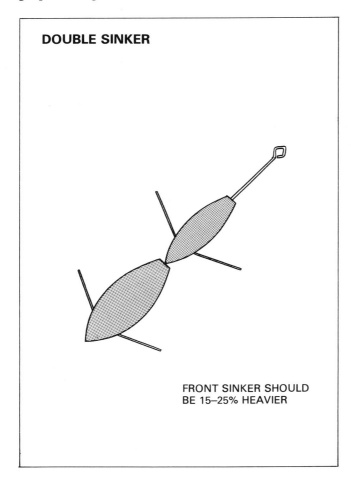

DOUBLE SINKER

FRONT SINKER SHOULD
BE 15–25% HEAVIER

Double sinkers

An additional advantage of the long single tail wire is that two lead bodies, each with grip wires, can be moulded one behind the other. Use your normal 3–6 ounce moulds to produce double sinkers between 6 and 12 ounces. It pays to use sinkers at least an ounce different in weight, with the heavier body at the front. Short aerodynamic shapes are best, thus Beachbomb and Aquapedo moulds reign supreme. Armed with 10 ounces-plus of double bomb and two sets of grip wires, you can tackle the heaviest seas with confidence.

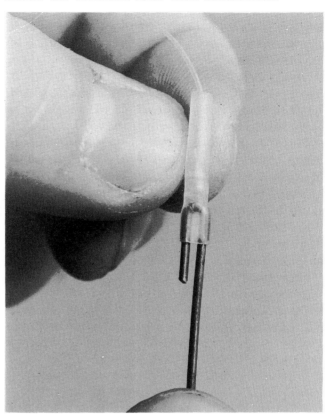

Sleeve attachment 1. *Bend a tight "U" in the wire. Tie the leader directly to the wire with a Uni-knot.*

Sleeve attachment 2. *Protect the knot and close the wire bend with a piece of tight fitting plastic tube. This is a cheap and highly effective way to secure a surfcasting sinker.*

Hooks

Hooks are used to present baits and trap biting fish; that much holds true for any kind of fishing. Casting from the shore presents its own difficulties, most of them related to long distance. Hooks which control baits and hook fish at 50 yards may prove useless at 100 yards. Beyond 150 yards it is extremely difficult to catch fish at all unless your hooks are close to perfect.

The first hurdle is bait preservation. Does the worm, fish strip or peeler crab stay on the hook, or does it explode in mid-cast? If a cast holds together, does the weight of the hook upset a bait's action underwater? Some fish ignore a piece of worm anchored by thick stainless steel but will snatch the same bait threaded on narrow gauge wire.

The teeth of rays, smoothhounds and dogfish are flat and strong. Powered by massive grinding muscles capable of pulverising shellfish and hard crabs, a big fish's jaws literally crush medium-weight hooks. Fine-wire Aberdeen hooks used extensively in match fishing last but a few seconds.

Tope and conger eels crush and cut their prey. A strong hook is essential, and this time it needs the support of a wire trace. However, a substantial hook is no good unless razor sharp—tope especially are hard to hook at long range. Conger are a short to medium range species, but they too require a fair impact to sink the barb. Blunt hooks skid off their rubbery jaws.

There are fish that suck and nibble a bait, and some that swallow whole. Short shank hooks are good enough for wide-throated species which can be unhooked with forceps or pliers. Long shank hooks are better for flatfish and other narrow jawed fish which swallow a hook right down; you can still reach the end of the shank for unhooking. Sometimes it pays to tie on a fine wire hook which can be deliberately pulled straight. There is no easier and kinder way to unhook a deeply impaled flounder, sole or dab.

Tying and whipping, snood modification and bait clips contribute to better casting and bait protection. Simple alterations in hook design and size make life a lot easier on the beach. One problem remains: how to drive home a hook at long range. Striking is useless. At even 75 yards a powerful sweep of the rod shifts the hook only a few inches and generates a point pressure of less than 12 ounces.

Special traces and grip wire sinker allow us to reverse the process so that the fish hooks itself, but it can do so only if the hook is sharp, easily sunk beyond barb depth and capable of taking a firm grip in soft tissues as well as hard. The right choice of hook turns 9 bites out of 10 into hooked fish. The wrong one is a total failure.

No hook is beyond criticism. There are plenty of really bad ones, half a dozen which excel, and a reasonable selection of middle of the road designs which are neither atrocious nor inspiring. And to be truly successful any hook must be chosen in relation to a *combination* of bait size, casting range, species, hooking power and strength. Compromise is usually necessary, and for that reason alone very few anglers are without their individual preferences. However, there is a broad consensus about the hooks that are worth buying and those which are completely useless. Very few match fishermen would use the sliced beaked design, but everyone would have a few blue Aberdeens in his bag.

PATTERNS, SIZES AND APPLICATIONS

Fine wire Blue Aberdeens

These are something of a cult hook. Extremely sharp, thin in the wire and modestly strong, they are *the* hook for small fish and delicate baits. Long range fishing for dabs, pouting, whiting and even shy codling is enhanced by a blue Aberdeen. Smaller sizes—size 6 to 1/0— are used all around the British coast for competition work and general pleasure fishing. Some anglers take the view that unless you are fishing specifically for big cod, conger or rays, there is really no need to use any other design of saltwater hook. There are several types of Aberdeen hook, many of which are available in blued steel. The one usually referred to as a genuine Aberdeen Blue is the plain shank (no ring or spade) Mustad 3730A. Aberdeen Blues can be pulled from a fish's throat and re-bent into shape, a most useful trick in high-speed match fishing.

Ringed Aberdeen hooks

These offer improved strength at the slight sacrifice of sharpness and penetration. They are stocked by most dealers and commonly available in the size 6–8/0 range, which covers every

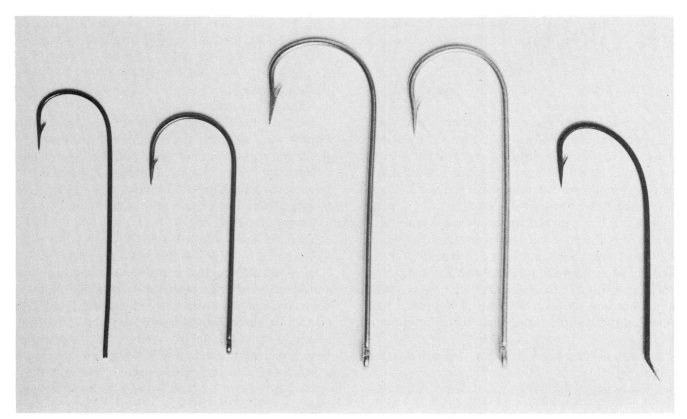

Lightweight shore hooks. Right to left: Breakaway Spearspade, Au Lion d'Or 1322, Mustad Aberdeen 3282, Partridge Aberdeen Z10, and the classic blue Aberdeen 3730A from Mustad.

requirement. Above all they are an excellent general purpose hook for worm presentation, sandeels and fish strips. Whiting, flatfish, bass and cod are hooked and held without much risk of struggling free. Be careful of hauling heavy fish through strong surf—there is a limit to the insurance provided by the relatively slim, modestly tempered wire. Mustad 3282 are popular, usually in silver and with neat eyes for direct trace attachment.

Au Lion d'Or (model 1322) hooks from France are similar to the Mustad Aberdeen. The wire is slightly thicker and much tougher, making the larger sizes a particularly wise choice for winter cod. Few shops have them in stock. The finish looks like satin chrome; whatever it is, the hook is fairly stain resistant and can be used several times before rust sets in.

The sharpest, strongest and best tempered Aberdeen is made by Partridge of Redditch, England. Most sizes are available, and as the hook gains popularity because of its sheer quality, more and more tackle shops sell them. The model number is Z10, sizes 8 to 4/0. A shorter shank version is available under code Z9A in sizes 6 to 3/0. Both models are bronzed and eyed. Patridge have recently introduced a blue steel Aberdeen, Z12, which is lighter than the Z10, plain shanked and sized 8 to 4/0. Quality, temper and sharpness

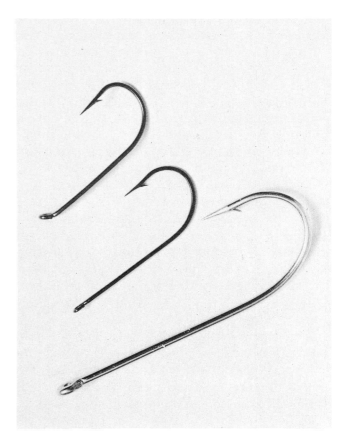

Strong and medium weight hooks for shore fishing. Right to left: Partridge, Kendal, Kirby, Extra-strong (Z22), Mustad Viking 79515 and Partridge Flashpoint Z5.

183

are higher than Mustad's blue Aberdeen—the two brands are set for major confrontation in the sea match world.

Mustad Viking, Spearspade, Spearpoint and Patridge Flashpoint

These hooks lie midway between the delicate accuracy of Aberdeens and the large, rugged sea hooks which are all power and no finesse. There is no reason why any of these models should not be substituted for Aberdeens except for fishing fragile baits like white ragworm.

Mustad Vikings are produced in a number of basically similar models. Numbers 79510 and 79515, its successor, are classic hooks for big cod and bass. Forged, well tempered, sharp and medium-weight in the wire, they accept bunches of worms, squid and whole crabs with ease. Many sizes are available, and the most popular lie between size 2 and 4/0.

Breakaway Tackle's Spearpoint and Spearspade hooks are manufactured by Patridge. Essentially the same hook with either a small eye or extended spade, they are offspring of traditional low-water salmon hooks. Needle sharpness and high strength in relation to wire diameter are two key features of the range. Rather than rely on size numbers alone, Breakaway Tackle grade their hooks according to species: cod, bass, whiting and dab. Beginners particularly welcome the neat packaging which carries tying instructions and selection guide.

Many cod anglers believe that an extended shank promotes better long-range hooking. Breakaway and Vikings are borderline in this respect, and thus rejected by a section of the cod fishing community. Patridge offer a reasonable alternative in the Z5 Flashpoint series, sizes 6 to 7/0. Bronzed, forged hooks with round bend and small turned-down eyes, they are exceedingly sharp and adequately tough.

An appropriately sized hook from this group will handle the majority of baits used from the surf and should easily land most species of fish from dabs and soles, through codling, dogfish and bass, right up to medium-weight rays, tope and conger eels.

Heavy duty hooks

These are seldom strictly necessary for British surf fishing but may prove essential for overseas sport. Mustad produce a vast array of models and sizes. O'Shaughnessy and Seamaster are fine examples. Closer to home, the Partridge Kendal Kirby Extra Strong (Z22) is well worth considering. Scalpel-sharp point, round, offset bend and realistically slim, nickel plated shank are a challenge to any

tope and conger eel. Were it exported to America, drum and striper fishermen might find it a realistic alternative to the standard surf hooks. Penetration is markedly superior to most large books—a tremendous advantage with hard-mouthed species at medium to long range.

Do you really need a big strong hook? This depends on where you fish and the chances of hooking a monster. In general, surf fishermen underrate their tackle. Small hooks are not necessarily inferior; and there is some truth in the theory that hook size and power should be reduced to match main line and trace breaking strains. Why use a hook of 300 pounds breaking strain on 20 pound test tackle?

Hooks are subject to enormous leverage and crushing pressures. It is unrealistic to expect a weak hook to deal with very big, hard fighting fish. However, sometimes the size of a hook is its own worst enemy. Angles of barb, point and shank, bend circumference and wire diameter sometimes make it easier for a big fish to break away from or even straighten a large hook. Small hooks—provided they are reasonably strong in the wire and well made—sink in much deeper, so that fighting stress is transferred from the point to the back of the bend, a far more solid foundation.

Tests suggest that a small hook set deep is much more reliable and actually stronger than a big hook

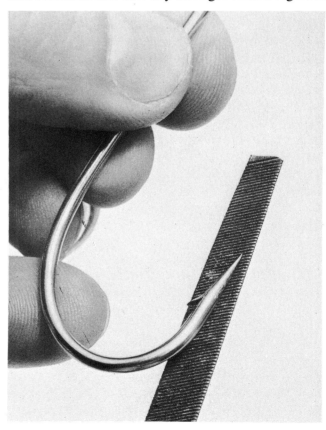

Sharp hooks catch more fish. A file or slip stone soon corrects blunt points caused by sand and stones.

Snelling 1. *Fold a loop about six inches in diameter and lay it alongside the hook shank.*

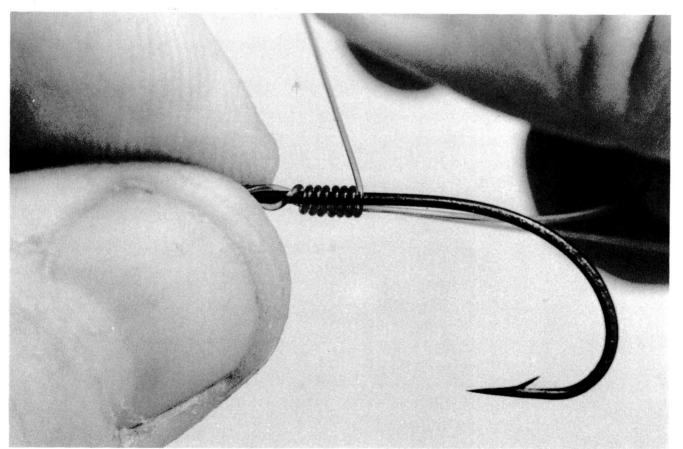

Snelling 2. *Hold the left hand end of the loop between right finger and thumb, and whip it neatly around the shank and double strands of nylon. Put in at least six full turns.*

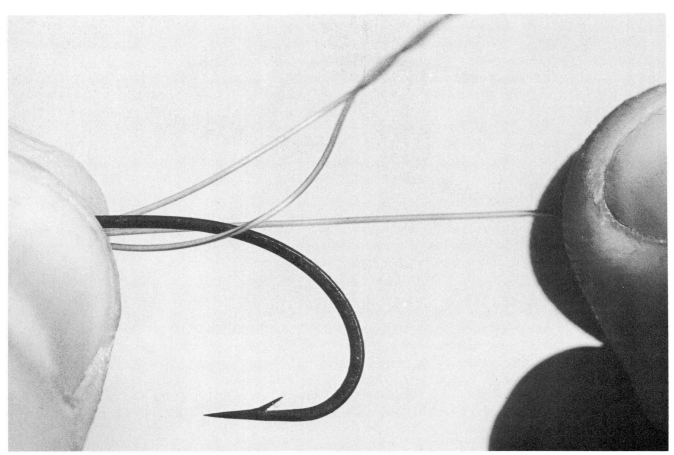

Snelling 3. *Carefully slide your left finger and thumb over the coils and pinch them to the shank. Now pull on the spare end of nylon to tighten the knot.*

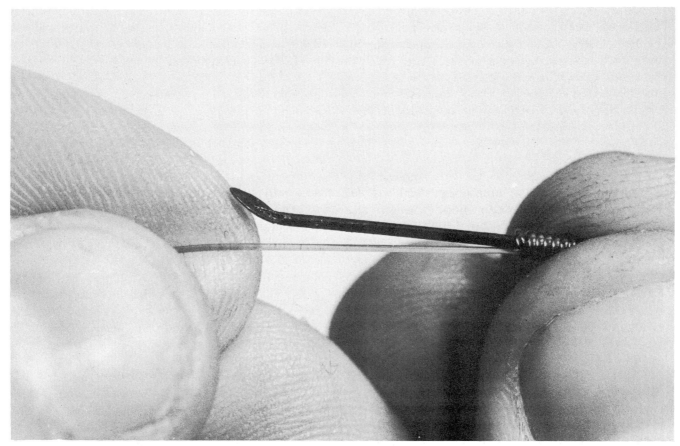

Snelling 4. *Swap over your hands so that right finger and thumb now hold the knot coils. Pull on the snood to further tighten the knot.*

186

Snelling 5. Slide the knot close to the spade end. Pull the knot tight with pliers. Finally trim the loose end.

sunk only to barb depth. There is another factor: hooks affect a bait's action on the seabed. Instead of rolling with the current, baits on big, coarse hooks hold fast in the sand by the sheer weight of the hook. Some fish are not concerned with the unnatural reaction; others swim right past. If everyone around you is catching fish while your bait lies ignored, try changing to a smaller or lighter hook. Hook weight is more deterring than an exposed shank.

Hook attachment

Hooks are manufactured with plain shanks, eyes and spade-end tags. Sometimes there is no apparent balance between hook design and attachment system—hooks are for the most part the result of traditional craftsmanship. Anglers too have their preferences: some match anglers insist on a spade end while others choose the same hook with an eye. There are definite advantages in spades and plain shanks, but for beginners the eyed hook is best because it is so easy to tie to the trace. Whipping and snelling are more demanding, and in many cases the extra work is hardly justified for general fishing.

Whipped hooks

A fine wire, needle sharp Aberdeen Blue supports the most fragile worm bait. The delicate white

ragworm loses only a drop of blood when the point and barb are inserted. A whole worm threads neatly up the shank and on to the trace. Hardly damaged by the hooking process, it casts well and retains all its attractive juices.

The same worm slips neatly on to an ordinary eyed Aberdeen or Viking hook, threads smoothly on to the shank, then stops fast against the eye and knot. The smallest eye effectively trebles shank diameter, and worms cannot be threaded on to the trace without splitting the body wide open. Blood and juices are lost; the bait explodes in mid-cast.

Aberdeen Blues are super-glued and whipped so neatly to the trace that a worm's body hardly expands as it slides into position. There is no particular skill in whipping plain shanked hooks, but it is not easy to produce a reliable bond between shank and trace unless you work carefully. No matter how tightly you whip, thread tension alone will not anchor the components. Nylon and metal must first be bonded, then whipped, and finally sealed. Try this technique (see the photographs for close-up details):

1) Clean the hook shank with methylated spirit to remove grease. Spread a thin smear of superglue along the back of the shank. Lay on a nylon snood and hold the two in close contact until the glue sets.

187

2) Trim off the nylon with a sloping cut and whip it to the shank with medium weight Gudebrod rod thread. Tie off the whipping with the normal rod maker's tuck. Check the alignment of snood and shank and adjust if necessary. They must lie parallel.

3) Smear superglue over the entire whipping and leave it to dry. Adhesive seeps into the threads and fuses shank, thread and nylon into one smooth layer. Because of the sloping cut made in the nylon, the whipping is nicely tapered for easy bait threading. After a few hours' drying the hook is ready to use.

Superglue is not waterproof. In time, saltwater eats into the whipping and breaks the bond. This is seldom a problem in everyday beach fishing; hooks never last that long. It is possible for hooks stored in a damp tin to gradually lose strength, so if you go fishing infrequently, add a smear of varnish to the whipping for extra protection. Do not take chances: good whippings are as strong as eyes and spades, but bad ones are the worst possible way to attach hooks to snoods.

Ordinary Aberdeens and some lightweight Vikings and Spearpoints may be whipped. Cut off the eye or spade and use the standard whipping technique after cleaning the shank and perhaps roughening it slightly with a file for a better key. Take care when trimming the hook shank. Snipping off with pliers produces a sharp edge which would cut the snood. Grind the end of the wire square across on a slipstone.

Best results are ensured by matching hook wire to nylon snood diameter. They should be fairly similar otherwise either the snood slides out or the hook pulls from under its tube of whipping. Matt-finish brands of monofilament like Sylcast and Stren bond better than shiny, cheap lines. If necessary though you can key the nylon by gently pulling it through folded abrasive paper.

Eyed hooks
Eyes are an excellent link between hook shank and trace. Nothing is easier to tie or more reliable. Where tackle strength outweighs bait disruption, an eyed shank outfishes every other hook. Several knots may be used, and with wire traces you have the choice between tying, twisting and crimping.

There are anglers who spend hours experimenting with knots. According to them, certain knots are superior in terms of impact resistance and overall strength. They can show you clear evidence that a tucked blood knot is far from the ideal choice. That may be so in the laboratory, and might even prove correct in ideal fishing conditions. Given warm, dry hands, plenty of time to retie if necessary and perfect lighting, anyone can learn to make those complicated super-knots so often written about yet so seldom used.

Icy fingers, slippery tackle and no time for hesitation are another matter. Then it pays to tie the good old tucked blood knot, Uni-knot or Palomar. It is better to hit the target every time with a 80-90 percent strength knot than to struggle with that elusive 99 percent hitch that goes wrong four times out of five. After practising for 10 minutes, most beginners can tie simpler knots reliably. Coils snug down neatly, and the knot stays firm under pressure. If you tie 6 tucked blood knots and test each for strength, each one's breaking point should be within 5 or 10 percent of maximum value.

Palomars and Uni-knots show a similar pattern. But 6 examples of a more critical knot might test out this way: 95 percent, 97, 95, 55, 90 and 70. If all goes well, the knot is indeed superior. Now and again it falls flat; in accordance with Murphy's Law, that's the time you will hook a king-size bass or cod.

The tucked half blood knot is good enough for general fishing. Better still, use the Uni-knot which

Small fish are an important part of modern shore fishing. It pays to scale down your hooks accordingly.

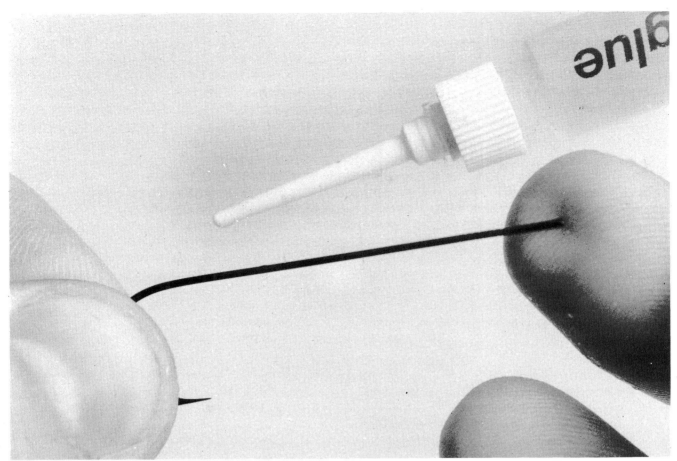

Whipping 1. Smear superglue down the shank. If necessary, first clean the wire with methylated spirit or Ajax.

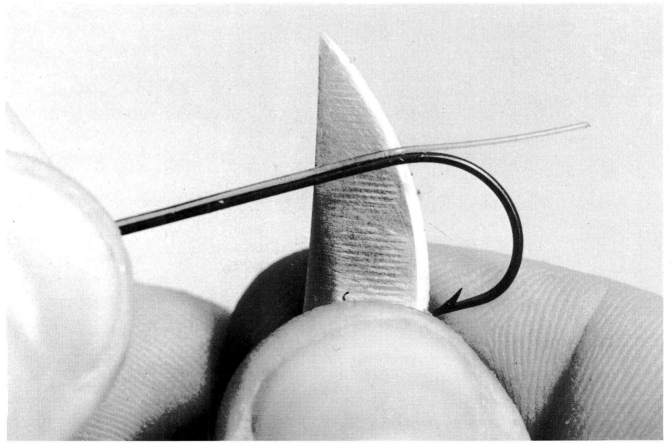

Whipping 2. Lay the snood on the shank and leave it to bond. Trim the end of nylon close to the bend with a tapering cut.

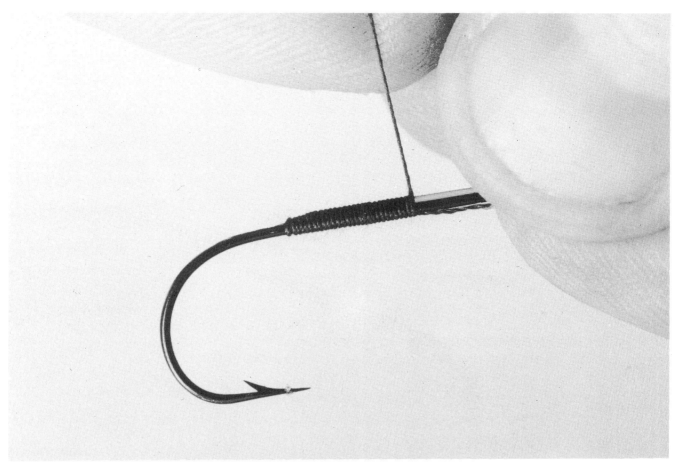

Whipping 3. Begin whipping the shank with ordinary sewing thread or Budebrod rod thread.

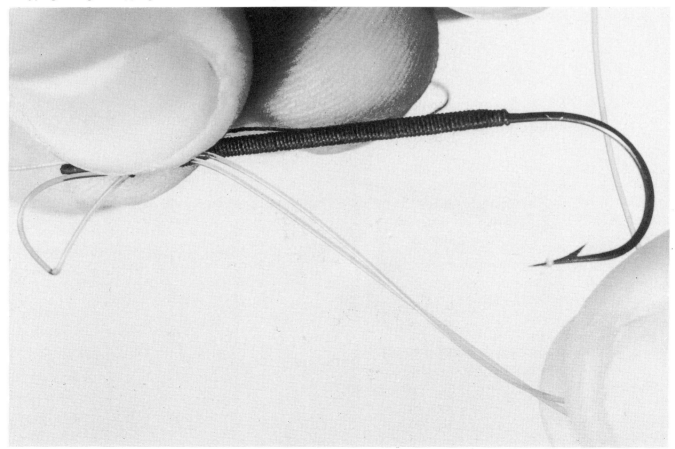

Whipping 4. Tie off the thread with the normal rod maker's tuck.

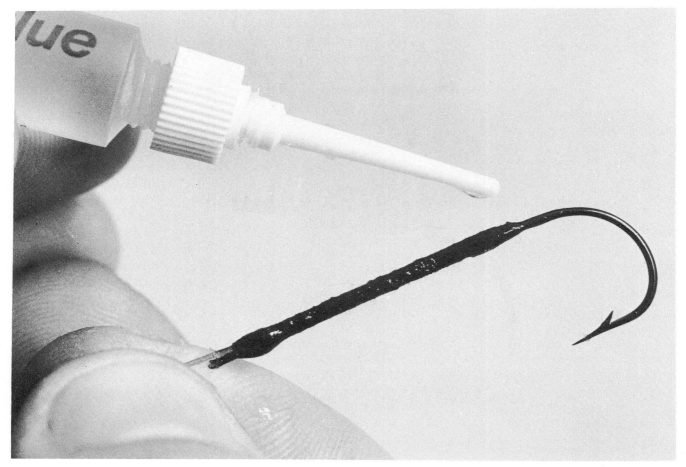

Whipping 5. Adjust the shank and snood so they lie parallel, then seal the threads with superglue.

is slightly stronger provided the coils fall neatly into place. A little practice develops the skill necessary to tie the knot with your eyes closed. Make sure the coils align correctly *before* you tighten the knot, otherwise they ride over each other and skid free. The Palomar also depends on sensible practice and care in smoothing its parallel coils before you pull them tight. Its great advantage is the double run of nylon around the hook eye. The spare end of Uni-knots and Palomars lies parallel to the snood, whereas a sprig of nylon juts out at right-angles from the blood knot barrel. Mostly it makes no difference, but with soft worm baits the blood knot may cause some damage.

Snelled hooks

Spade end hooks are attached with a special snell which is easy to tie once you see it done, and on the whole makes a reasonably reliable, tough joint. A traditional favourite of commercial fishermen, the spade hook/snell combination is much faster to tie than a plain shank whipping (which can be used on a spade end hook if you prefer). Spade end hooks are cheaper than eyed models; looking at it the other way, only cheap hooks are spaded. Keen surf men steer clear.

I see little reason for snelled hooks in beach fishing. Either proper whippings or knotted eyes are much better. However, one advantage of the system is that it holds the hook shank straight out from the trace, whereas an eyed hook tends to fold. Sometimes bait presentation is enhanced by a straight joint, and in those circumstances a snell is preferred. Spade ends are not necessary; the hitch can be tied just as easily on an eyed hook. Either treat the eye as an ordinary spade, or thread line through beforehand. As long as the trace nylon is fairly thin, a snell will not damage threaded worms.

Looped-on hooks are a satisfactory means of baiting with sandeels and sprats. Tie a trace-end loop long enough to slide through the eye and around the hook bend. Push the loop into the eye, attach the bait, take the loop around the hook and bait; halfpay draw the loop into the eye. Tuck the fish's tail under the double strand, then pull the knot tight.

Hook modification

Cutting off eyes has already been discussed. It opens up the field for whipping stronger hooks than Aberdeen Blues. Why bother? It means you

191

can avoid bursting worms against the normal shank eye yet still choose a reasonably strong wire. At the same time you can modify shank length. Trimmed down by a few millimetres, long shank Aberdeens are more suited to short, bulky baits like crabs and shellfish.

An offset hook point definitely increases hooking power. Many otherwise excellent surf-casting hooks are manufactured with straight shanks only. If the wire is well forged and highly tempered, it is a mistake to offset the bend. Softer hooks are modified by a slight twist with pliers. It does not matter whether a bend is offset left or right.

You can take the process one stage further. If you think that a size 1 Aberdeen should be thicker in the wire, reform a smaller bend in a standard 2/0 hook. Some Aberdeens are soft enough for safe bending as long as you leave the point alone.

Hooks are usually over-long in point and barb. A minute's work with a file and slipstone reduces the metal and creates a much sharper, secure point. Patridge hooks never need this modification. One star attraction of the range is the excellent design of the sharp end.

Sharpening hooks
Again with the notable exception of Partridge and Breakaway, most of the world's surfcasting hooks are supplied relatively blunt, or at least subject to wide variation. Before using any hook, and from time to time while fishing, touch up the point with a file or slipstone. Absolute sharpness is difficult to maintain because of sand and stone abrasion.

An ideal hookpoint is chisel shaped and relatively short, not round and long like a needle. Short points last much longer, and they do not skid off or fold over anywhere near as easily when a fish bites. It takes but a few strokes of the file 3 or 4 times a day to keep your hook in perfect condition. A small price to pay for peace of mind and better sport.

Traces and Accessories

There are no world-wide standards for traces and terminal rigs. Every country develops its own themes. Fishermen 50 miles along the coast probably use a different rig from your own. Species and sea conditions, baits and tackle influence trace and accessory design. The seasons bring their own changes: a rig for summer fishing might be entirely useless on the same beach in January.

Experiment is the key to successful bait presentation. It really does pay to ring the changes with trace length and breaking strain, paternoster arrangement, sinker weight, hook size and how baits are cut. Sometimes bass ignore ragworms presented on paternoster snoods yet bite freely on a single hook rig allowed to wash over the seabed. Cod often take an opposite view: well anchored baits on short paternoster snoods attract five fish to the running leger's one.

Little can be predicted. Surf fishing changes from day to day, and sometimes morning tides fish differently from late evening tides. What a surf man needs above all is a sound background knowledge of how rigs work and how they are best constructed. Simplicity is the underlying theme.

Paternosters account for the vast majority of fish hooked in the surf, short range or at maximum distance. Paternosters are easy to tie, versatile and they definitely reduce bait explosion. Set properly in the tide, a paternoster virtually guarantees that boldly biting fish hook themselves.

The rig is assembled around a central core of heavy-duty nylon at least as strong as the shock leader. Knotting inevitably reduces line strength, so for safety it is better to use a paternoster breaking strain 10 percent above that of your shock leader. In practical beach terms that means tying traces in 35–55 pound monofilament to match 3–5 ounce sinkers. Sometimes even stronger line is required to withstand sand abrasion or to stiffen the core so that hook snoods remain separated. Nothing is worse than a paternoster that tangles into a ball of nylon as soon as it hits the seabed.

Hooks are attached to a paternoster core by lengths of nylon called snoods. Length and breaking strain vary with hook specification, bait selection and species likely to attack. There are no definite rules here, and fish themselves switch preferences with time and tide. Work on the

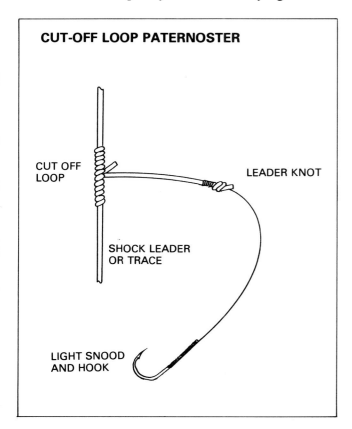

CUT-OFF LOOP PATERNOSTER

CUT OFF LOOP

LEADER KNOT

SHOCK LEADER OR TRACE

LIGHT SNOOD AND HOOK

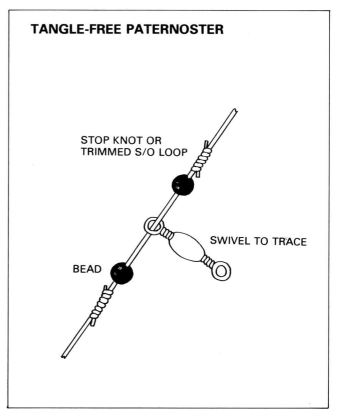

TANGLE-FREE PATERNOSTER

STOP KNOT OR TRIMMED S/O LOOP

SWIVEL TO TRACE

BEAD

principle that if the bait sits neatly on the hook and washes nicely in the tide, any snood is probably good enough. Snoods of 6–15 inch are a reasonable starting point; use 10–20 pound nylon for hooks up to 1/0, and 20–30 pound test for the larger sizes. Sharp teeth obviously require extra trace strength and perhaps even a wire snood.

The number of hooks depends on the length of trace you can handle and the size of fish. There is little point hooking big cod three at a time (even if you were that lucky) but on the other hand a match angler should not waste time snatching single whiting when a 3 hook rig might well attract two or three fish at once.

Pendulum and back casting are the most versatile methods of handling a paternoster because the sinker drop is usually well over 7 feet. Thus a trace up to 6 feet long can be accommodated without fouling the swivel in the rod tip ring or hitting the ground with the sinker; 6 feet allows an easy spread of three 9 inch snoods. Core attachment points are so far apart that hooks and traces never intertwine.

Nearly all paternoster problems are due to the method of tying on snoods. Tangles are the major fault, but strength is involved as well. Paternosters wrongly tied in even 60 pound nylon can snap in mid cast with potentially lethal results. A 5 ounce sinker whistling down the beach is no joke.

The plain stand-off loop is a valuable knot for general purpose fishing. Easy to tie, reasonably strong and adjustable for length, if offers an instant attachment point for snoods. You can tie a 3 hook paternoster in 2 minutes.

The loop itself stands off at right angles from the paternoster core and in heavy monofilament is stiff enough to support and hook. Extra stiffening may be necessary and is best achieved by cutting plastic sleeves 0.25 in longer than the loop and slipping them over it. The extra quarter inch supports the snood knot and prevents its swivelling out of alignment. Old Biro refills, stripped electrical flex and model aeroplane fuel tube are effective stiffeners. 1–3 inch loops are about right for most rigs.

Cut stand-off loops. Heavy nylon is stiff enough in itself to support a lightweight hook, snood and bait. Snip the top half of an ordinary loop about 0.25 inches from the knot coils. Straighten the stand-off section of nylon and tie on the snood with a shock leader knot. Snood and cut loop stand well away from the centre core, and the rig is adequately strong for most species of fish up to 5 pounds. Bait presentation is particularly neat with

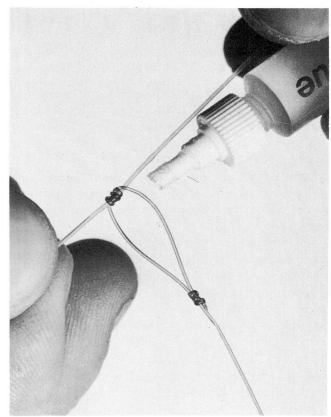

Uni-knot snood tied directly to the leader and super-glued in place.

Aberdeen Blue hooks. Tangles are virtually eliminated in snoods less than 9 inches long.

Tangle-free casting of long snoods is a little more difficult. You could consider a swivelling rig which, although more expensive and slower to tie does offer one of the best solutions to the eternal problems of big baits cast on 12 inch-plus snoods. Two or three hook paternosters are made this way, but for cod and big bass it is better to use one bait.

Method A

Tie a 5 or 6 turn stand-off loop at the correct height on the centre core. Cut off the loop to leave just the knot barrel. Slide on a small bead, a swivel, then a second bead. Sandwich the beads and swivel with a second cut-down loop tied about 2 inches from the first. Knot barrels prevent the beads from sliding out of position, and beads buffer line from swivel pressure when a fish takes hold. Snoods and hooks are the same as for a normal paternoster rig.

Method B

Two knots in the paternoster core must introduce weakness. Very powerful casters are acutely aware of a potential snap-off. Instead of tying and cutting stand-off loops, they retain beads and swivel with two separate nylon stop-knots bound tightly to the

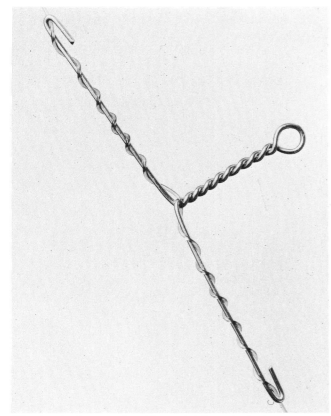

Simple wire boom twisted from stainless steel wire.

heavy core and usually further secured by a dribble of superglue. At worst, the stoppers slip under heavy pressure—a small price to pay for extra insurance against killing your neighbour.

Wire booms twisted on to the paternoster are the old fashioned way to attach snoods. The main objection is excessive air resistance, but there are small diameter stainless steel wire booms on sale that minimise the risk. Some booms have attachment points for the snood, others are purely supportive—the snood is still tied to the paternoster core. On the whole, you would do better not to bother about booms except for flounder and dab fishing, where for some reason they sometimes appear to increase the catch.

Bare snoods may be tied direct to the paternoster core. Most good knots will suffice, but there is a special system based on the Uni-knot which produces a neat stand-off. Tie the snood to the core with a Uni-knot, and be sure to leave a spare end of line at least 4 inches long. Tie this free end back against the main snood with another Uni-knot. A type of triangular boom results, stiff enough to support hook and baits. The snood slips under high pressure, but you can avoid most problems by gluing the first Uni-knot to the heavy nylon. The rig is extremely cheap to make and

therefore ideal for rough ground fishing where tackle losses are high.

Keeping baits on

All terminal rigs tend to rip off baits in mid cast. Paternosters are worse than most because they are the best rig for long distance work and thus subjected to higher stress. In standard form with snoods dangling, any rig will smash soft baits to pieces. Bait clips and snood restraints are essential for top results. These two accessories are so important that many anglers incorporate them in every trace they tie. For what little it costs, why do less?

Bait clips are blunt, shallow hooks which strap to the paternoster core and interlock with the baited hook for casting. The distance between hook and clip is adjusted so that the arrangement holds together while the rig is held straight by the sinker's weight but unfastens when the core buckles in contact with the sea. Anchored close to the terminal rig throughout the cast, baits are less likely to tangle and burst. Reduced air drag adds many yards to the cast—as much as 10 percent with bulky tackle.

Bait clips are made from a scrap of stainless steel wire or cut-down hooks. Either whip the shank to the paternoster core or fix it on with a piece of

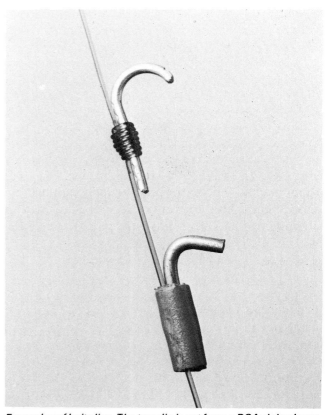

Examples of bait clips. The top clip is cut from a DCA sinker loop; the other is bent from scrap brass wire. Whippings are more secure, but plastic sleeves allow instant adjustment.

195

rubber tube just large enough in diameter to accept heavy nylon and wire clip with a firm push fit. The clip should be free to slide under moderate pressure so that you can adjust the interlocked hooks to a suitable pressure. Trial and error is the only way to find the best settings for clip and snoods. One clip is required for each snood on the paternoster. Fix the baits up or down the trace as you prefer. The best in-flight position for a single bait is just behind the sinker.

Tying on sinker and leader

Knotting a trace directly to sinker and leader is bad practice. Knots tend to slip under full-power casting pressure, and the sinker knot is wide open to seabed abrasion. After three of four casts and retrieves over sand and shingle, a direct sinker knot is too weak to withstand one more big cast.

Swivels and split rings are ideal intermediary links. Either is acceptable. Split rings are cheap, reliable and very strong. Swivels are probably unnecessary in general surf angling even with fixed spool reels which twist line. Very few if any swivels comb out twists. Most of them are little more than expensive substitutes for a split ring, and less reliable.

If you must use swivels, buy the best: Dexter and Berkeley are as good as any. Swivels 0.5—1

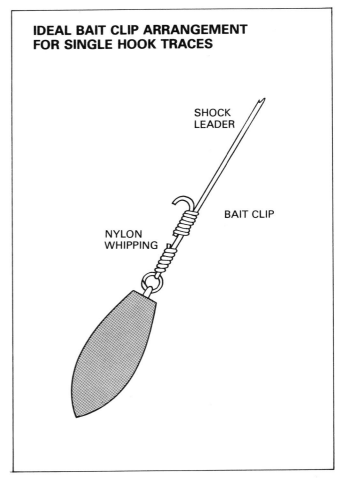

IDEAL BAIT CLIP ARRANGEMENT FOR SINGLE HOOK TRACES

SHOCK LEADER

BAIT CLIP

NYLON WHIPPING

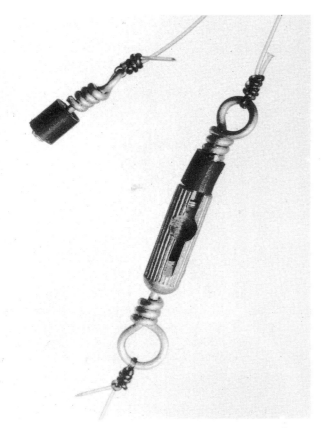

Dexter swivel with detachable loop for rapid trace changing.

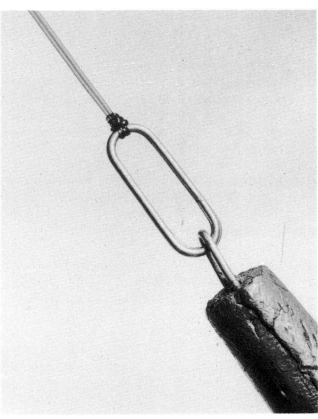

Stainless steel split ring and Palomar knot ensure firm sinker attachment and safe casting.

inch long are suitable for all-round beach work. Which split rings? Mustad Ovals 0.375–0.75 inches long are superior to any other. Guard against cheap rings that pull open under moderate pressure. The same goes for link swivels: most of them are bad news, and the worst are potential killers. Some Oriental link swivels of the safety pin type burst open at 10 pounds pressure.

A plastic-sleeved knot is an acceptable alternative for sinker attachment. Mould your sinkers with narrow tail loops. Thread an inch of rubber tube on to the lower end of the terminal rig, tie the nylon straight to the sinker loop, then pull the tube down to cover the knot barrel and wire. The sleeve buffers line and knot from seabed abrasion, eliminating the need for a swivel or split ring. Long-tail sinker wires can be bent into a tight 'U'

instead of a closed loop, then tied the same way. With the sleeve in place, there is no danger of the knot slipping free.

Quick-change attachments are standard equipment in match fishing. Two traces are used, one on the rod, the other prebaited and hung on the rod rest. Instead of rebaiting the original trace when you retrieve it—with or without fish on the end—unclip the whole rig, replace it with the spare one, and re-cast immediately. Fresh baits are back in the water within seconds. Time saved means more fish caught, especially when fish swim downtide in small shoals which may be in casting range for only 10 minutes at a time.

A plain swivel on the end of a leader, plus a safety-pin link clip on each end of the trace work

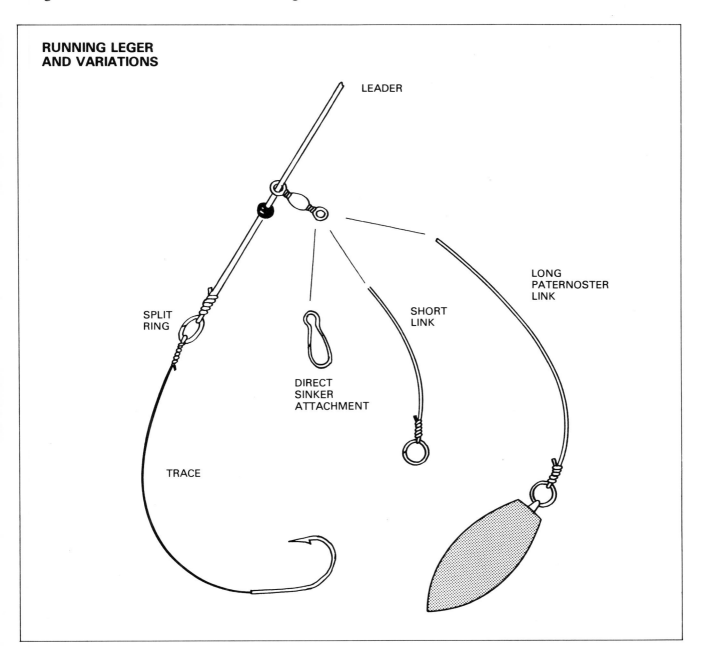

RUNNING LEGER
AND VARIATIONS

LEADER

SPLIT RING

DIRECT SINKER ATTACHMENT

SHORT LINK

LONG PATERNOSTER LINK

TRACE

well enough. Check the quality of the components before you start to cast big sinkers at full power. Even better are the new detachable swivels marketed by Dexter Products. One loop lifts out of the swivel barrel. One swivel and two spare ends serves the same purpose as conventional quick release gadgets and are much stronger and safer.

Snood stoppers are a neat way to prevent baits slipping from the hook and up the snood towards the stand-off loop. Most baits slip under full casting power and even bait clips cannot save them. In fact, clips aggravate the situation. Whip a few turns of stiff nylon to the snood just above the hook, trim the rear end short and leave the other—the one nearer the hook—about 0.25 inches long. Worms and other baits skidding up the shank are trapped by the whisker of free nylon. If a high proportion of your bites never develop into hooked fish, bait slip may well be the reason.

Specialised traces
Running legers are a waste of time and money for general surfcasting. The theory of a free-running trace is defeated by distance and tidal current; and most fish take paternostered baits equally well anyway. Short range fishing for rays and conger

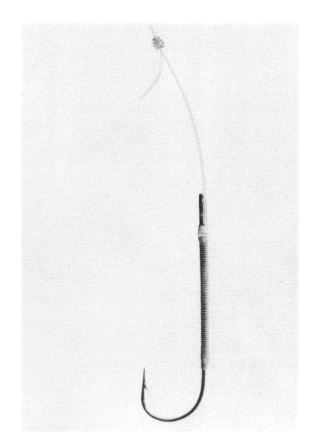

A whisker of stiff nylon tied above the hook prevents bait slip and missed bites.

eels are the main exception. Here, delicacy of presentation is boosted by a straight through trace and a sliding sinker.

Complicated and expensive booms like Clements and Kilmore are unnecessary. Thread a plain swivel on to the leader, then connect trace to leader with a second swivel or a split ring. Attach the sinker to the sliding swivel and your rig is complete. Sinkers are either hitched on with a link clip or split ring, or simply tied on with a short insert of nylon monofilament. If you are worried about the sliding swivel digging into the trace swivel knot, keep them apart with a nylon bead.

Running legers are more useful when modified for specialist work. On rough ground, tie the sinker to its swivel with weak nylon. If a sinker fouls the bottom its weak link, called a rotten bottom, breaks first. Sometimes it operates like a dream; as often as not the hook snags instead, in which case you lose the lot. A rotten bottom is most useful when the sinker snags after a fish is hooked. Snap off the weak nylon and resume the battle.

Shorten the trace, extend the nylon link between sinker and slider, and you are back to the tangle-free paternoster theme. A free-running trace is unimportant in most circumstances, but its swivel does prevent tangles. There is no great

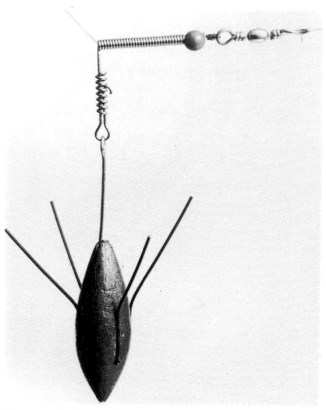

Home-made clips or plain swivels are just as good as the traditional booms and much cheaper.

advantage in doing it this way, but it does mean you can change from a running trace to a paternoster in seconds. For hard casting the nylon link must be at least the same breaking strain as the leader itself.

Very long traces rigged paternoster or rúnning style are sometimes useful for shy-feeding species for for presenting baits just off the bottom. Under normal conditions it is impossible to cast a 10 or 12 foot trace. But if you rig 2 bait clips on the leader, say 6 feet apart and facing away from each other, a long trace can be taken over the top clip and the baited hook fixed below. Both clips release when the sinker hits the water, and the whole trace floats cleanly into the tide. If necessary buoy the hook with a sliver of cork or polystyrene foam. At least it holds the crabs at bay.

Knots for trace assembly and general fishing

New knots appear every season. Most claims are wildly exaggerated, and after a few months everyone returns to the old faithfuls—blood knots, leader knots, bimini twists, palomars and uni-knots. As I have already explained, ease of tying and reproducibility are just as important as ultimate tensile strength. In my view there is a lot of nonsense written about knots, and I sometimes wonder why so many writers set themselves up as knot experts. For the money I suppose.

Anyway, I have deliberately cut the list to the bone. All these knots are perfectly safe for surf fishing. If one fails, the reason is either lack of practice on your part, or some failure in the line. Perhaps the sharp edge of a swivel or seabed abrasion had already damaged the nylon. It is true that some knots are stronger under laboratory conditions, but here we are solely concerned with the reality of surf fishing.

All these knots stand up to the rigours of casting and fishing, but wouldn't it be nice if one knot could handle everything—reel line, leader, traces and hooks? Try working out your tackle on the Uni-knot system. You may be convinced, as I am, that it really is the universal nylon monofilament hitch.

Blood knot

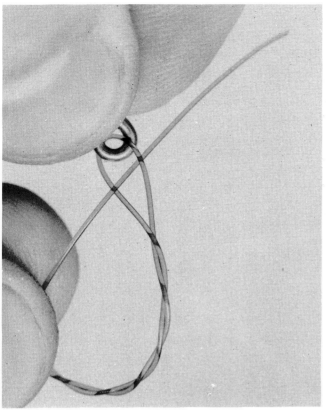

Blood knot 1. *Push the line through the ring and double back about 4 inches. Twist the strands around each other six times and push the spare end through the formed loop.*

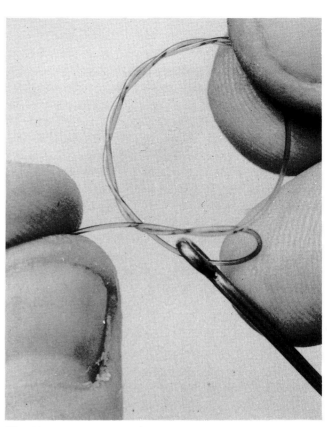

Blood knot 2. *Now tuck the end of line through the main circle of the knot.*

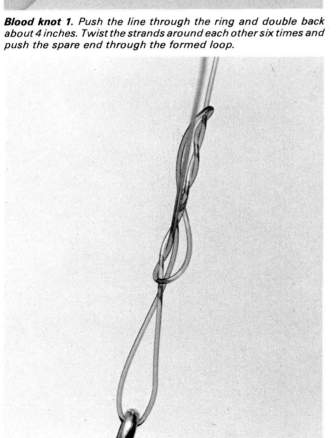

Blood knot 3. *Pull gently on the knot until the coils fall neatly in place. Then lick the knot to lubricate the material. Friction burns dry line.*

Blood knot 4. *Pull the knot tight and trim off the end. Leave about 0.125 inches free in case the knot slips under pressure.*

Leader knot

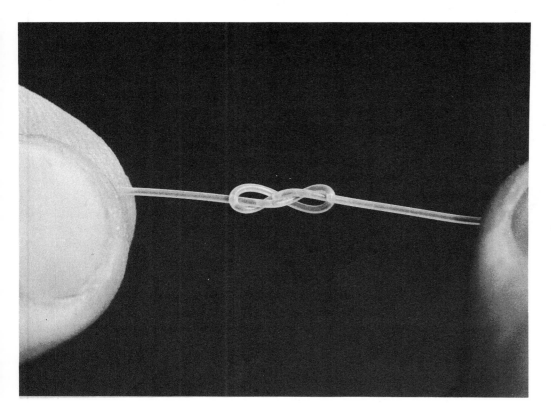

Leader knot 1. *Tie a half hitch in the leader and pull it tight enough to form a figure eight.*

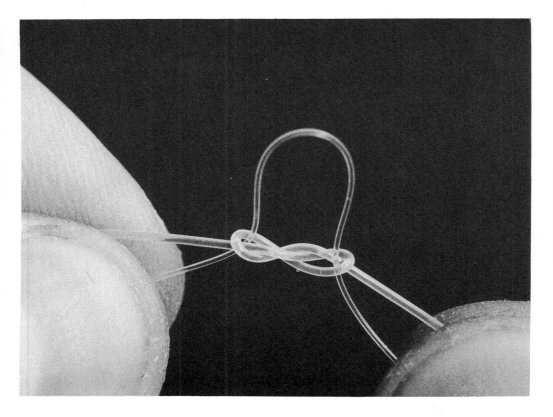

Leader knot 2. *Push the main line through the figure eight. Notice that the main line feeds in and out parallel with the ends of the leader itself, not on the opposite side of the loops.*

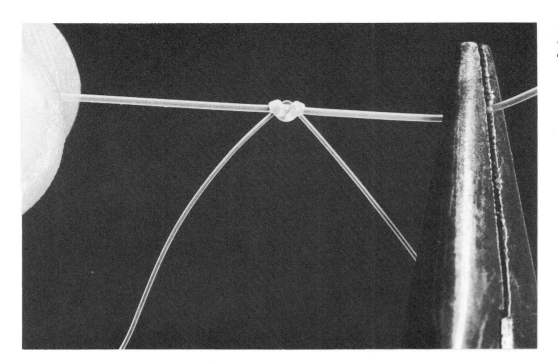

Leader knot 3. Pull the leader hitch tight with pliers.

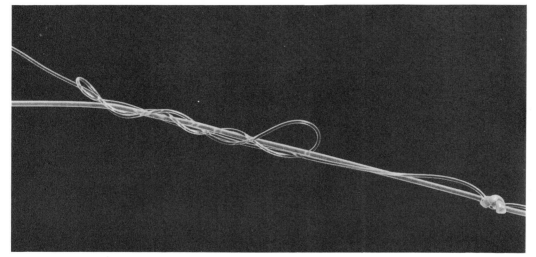

Leader knot 4. Tie a Uni-knot in the main line. Pull it tight enough to settle the coils. Then slide it up to the other knot.

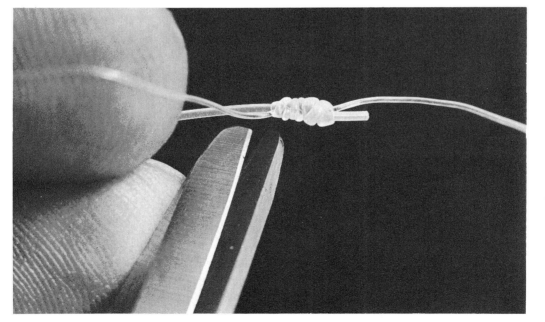

Leader knot 5. Pull the two knots snugly against each other and trim the ends. The Uni-knot is trimmed quite close but the leader end is left 0.125 inches long to insure against slipping.

Uni-knot

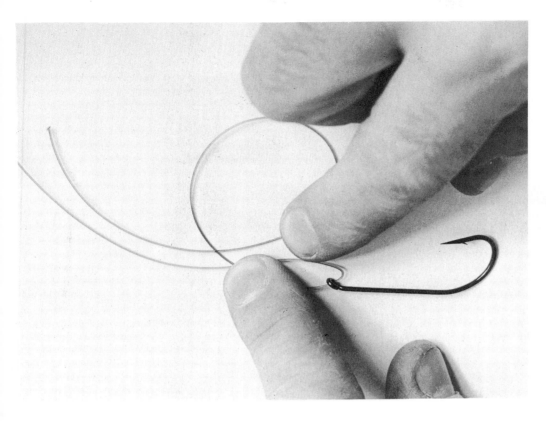

Uni-knot 1. *Pass six inches of line through the eye, double it over, then form a loop.*

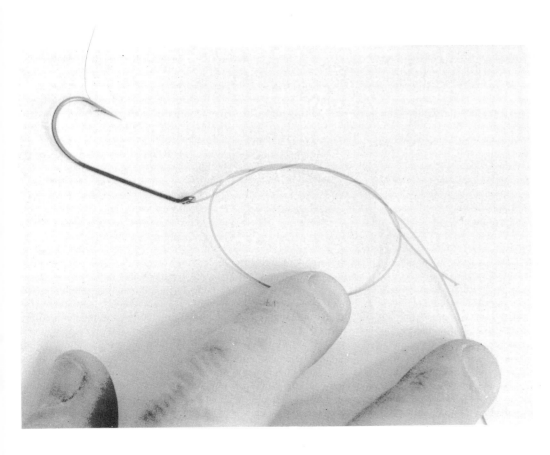

Uni-knot 2. *Lay the loop next to the main part of the line. Wrap the spare end of nylon around the two parallel sections of line. Use at least six full turns.*

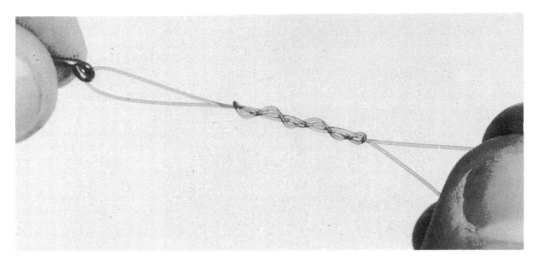

Uni-knot 3. Pull the ends of the line to form the knot barrel. When the coils fall into place, lick them and pull the knot tighter.

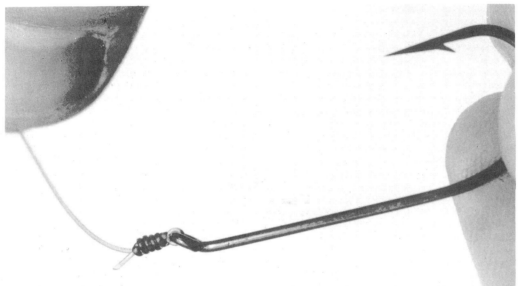

Uni-knot 4. Slide the knot close to the hook eye, then pull fully tight. The Uni-knot is also excellent for tying together two pieces of nylon.

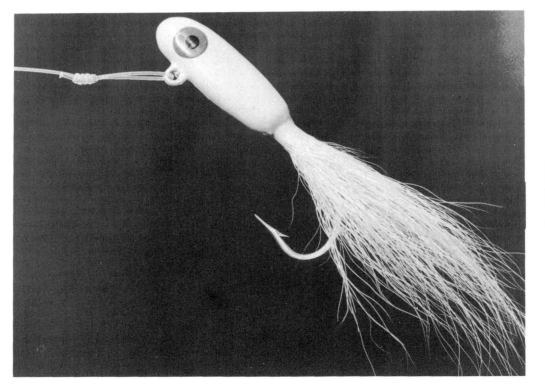

Uni-knot 5. Tightening the coils slightly away from the lure attachment eye forms a secure loop of nylon which enhances underwater action.

Stand-off loop

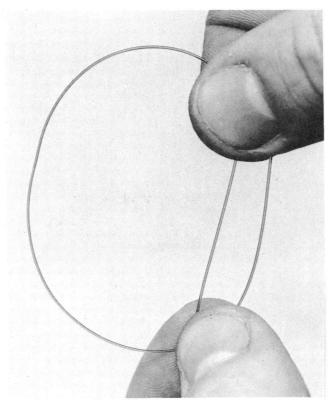

Stand-off loop 1. *Form a loop in the trace at the appropriate point for snood attachment.*

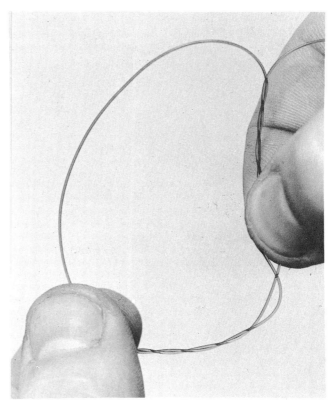

Stand-off loop 2. *Twist the parallel strands around each other six or seven times.*

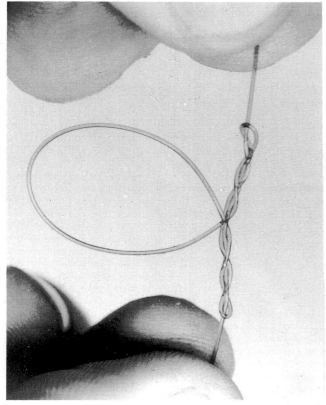

Stand-off loop 3. *Push the opposite side of the main loop through the middle of the twisted section and gently pull the coils into place.*

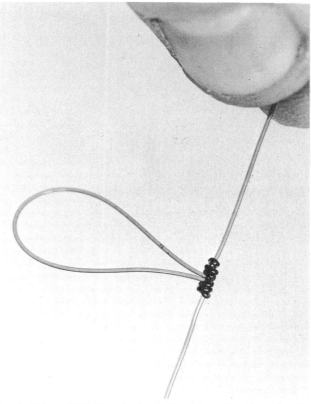

Stand-off loop 4. *Tighten the knot after lubricating the nylon to avoid friction burns. Stand-off loops sometimes slip so much that the loop disappears. Put in plenty of twists, and tighten the knot very slowly. Some brands of nylon skid worse than others.*

Palomar knot

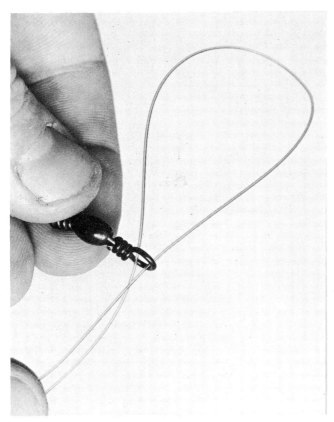

Palomar knot 1. *Double 6 inches of line and push into the swivel loop.*

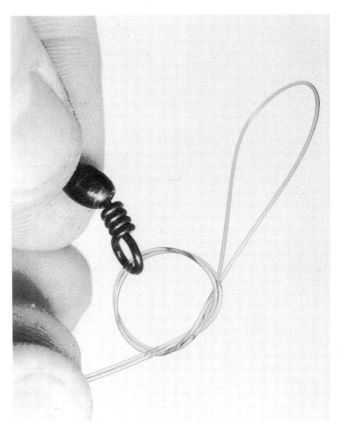

Palomar knot 2. *Tie a half hitch, and make sure that the loop is big enough to slip around the lure, sinker, hook or whatever.*

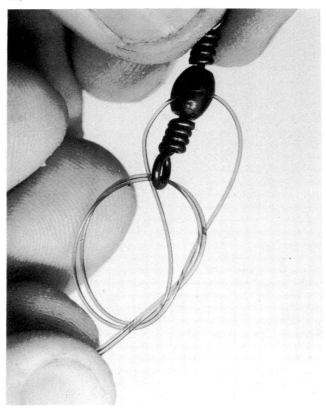

Palomar knot 3. *Pass the loop around the swivel, then gently draw the knot tight. The coils must pull down evenly or the knot slips.*

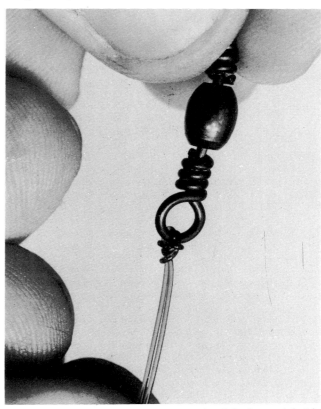

Palomar knot4. *Tighten the knot and trim. It looks weak but is actually one of the strongest monofilament knots.*